THE SECOND WORLD WAR IN 100 OBJECTS

THE STORY OF THE WORLD'S GREATEST CONFLICT
TOLD THROUGH THE OBJECTS THAT SHAPED IT

MAJOR GENERAL
JULIAN THOMPSON CB OBE
AND
DR ALLAN R MILLETT
SENIOR MILITARY ADVISOR FOR THE
NATIONAL WORLD WAR II MUSEUM

CARLTON

THIS IS A CARLTON BOOK

Published in 2012 by Carlton Books Limited
20 Mortimer Street
London W1T 3JW

10 9 8 7 6 5 4 3 2 1

A CIP catalogue record for this book is available from the British Library.

ISBN 978 1 78097 103 2

Printed in Dubai

CONTENTS

INTRODUCTION

The 100 objects in this book all have a vital connection with the Second World War. Some were conceived before that war, and others during it, but all formed an essential part of the "tapestry" of that conflict. My aim in this book was to produce pictures and text that would resonate with readers whether they were experts on the Second World War or approaching the subject for the first time. I chose objects only, not people. My choice ranges from the biggest object, the Atlantic Wall, to an ampoule of penicillin. Among the big objects, I include the Maginot Line, the two Mulberry Harbours and the Bridge over the River Kwai, or to give it its proper name at the time; the Mae Klong. The smaller objects include Churchill's cigar and insignias for the SAS, Popski's Private Army, the SS and the Desert Rats, as well as Australian divisional patches.

I wanted to include objects associated with the Germans, Japanese and Italians, as well as British, American, Russian, French, Australian and other Allied nations who used some of the same equipment. Three of the most famous tanks of the war appear here: the Russian T-34, the German Tiger and American Sherman; this last used extensively by the British as well. The Italians were the first to use human torpedoes to attack ships; other nations quickly followed suit, and their torpedoes appear in the book as well. Numerous vehicles became famous in the Second World War, none more so than the ubiquitous Jeep, though the amphibious DUKW (Duck) was probably a close second. Arguably the most deadly anti-tank gun of the Second World War, the German 88-mm appears in both its guises: anti-tank and anti-aircraft.

Several documents appear in the book. Right at the beginning is the piece of paper that Neville Chamberlain waved for the crowd to see when he returned to London from meeting Adolf Hitler in Munich, telling them that this guaranteed "Peace in our time". Just 11 months later, Hitler issued his first war directive ordering the invasion of Poland and the Second World War had begun. The third document, created by President Roosevelt and Prime Minister Churchill on board HMS *Prince of Wales* at Placentia Bay Newfoundland in August 1941, became adapted as the Charter of the United Nations – which is also reproduced here. The final document did not see the light of day until a month after it was written: a note penned by General Eisenhower to be used in the event of the 6 June 1944 Normandy landings failing.

As well as the Spitfire, among the other aircraft depicted in the book the famous "Flying Fortress" B-17 bomber, the Mustang, the BF109 Messerschmitt and the Zero all appear, along with the "String bag" Swordfish and the Lancaster bomber. The carrier USS *Enterprise* (the celebrated "Big E") is here, along with HMS *Hood*, the *Graf Spee* and the "little ships" of Dunkirk.

I hope that readers will enjoy reading about the chosen items in *The Second World War in 100 objects*, and find the book both informative and perhaps that it throws a light on some generally less well known facts.

Julian Thompson

ABOVE: One of the most iconic items of the Second World War, the British Mark III combat helmet.

1 Peace in Our Time

On the afternoon of 30 September 1938, the Prime Minister of the United Kingdom, Neville Chamberlain, left Munich in a British Airways Super Lockheed Electra and landed at Heston airport, near today's Heathrow. A huge crowd greeted him. Facing a battery of microphones, he waved a piece of paper, saying, "This morning I had another talk with the German Chancellor, Herr Hitler, and here is a paper which bears his name as well as mine." The police cleared a route through the mob to enable him to drive to Buckingham Palace, where he appeared on the balcony with the King and Queen. That evening, he addressed a crowd from an upper window in Downing Street: "My good friends, this is the second time in our history that there has come back from Germany to Downing Street peace with honour. I believe it is peace in our time."

Chamberlain's visit to Munich was his third trip to see Hitler in 15 days as a result of a crisis concerning Czechoslovakia. In 1938 Czechoslovakia's total population of around 14 million included some three million German speakers, most whom lived in an area known as Sudetenland. In early September, the Sudetenlanders, stoked by Hitler's inflammatory speeches and with strong Nazi support, rioted, demanding union with Germany. By 15 September the Czech authorities had restored order, but there was an atmosphere of mounting tension across Europe.

That day, Chamberlain flew to the Berghof, Berchtesgaden, to persuade Hitler not to invade Czechoslovakia. He proposed that where more than half of the population desired union with Germany they should be granted their wish, to which Hitler agreed. The French reluctantly joined the British in putting pressure on President Beneš of Czechoslovakia to agree. Chamberlain returned to London, but Hitler, in a classic blackmailer's ploy, said the concessions were insufficient.

On 22 September, Chamberlain flew to meet Hitler at the Dreesen Hotel in Bad Godesberg, one of Hitler's favourite watering holes. Chamberlain was inclined to concede to Hitler's demands, but was opposed by his own Cabinet. On 23 September the Czechs mobilized and the British Royal Navy was deployed to war stations. Britain prepared for war. Chamberlain broadcast on 27 September: "How horrible, fantastic, incredible it is that we should be digging trenches and trying on gas-masks here because of a quarrel in a faraway country between people of whom we know nothing."

An appeal to Benito Mussolini, First Marshal of the Empire of Italy, to mediate signalled to Hitler that the French and British would crumble. On 29 September, Chamberlain flew to Munich along with Édouard Daladier, the French Prime Minister. They met Hitler and Mussolini at the Führerbau, the new neoclassical Nazi party headquarters. Here they accepted terms put forward by Mussolini but drafted by the German Foreign Office, conceding virtually all Hitler's demands. The next morning Chamberlain met Hitler in his private apartment, for what the former described as "a very friendly and pleasant talk", during which they signed the paper that Chamberlain showed at Heston.

German troops occupied Sudetenland immediately. They delayed occupying the rest of Czechoslovakia until May 1939, Hitler declaring, "I shall not occupy Prague for six months or so. I can't bring myself to do such a thing to the old fellow at the moment."

Strategic experts still disagree over whether the year's delay before the outbreak of the Second World War benefitted Germany or the Allies. Perhaps Chamberlain's climbdown caused Hitler to underestimate the British, to his ultimate cost. In August 1939 he said to his generals, "Our enemies are small worms. I saw them at Munich."

We, the German Führer and Chancellor and the British Prime Minister, have had a further meeting today and are agreed in recognising that the question of Anglo-German relations is of the first importance for the two countries and for Europe.

We regard the agreement signed last night and the Anglo-German Naval Agreement as symbolic of the desire of our two peoples never to go to war with one another again.

We are resolved that the method of consultation shall be the method adopted to deal with any other questions that may concern our two countries, and we are determined to contimue our efforts to remove possible sources of difference and thus to contribute to assure the peace of Europe.

Neville Chamberlain

September 30, 1938.

LEFT: Chamberlain at Heston airport on 30 September 1938 on his return from Munich.

ABOVE: The paper with Hitler's and Chamberlain's signature.

OVERLEAF: Chamberlain greeted by an SS guard of honour on his arrival at Munich. The German foreign minister von Ribbentrop is on Chamberlain's left.

2 Führer Directive Number 1

From the moment Adolf Hitler became Chancellor of Germany in January 1933, he had directed the country's armed forces with political aims, ordering a programme of rearmament in direct violation of the terms of the Treaty of Versailles (1920) and readying the military for a series of aggressive actions aimed at constructing a Greater German Reich. His direction of (and interference in) military affairs was characterized by a series of directives to the army. More general and forward-looking than simple orders, these *Führerdirektivs* tended to be of a strategic nature, beginning in autumn 1933 with the "Directive for the Armed Forces in the Event of Sanctions" and continuing in March 1938 with a "Directive 1" which ordered the Anschluss that annexed Austria. To enable his will to be transmitted throughout the armed forces with a minimum of political interference or modification by the traditional military hierarchy, on 4 February 1938 Hitler replaced the old Defence Ministry with the OKW (*Oberkommando der Wehrmacht*, High Command of the Armed Forces) headed up by one of his own placemen, General Wilhelm Keitel (an officer so unpopular with operational officers for his slavish subservience to Hitler's will that he became known as *Lakeitel*, "lackey").

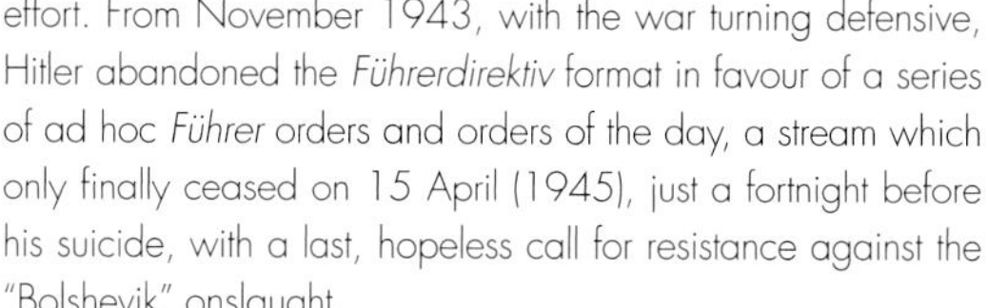

Plans for the projected assault on Poland (known as "Case White") were first circulated on 3 April 1939, but the assault was delayed until the autumn to give time to isolate the country diplomatically and to broker the agreement with the Soviet Union on Poland's dismemberment which bore fruit with the Nazi-Soviet Pact of 24 August.

By the fourth week in August, all was ready; Hitler gambled that France and Britain would lack the political will to intervene on behalf of Poland, and this is reflected in the first of a new series of *Führerdirektivs*. Directive Number 1, dated 31 August 1939, self-servingly summarized the scenario in its opening words: "Since the situation on Germany's eastern frontier has become intolerable and all political possibilities of peaceful settlement have been exhausted, I have decided upon a solution by force." A brief invocation of Case White as the template for the coming operation against Poland is followed by a much longer section concerned with the West. Germany's armed forces are ordered at all costs to respect the neutrality of Holland, Belgium, Luxembourg and Switzerland and warned that the blame for hostilities opening in western Europe must be laid firmly at the door of Britain and France. Whenever, however, either of those two countries might engage in aggressive moves against Germany, then the neutrality of the others could be violated with impunity in order to outflank the French defensive positions.

The declarations of war by Britain and France against Germany on 3 September provided Hitler with this pretext, leading to the issue of *Führerdirectiv* 2 ("For the Conduct of the War") the same day. The series continued until Directive 51 (of 3 November 1943), which gave orders for the disposition of the army to fight against the Allied opening of a second front in the West. Long before this, the style of the directives had turned from strategic judgments to Hitler's more typical micromanaging of operational military matters, which undercut operational officers' authority and undermined any rational direction of the war effort. From November 1943, with the war turning defensive, Hitler abandoned the *Führerdirektiv* format in favour of a series of ad hoc *Führer* orders and orders of the day, a stream which only finally ceased on 15 April (1945), just a fortnight before his suicide, with a last, hopeless call for resistance against the "Bolshevik" onslaught.

ABOVE: The German invasion of Poland, 1 September 1939.

RIGHT: Hitler's Directive Number 1, issued on 31 August 1939, ordered the invasion of Poland.

C-126 a

Der Oberste Befehlshaber der Wehrmacht

OKW/WFA Nr. 170 /39 g.K.Chefs. L I

Berlin, den 31.8. 39.

8 Ausfertigungen

2. Ausfertigung.

Weisung Nr. 1

für die Kriegführung.

1.) Nachdem alle politischen Möglichkeiten erschöpft sind, um auf friedlichem Wege eine für Deutschland unerträgliche Lage an seiner Ostgrenze zu beseitigen, habe ich mich zur gewaltsamen Lösung entschlossen.

2.) Der Angriff gegen Polen ist nach den für Fall Weiss getroffenen Vorbereitungen zu führen mit den Abänderungen, die sich beim Heer durch den inzwischen fast vollendeten Aufmarsch ergeben.

Aufgabenverteilung und Operationsziel bleiben unverändert.

Angriffstag: 1.9.39.

Angriffszeit ....

Diese Zeit gilt auch für die Unternehmungen Gdingen - Danziger Bucht und Brücke Dirschau.

3.) Im Westen kommt es darauf an, die Verantwortung für die Eröffnung von Feindseligkeiten eindeutig England und Frankreich zu überlassen. Geringfügigen Grenzverletzungen ist zunächst rein örtlich entgegen zu treten.

Die von uns Holland, Belgien, Luxemburg und der Schweiz zugesicherte Neutralität ist peinlich zu achten.

- 2 -

C-126 a

- 2 -

Die deutsche Westgrenze ist zu Lande an keiner Stelle ohne meine ausdrückliche Genehmigung zu überschreiten.

Zur See gilt das gleiche für alle kriegerischen oder als solche zu deutenden Handlungen.

Die defensiven Massnahmen der Luftwaffe sind zunächst auf die unbedingte Abwehr feindl. Luftangriffe an der Reichsgrenze zu beschränken, wobei so lange als möglich die Grenze der neutralen Staaten bei der Abwehr einzelner Flugzeuge und kleinerer Einheiten zu achten ist. Erst wenn beim Einsatz stärkerer franz. und engl. Angriffsverbände über die neutralen Staaten gegen deutsches Gebiet die Luftverteidigung im Westen nicht mehr gesichert ist, ist die Abwehr auch über diesem neutralen Gebiet freizugeben.

Schnellste Orientierung des OKW über jede Verletzung der Neutralität dritter Staaten durch die Westgegner ist besonders wichtig.

4.) Eröffnen England und Frankreich die Feindseligkeiten gegen Deutschland, so ist es Aufgabe der im Westen operierenden Teile der Wehrmacht, unter möglichster Schonung der Kräfte die Voraussetzungen für den siegreichen Abschluss der Operationen gegen Polen zu erhalten. Im Rahmen dieser Aufgabe sind die feindl. Streitkräfte und deren wehrwirtschaftl. Kraftquellen nach Kräften zu schädigen. Den Befehl zum Beginn von Angriffshandlungen behalte ich mir in jedem Fall vor.

- 3 -

C-126 a

- 3 -

Das Heer hält den Westwall und trifft Vorbereitungen, dessen Umfassung im Norden - unter Verletzung belg. oder holländ. Gebietes durch die Westmächte - zu verhindern. Rücken franz. Kräfte in Luxemburg ein, so bleibt die Sprengung der Grenzbrücken freigegeben.

Die Kriegsmarine führt Handelskrieg mit dem Schwerpunkt gegen England. Zur Verstärkung der Wirkung kann mit der Erklärung von Gefahrenzonen gerechnet werden. OKM meldet, in welchen Seegebieten und in welchem Umfang Gefahrenzonen für zweckmässig gehalten werden. Der Wortlaut für eine öffentl. Erklärung ist im Benehmen mit dem Ausw. Amte vorzubereiten und mir über OKW zur Genehmigung vorzulegen.

Die Ostsee ist gegen feindl. Einbruch zu sichern. Die Entscheidung, ob zu diesem Zwecke die Ostsee-Eingänge mit Minen gesperrt werden dürfen, trifft Ob.d.M. ~~bleibt vorbehalten~~.

Die Luftwaffe hat in erster Linie den Einsatz der franz. und engl. Luftwaffe gegen das deutsche Heer und den deutschen Lebensraum zu verhindern.

Bei der Kampfführung gegen England ist der Einsatz der Luftwaffe zur Störung der engl. Seezufuhr, der Rüstungsindustrie, der Truppentransporte nach Frankreich vorzubereiten. Günstige Gelegenheit zu einem wirkungsvollen Angriff gegen massierte engl. Flotteneinheiten, insbes. gegen Schlachtschiffe und Flugzeugträger ist aus-

- 4 -

C-126 a

- 4 -

zunutzen. Angriffe gegen London bleiben meiner Entscheidung vorbehalten.

Die Angriffe gegen das engl. Mutterland sind unter dem Gesichtspunkt vorzubereiten, dass unzureichender Erfolg mit Teilkräften unter allen Umständen zu vermeiden ist.

Verteiler:

OKH	1. Ausf.
OKM	2. "
R.d.L.u.Ob.d.L.	3. "
OKW:	
Chef WFA	4. "
L	5.-8. "

3 The Yellow Star

The yellow six-pointed Star of David with the word *"Jude"* (Jew) is universally known as a badge worn by Jews as part of their victimization by the Nazis. Although the persecution of Jews in Germany began as soon as Hitler came to power in 1933, they were not required to wear a badge or other sign marking them out from the rest of society. But yellow stars of David were painted on the windows of Jewish-owned shops as early as 1 April 1933, the date on which the Nazis declared a boycott on these premises. This offensive graffiti does not appear to have been officially organized, because the matter of special Jewish badges had not yet been a subject for discussion among Nazi leaders. More likely, ordinary rank-and-file Nazi party members and probably the SA (*Sturmabteilung* or Stormtroopers) recipitated the paint-daubing ploy and the idea caught on, spreading quickly around Germany thanks to the media, especially the radio.

On 7 November 1938, Ernst vom Rath, Third Secretary at the German Embassy in Paris, was assassinated by Herschel Grynszpan, a Polish Jew. In retaliation, Reinhard Heydrich, Chief of the Sicherheitsdienst – Security Service (SD) – ordered the destruction of all places of Jewish worship in Germany and Austria. This action had long been prepared; the murder of vom Rath merely provided the excuse to begin the atrocity on the night of 9 November. As well as demolishing 177 synagogues, bands of Nazi hooligans destroyed an estimated 7,500 Jewish shops. Streets in every town were covered in broken glass, and the event was named *Kristallnacht* (Crystal Night, or Night of Broken Glass). On 12 November, at a meeting of Nazi leaders, Heydrich suggested a special badge for Jews. But no action was taken for nearly a year.

It was not until after the defeat of Poland in September 1939 that Jewish badges were introduced in the German-occupied sector (the Soviet Union occupied the eastern part of Poland). To begin with, there was no laid-down policy, and it was left to individual Nazi officials whether to issue orders that Jews in their area of jurisdiction were to wear badges. The designs varied from place to place. However, on 23 November 1939, Hans Frank, the German Governor General of Occupied Poland, ordered that all Jews above the age of ten were to wear a white armband with a yellow Star of David on their right arm. By December 1942, more than 85 per cent of the Jewish people in Poland had been transported to extermination camps. This figure included Jews living in the former Soviet Polish territory, as by now the Russians had been pushed out following Hitler's invasion of Russia in June 1941.

An instruction published on 1 September 1941 had ordered all Jews in Germany and Poland to wear the yellow Star of David with *"Jude"* inscribed on it, on the left side of the chest. This order was then extended to include Jews in most occupied territories and countries. There is a legend that when Jews in Denmark were ordered to wear the star, King Christian X wore one and his example was followed by the whole population, Jew and Gentile, causing the Germans to rescind the order. In fact, the Germans never required Danish Jews to wear the star. What is not legend is the reaction by the Danes to discovering that 7,500 Danish Jews were about to be deported to death camps. Most of these Jews were hidden by their neighbours, and many were subsequently smuggled out to Sweden.

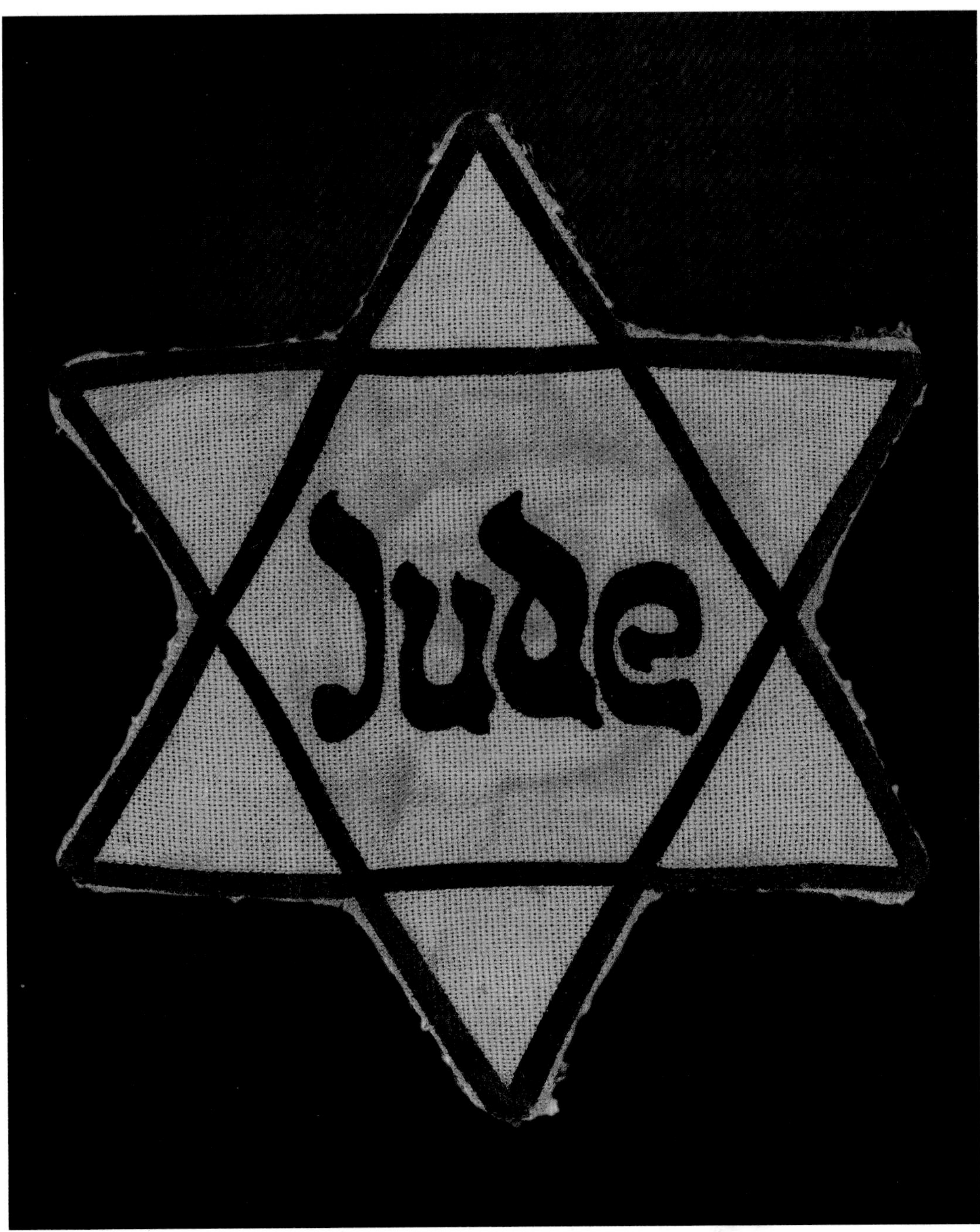

LEFT: French Jews after being rounded up in Paris and held in a covered cycling stadium, photographed in a transit camp, at Drancy north east of Paris in July 1942. From here they were taken by train to extermination camps in the east.

ABOVE: The yellow Star of David.

4 The Enigma Machine

Enigma is the codeword for a cipher machine based on a design by Dutchman, H A Koch. His ideas were developed by a Berlin engineer, Dr Arthur Scherbius, who first marketed it in 1923. By 1929 both the German army and navy had purchased different versions of it. Later it was bought by the Luftwaffe, the SS (*Schutzstaffel* or Protection Squadron), the *Abwehr* (the German secret service) and the *Reichsbahn* (German state railways). The machine consisted of a set of three rotating discs, called rotors, connected to a keyboard and a series of electrically powered lights. When a key was pressed the rotor would turn, and a display lamp would illuminate a letter.

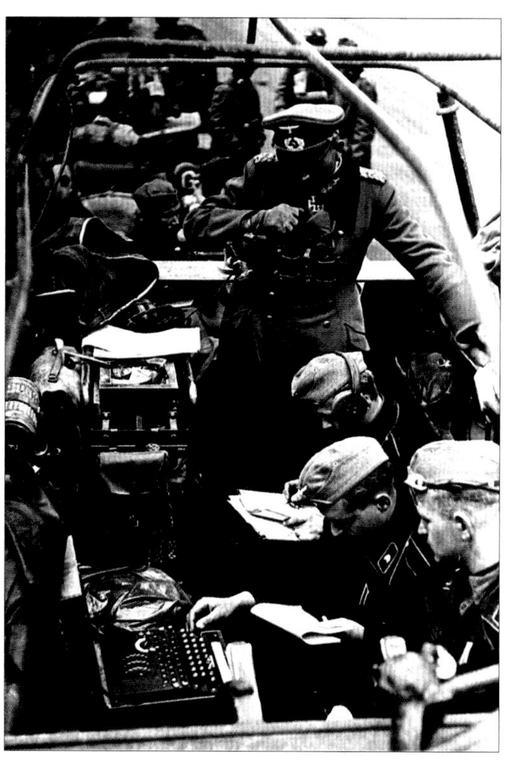

To encrypt a message, the operator would press the alphabetical key for the initial letter of the message, for example B, and the X lamp might light up. In earlier versions of Enigma, the operator copied down the resulting series of letters on to a message pad. Eventually the message would consist of an apparently meaningless jumble of letters, which in turn were transmitted by radio. The enigma operator at the receiving end would adjust his machine to the settings of the day and decrypt the message in the same way.

Throughout the Second World War, the Germans believed that the Enigma was unbreakable because for every signal sent there were millions of possible solutions. Every day the rotor settings were changed, and possessing a machine was only part way to breaking the code; you had to know what the day's setting was. The limitations to Enigma were that there are only 26 letters in the alphabet, that no letter could stand for itself, and that there were no numeral keys, so figures had to be spelled out.

The Poles acquired an Enigma machine and started reading some German signal traffic as early as 1932. They passed on the information to the French in 1939, and the British in 1940. The British Government Code and Cypher School at Bletchley Park began to break the Luftwaffe Enigma codes during the Norwegian and French campaigns of 1940, but took longer to read the German navy traffic. During the Battle of Britain (10 July–31 October 1940), most Luftwaffe traffic was sent over landlines, and consequently could not be read by Bletchley Park. The gravest crisis for the Allies arose during the Battle of the Atlantic when Admiral Dönitz's U-boat command began to use a fourth rotor on their Enigma machines, hugely multiplying the complexity of the enciphering of messages. The new German system was codenamed "Shark". Brilliant work by Bletchley Park eventually resulted in the deciphering of much of the U-boat command signals, and eventually the breaking of "Shark", assisted by the fact that Dönitz controlled his U-boats so precisely that he transmitted a huge volume of radio traffic, believing "Shark" to be unbreakable.

A number of Enigma machines were captured during the Second World War, but these only provided a partial

OPPOSITE: General Heinz Guderian commanding XIX Panzer Corps in his command half-track during the Battle of France 1940 with an Enigma Machine.

RIGHT: A three-ring Enigma cypher machine in wooden transit case, circa1930s.

breakthrough in reading German signal traffic. In March 1941, during a Commando raid on the Lofoten Islands off Norway, the German trawler *Krebs* was taken, with two Enigma machines and the current settings. In May 1941 and July 1941, the British captured two German weather ships, acquiring their codebooks for the following months. In May 1941, U-110 was forced to the surface, and sailors from HMS *Bulldog* boarded and seized her Enigma machine and codes before she sank. In October 1942, HMS *Petard* depth-charged U-559 to the surface and captured the latest codebooks. In June 1944, sailors from the USS *Pittsburgh* boarded the surfaced U-505, capturing her codebooks.

The work of Bletchley Park in breaking the German cyphers was greatly assisted by the invention of the "Bombe", an early form of computer.

5 The SS Insignia

Although there were a multiplicity of SS badges depending on the type of uniform worn and the unit, two themes were common: the double lightning flash and the death's head. The SS, short for *Schutzstaffel*, literally meaning "defence echelon", began its existence as the black-shirted personal guard for Hitler. Heinrich Himmler, a chicken farmer by trade who had never served as a soldier or heard a shot fired in action, was appointed by Hitler to command this guard. It was formed from the SA, the brown-shirt storm troopers of the Nazi party who had played a leading part in bringing Hitler to power. From small beginnings the SS was expanded into a very large force, an alternative army, whose main task in Himmler's eyes was to ensure the continuing existence of Nazi power.

The name *Schutzstaffel* was abbreviated to SS, depicted as a double lightning flash in imitation of ancient runic characters. This double flash was worn on a black collar patch, often just on one side of the collar. Although it became the insignia for all SS units, at first it was confined to members of Hitler's guard, the *Leibstandarte* Adolf Hitler, which after Hitler's accession to power moved from Munich to take over bodyguard duties from the Army Chancellery Guard in Berlin.

The other badge worn by the SS, usually on the front of their caps below the German eagle, was the death's head, the *Totenkopf*. This, with their black uniforms, was a copy of the outfit and headdress worn by the Life Guard Cavalry of the Prussian kings and German emperors, the "Death's Head" Hussars or *Leibhusaren*. In addition to collar and cap badges, the SS took to wearing cuff bands to denote their unit: the *Leibstandarte* Adolf Hitler wore one embroidered Adolf Hitler; the 2nd SS Panzer Division (*Das Reich*) wore a *Das Reich* cuff band, and so on.

From its original strength of 117 men, the Leibstandarte soon expanded into two battalions commanded by Sepp Dietrich, Hitler's personal bodyguard and chauffeur. On 30 June 1934 the Liebstandarte took part in the night of the "Long Knives" when Hitler ordered the elimination of Ernst Röhm, the Chief of Staff of the SA. The executioners led by Dietrich, and several Liebstandarte NCOs (non-commissioned officers) including the Drum Major killed six SA men in Munich, and three in Berlin. One of the motives behind these murders was an unspoken agreement between Hitler and the army that the SA would not become a rival army. The SA did not, but the SS most certainly did.

During 1934–35 more SS units were formed into SS-*Verfugüngtruppe* (SS-VT), or Special Purpose Troops, including two new *Standarten* (regiments), the Germania and the Deutschland. A motorized battalion of the *Leibstandarte* led the German occupation force into Austria in March 1938. In July 1938, Hitler announced that all SS-VT *Standarten* would form part of the army in war. By 1943, the *Leibstandarte* had become the 1st SS Panzer Division *Leibstandarte*, and the *Deutschland* and *Der Führer* the 2nd SS Panzer Division *Das Reich*. Eventually there were almost a quarter of a million SS troops in 38 divisions of the Waffen SS, as the SS-VT came to be called. So much for Hitler's promise to the army. The Waffen SS acquired a reputation as fanatical and highly competent soldiers in the Second World War, but this should not obscure the fact that they carried out numerous atrocities against both soldiers and civilians, notably in Russia and France. The SS even had a slang word for it, *rabatz*, meaning "having fun killing everyone in sight".

Even more notorious for their atrocities were the concentration-camp guard units, the SS-*Totenkopfverbände* (SS-TV), a separate part of the SS from the Waffen although they did provide the manpower for the 3rd SS Panzer Division Totenkopf. Unlike the Waffen, the SS-TV wore a death's head insignia on their tunics. Under the direction of the murderous ex-chicken-farmer Himmler, they enslaved and murdered millions.

LEFT: The Nuremburg Rally 1933. The motto on the standards is "*Deutschland Erwache*" (Germany Awake).

ABOVE: An SS insignia in bronze, with silver-plated runes.

6 The Stuka

The Stuka Junkers 87 bomber was designed to provide close support for the German army. It was inspired by the experience of the First World War when, by 1918, the German army was on the receiving end of fire delivered by the Royal Flying Corps and later the RAF in support of the British Army. The Germans further developed the techniques for this tactic, in stark contrast to the British. By 1939, the RAF was paying lip service to close air support of ground forces in the interests of pursuing an independent war strategy which disregarded the needs of the other two services. The German tactical doctrine of pushing their armour far ahead carried with it the risk that the tanks would outrun their artillery support. Tactical air support would fill the gap, especially the Stuka dive-bomber.

The Stuka's dive-bombing attack was especially effective in towns, and against vehicles on roads, when these were all lined up like ducks in a row. It was not so effective against infantry well spread out in open country, but it took a long time for troops to realize this. The psychological terror effect was enhanced by a wind-driven siren mounted on the fixed undercarriage which gave out a loud wailing scream as it dived. The technique used by the Stuka pilots was to put the aircraft into a steep dive from about 1,800 metres (6,000 feet), aiming the aircraft at the target using his ailerons to keep it aligned, while the dive brakes automatically kept the dive at the correct angle. As soon as the bombs were released, usually at about 275 metres (900 feet), an automatic recovery system pulled the Stuka out of its near-vertical dive. The G-force on the aircrew was around force six. Stukas often dropped their bombs within a few metres of the target, and even achieved direct hits. This was something a conventional bomber could only achieve by sheer luck.

The Stuka was fitted with a twin-barrelled rear-firing twin machine gun but, with a fixed undercarriage and gull wings, the aircraft was slow, and its rear gun gave little protection against well-flown modern fighters. The Stuka was especially vulnerable during the pull-up from its dive. The Spitfires and Hurricanes created such mayhem among the Stukas when they took part in the Battle of Britain that they were withdrawn from that particular contest.

The Stuka was used to great effect in Russia and in North Africa, in the role for which it was intended, destroying a significant number of tanks. The Stuka's successful time in North Africa came to an end when the RAF regained air superiority in early-to-mid-1942.

The Stuka also had a very long run of success at sea, especially in the Mediterranean, operating from airfields in Italy, the Greek Islands and the North African coast. This was partially the result of the fact that the Royal Navy did not have a really effective carrier-borne fighter until it acquired American Grumman Hellcats in 1944. That in turn was because aircraft procurement for the Royal Navy in the interwar years was in the hands of the RAF, resulting in a run of poor-performance aircraft ordered by a service that had no interest in carrier warfare – unlike the situation prevailing in the US and Japan.

Stukas inflicted heavy casualties, ship losses and damage to British convoys transiting the Mediterranean, especially those supplying Malta. They were also responsible for much damage in Malta itself, as well as to ships in the dockyard there, notably the carrier HMS *Illustrious*, in for repair. Stukas were used extensively in Crete in 1941, both in support of the German airborne landings and against ships evacuating the British troops when the island fell.

LEFT: Stukas over Stalingrad during the German assault on the city, September–October 1942.

ABOVE TOP: A Stuka (JU-87) starts a half-roll before a nosedive.

ABOVE BOTTOM: The Stuka was at its best in close support of ground troops, and in the anti-ship role, especially in the first half of the war, before the Allies gained air superiority.

7 Winter Skis

The Soviet Union invaded Finland on 30 November 1939 after the Finns refused to agree to territorial concessions demanded by the Russians in order to strengthen the defences of the Leningrad Military District. The Finnish Army consisted of ten divisions, which were short of many items of equipment, from artillery, mortars and radios to shells, but they were determined to defend Finnish independence, which had been gained from Russia after the Bolshevik revolution in 1917. The soldiers were well trained to use their initiative, and were at home in the forested terrain in both summer and winter. They could use their skis for mobility in snow, for example.

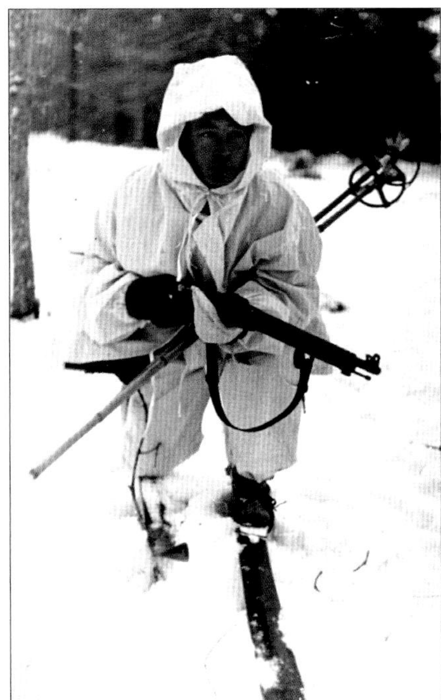

The Finns used the period of negotiations leading up to the Russian invasion to move to their defensive positions. Much of the 1,000-kilometre (620-mile) frontier was a trackless snow-covered wilderness of forests and lakes, impassable to a modern army. This allowed the Finnish commander, Carl Gustaf Emil Marshal Mannerheim, to concentrate six divisions along the 65-kilometre (40-mile) Mannerheim Line in the Karelian isthmus between Lake Lagoda and the Gulf of Finland, and another two on the 80 kilometres (50 miles) of Finnish frontier northeast of Lake Lagoda.

The Soviet Army deployed 26 divisions against Finland, comprising 1,200,000 men, with motor transport, plenty of artillery, 1,500 tanks and 3,000 aircraft. But it was a gravely flawed force, for Stalin's recent purges had stripped his army of good senior generals. Formation commanders were mainly sycophants terrified of their Communist Party apparatchik "political advisers" (ie minders). Soviet commanders were paralysed by indecision, fearing instant execution or, if they were lucky, the Gulag, should they demonstrate any initiative that departed from Soviet military doctrine. The solders were amazingly ill prepared for winter warfare. They had no white camouflage clothing, inadequate frost protection for vehicles and equipment, and no ski troops – crushing disadvantages in a campaign fought in sub-arctic weather.

A Soviet attack by one division at Petsamo in the north was halted in its tracks. Amphibious assaults at Helsinki, Hanko and Turku on the southern coast were repelled. The main Russian thrust through the Karelian isthmus with 12 divisions supported by armour resulted in stalemate, with heavy Russian losses. Initially the Finns, who had no experience of armoured warfare and no anti-tank weapons, were disheartened by Soviet tanks, but they quickly learned that these could be hunted down in the long winter nights using "Molotov cocktails", especially as Russian armour operated without infantry support.

In late December, the Finns counterattacked along the eastern front, where they outflanked Soviet road-bound formations by using ski troops moving through the forests. The Soviet reaction was to form isolated "hedgehog" positions which, although well defended, were small and could be picked off one by one. At Suomussalmi between 11 December 1939 and 8 January 1940, two Soviet divisions, outnumbering the Finns by four or five to one, were strung out along miles of track. They were too cumbersome to react to the slashing attacks by Finnish ski troops who cut the Russians to pieces. The Finns captured 65 tanks, 437 trucks, 10 motorcycles, 92 field guns, 78 anti-tank guns, 13 anti-aircraft guns, 6,000 rifles, 290 machine guns and large numbers of radios. It cost in addition 27,500 Soviet dead, 43 knocked-out tanks and 270 other vehicles destroyed. The Finns lost 900 dead and 1,770 wounded. On 1 February 1940, a reorganized Soviet Army under General Semyon

LEFT: Finnish soldier advancing with rifle at the ready, ski poles tucked under his arm.

ABOVE: Finns carrying out stem turns as they descend. The Finnish skill on cross-country skis made them far more mobile than their opponent infantry.

OVERLEAF: A posed picture of Finnish infantry in gas masks and white camouflage.

Timoshenko, reinforced by nine fresh divisions, bludgeoned the Finnish defences with a series of mass attacks, regardless of Russian casualties. On 13 February the Red Army broke through at Summa, and began to roll up the Finnish defences. On 12 March, the Finns agreed to peace terms.

The Soviet Union lost 200,000 dead and much equipment. Finland lost 25,000 dead and one-tenth of its territory. One of the major consequences of Soviet ineptitude in what became known as the "Winter War" was that Britain, the USA and especially Germany greatly underrated Russian military potential. In June 1941, at the start of Operation Barbarossa, Hitler thought that Russia would be a pushover. For several months after he invaded Russia, the British and Americans tended to share this view.

8 The *Admiral Graf Spee*

The "pocket battleship" *Admiral Graf Spee* was the last of three *Deutschland* class cruisers, laid down before Adolf Hitler came to power, while Germany still observed the terms of the Versailles Treaty of 1919. This treaty allowed Germany to build warships with a maximum displacement of 10,000 tons. In fact the class exceeded the displacement by 1,700 tons.

The *Admiral Graf Spee* and its sisters (*Deutschland* and *Admiral Scheer*) were not battleships, but heavily armed, thinly protected, long-range merchant raiders, stronger than any faster ship, and also faster than any other stronger vessels, except for the British battle cruisers *Hood*, *Renown* and *Repulse*. They were potentially a very serious threat. If the Germans had built all eight of the class, as permitted by the Treaty, three British battle cruisers would have been insufficient to match them – and the Washington Naval Treaty (6 February 1922) did not allow Britain to build any more battle cruisers.

On 21 and 23 August 1939, while diplomatic moves were being made to resolve the crisis over Danzig that eventually led to the outbreak of the Second World War, the *Admiral Graf Spee* and the *Deutschland* sailed from Wilhelmshaven for their intended areas of operations – the *Graf Spee* to the South Atlantic and the *Deutschland* to the North Atlantic. Their purpose: to strain British sea power by posing a constant threat to merchant-shipping routes. There were plenty of targets, because an average of 2,500 ships flying the Red Ensign were at sea on any given day. The two pocket battleships were permitted by Hitler to commence operations on 24 September, following the failure of his "peace initiative" after he had crushed Poland.

The *Deutschland* sank only two merchantmen before being recalled to Germany and renamed *Lützow*; it would never do if the "Germany" were to be sunk. Eventually, after the *Graf Spee* under Captain Langsdorff had sunk nine ships, Commodore Harwood with the heavy cruiser *Exeter* and light cruisers *Ajax* and *Achilles* located her 240 kilometres (150 miles) off the River Plate estuary in Uruguay, on 12 December 1939.

The *Graf Spee* was more heavily armoured than the *Exeter*, and with six 28-cm (11-in) guns in two triple turrets, and secondary armament of eight 15-cm (5.9-in) guns, outgunned the heavy cruiser, let alone the light cruisers with their 15.2-cm (6-in) guns. *Graf Spee* had 54,000-horsepower diesel engines which gave her a radius of action of 16,000 kilometres (10,000 miles) at cruising, even without refuelling from her attendant supply ship – more than twice the radius of a steam-turbine ship. She had a catapult-launched seaplane and search radar to scan the sea for victims or enemy warships. At this time very few British ships were fitted with radar.

Notwithstanding the disparity in size and gun power, Commodore Harwood ordered his ships to engage *Graf Spee* on two sides. A running battle ensued, with *Graf Spee* in Harwood's words "wriggling like an eel behind smoke screens". His fire was very accurate. *Exeter* was so badly damaged she had to retire, but the two light cruisers kept

LEFT: The *Admiral Graf Spee* after being scuttled on the orders of her captain.

ABOVE: The "pocket battleship" *Admiral Graf Spee* off Montevideo with some of her crew over the side inspecting damage after the Battle of the River Plate.

up the fire. Soon they too were so damaged that Harwood ordered them to disengage. Instead of turning to crush the two light cruisers, Langsdorff kept heading for Montevideo in Uruguay. Admittedly he had suffered two flesh wounds and been temporarily knocked unconscious. Once in Montevideo, a clever deception scheme by the British persuaded Langsdorff that a large force had now assembled and was waiting for him to emerge. The plan included the British Ambassador in Montevideo making considerable efforts to delay the *Graf Spee*'s sailing, to gain time for British reinforcements to arrive in the shape of the carrier *Ark Royal* and the battle cruiser *Renown*.

Langsdorff came to the conclusion that to engage in battle would lead to the certain loss of his ship and pointless sacrifice of his crew. Admiral Raeder, the Commander-in-Chief (C-in-C) of the German Navy, and Hitler both agreed that it was out of the question to accept internment of the *Graf Spee* by Uruguay.

At 16.15 hours on 17 December, the *Graf Spee* with a skeleton crew weighed anchor and moved slowly into the estuary of the Plate. At 7.36 pm, her ensign was hauled down. Twenty minutes later her structure was shattered by explosive charges. Amid billowing smoke and flames, she settled on a sandbank. The *Ark Royal* and *Renown* were still 1,600 kilometres (1,000 miles) away.

Three days later, Langsdorff wrapped himself up in the Imperial German Ensign (not the Swastika) and shot himself, having written in a final letter: "I alone bear the responsibility for scuttling the Panzerschiff *Admiral Graf Spee*. I am happy to pay with my life to prevent any possible reflection on the honour of the flag."

9 Churchill's Cigar

Many photographs of Winston Churchill depict him with a cigar either in his mouth or in his hand. There is even one of him at the controls of the aircraft that flew him home from Washington in January 1942, with a large cigar jutting out into the cockpit.

In November 1895, just ten days short of his 21st birthday, Churchill – who had graduated from Sandhurst at the end of the previous year and was now a second lieutenant in the 4th Hussars – accompanied his friend Reginald Barnes to Cuba, where Spanish forces were attempting to crush a rebellion by the islanders. Before leaving he persuaded the *Daily Graphic* to publish his reports on the insurrection. He also went to see Field Marshal Lord Wolseley, Commander-in-Chief of the British Army, who gave him clearance to see the Director of Military Intelligence (DMI), General Chapman. The DMI gave him maps and intelligence, and asked him to garner as much information as he could on a number of military matters, including the effect of the new metal-jacket bullet.

Few second lieutenants, then or now, would have sufficient clout to gain direct access to such elevated folk. It was an indication of the influence that Churchill had by virtue of his family connections. As well as bringing back information, he wrote to his mother, Lady Randolph Churchill, "I shall bring back a great many Havana cigars, some of which can be laid down in the cellars of 35 Great Cumberland Place" – his mother's new London home.

Churchill spent about a month in Cuba, where he filed five despatches for the *Daily Graphic*, saw some fighting and gained some sympathy for the rebel cause. On the soldierly qualities of Spanish troops, he told the *New York World*: "I make no reflections on their courage, but they are well versed in the art of retreat." During one attack, he was moving with General Valdez, who, as he later wrote to his mother, "drew a great deal of fire on to us and I heard enough bullets whistle and hum to satisfy me for some time to come". Bullets sound, as he reported to the *Daily Graphic*, "sometimes like a sigh, sometimes like a whistle, and at others like the buzz of an offended hornet". Churchill was never to lose the taste for being near the action, of which he was to see a great deal during his life. King George VI had to write and forbid him to be present off the Normandy beaches on 6 June 1944.

The other lifelong habit he acquired in Cuba was smoking cigars: Cubans. He was as good as his word to his mother, and brought a large stock back with him. For the rest of his life he smoked between six and ten a day. He wore a cigar cutter on his watch chain, but never used it, preferring to pierce the end with a match. He was also careless with his ash, and his clothes and carpets had numerous burn marks on them.

During the Potsdam Conference (16 July–2 August 1945) after the end of the War in Europe, Stalin told Churchill that he had taken to smoking cigars. Churchill replied that if a photograph of a cigar-smoking Stalin could be flashed across the world, it wo uld cause an immense sensation. On Churchill's return to England after the Yalta Conference (4–11 February 1945), he gave a banquet for King Ibn Saud of Saudi Arabia at Lake Fayyum in Egypt. He was told that the King, a strict Wahhabi Muslim, would not allow smoking in his presence. Churchill reported later: "I was the host and I said that if it was his religion that made him say such things, my religion prescribed as an absolute sacred ritual smoking cigars and drinking alcohol before, after and, if need be, during all meals and the intervals between them; complete surrender." The King, however, got his own back. Churchill was given a drink: "It seemed a very nasty cocktail. Found out afterwards it was an aphrodisiac," he reported.

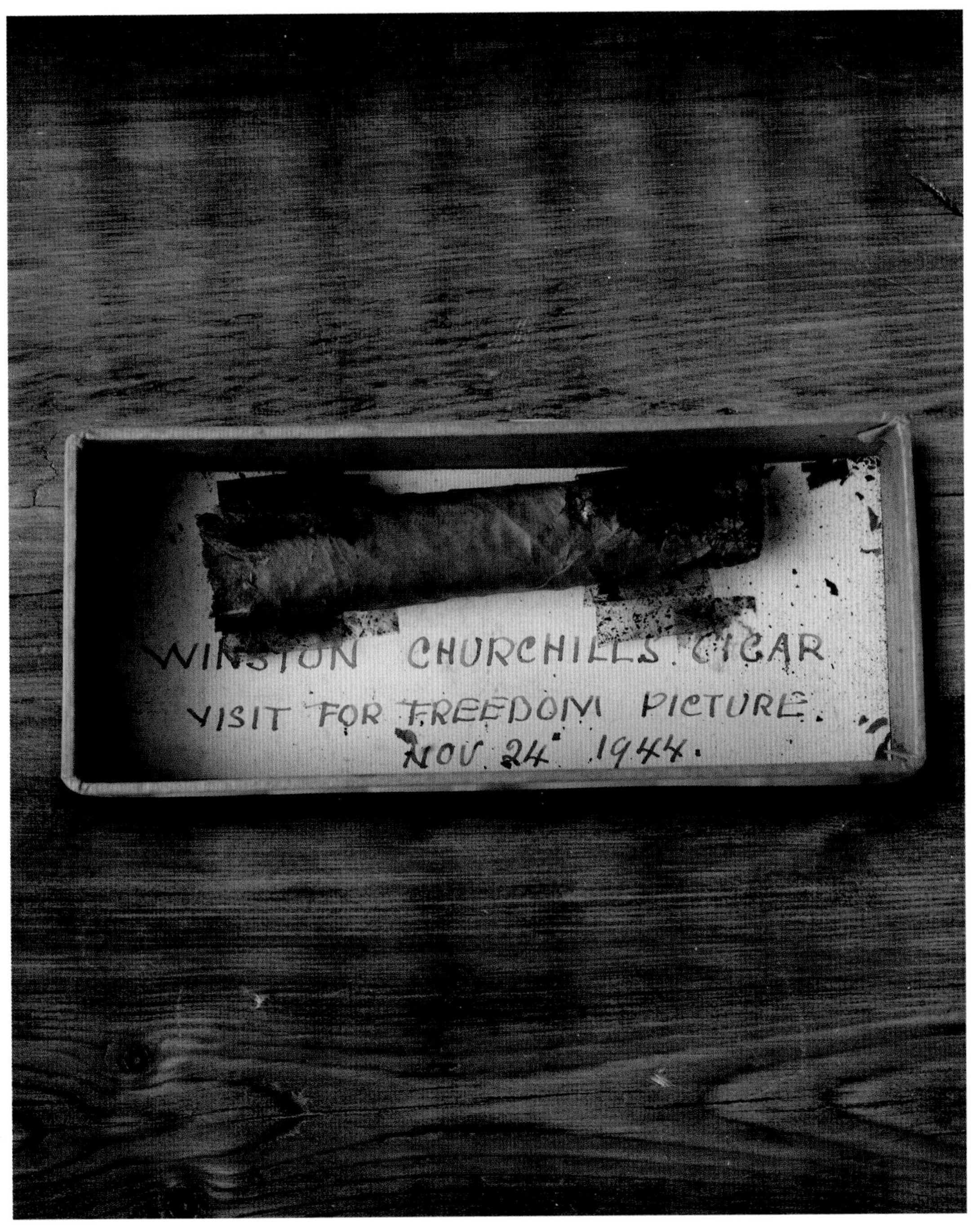

LEFT: Churchill in a "siren suit" smoking a cigar in his study.

ABOVE: A cigar half-smoked by Churchill sold at Bonhams on 17 January 2011.

10 The U-boat

The terms of the 1919 Treaty of Versailles specifically forbade Germany from owning any submarines – *Unterseeboot* (hence known as U-boats). However, in 1922, the Germans set up a design bureau at The Hague in the Netherlands to ensure that they did not fall behind in submarine development. Using yards in Rotterdam and in Helsinki in Finland, they constructed submarines for export to Turkey, Spain and Finland. A number of designs were prepared which would form the basis for future German submarines. The Germans also ran a secret submarine-crew-training programme in Finnish boats. Thus, when Hitler came to power in Germany, and revoked the Versailles Treaty, it was possible to begin the construction of submarines and expand the number of U-boat crews without delay.

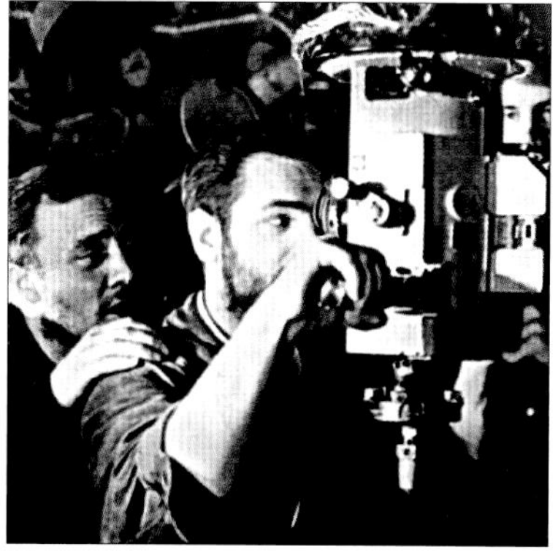

In January 1935, construction of U-boats began at Bremen in Germany. The first boats, Type 1 A, were based on those built for Finland and Spain. On 25 March 1935, Germany announced her intention to re-arm. Ten Type VIIA boats, based on earlier designs, were built within ten months. These were the basis of the highly successful Type VII B and VII C boats that became the workhorse of the German navy, and operated in the Battle of the Atlantic from 1939 to 1943.

Like the submarines of any navy in the Second World War, U-boats only dived when necessary. They had good endurance and surface speed when using their diesel engines. Using electric batteries when it dived, a typical submarine could motor for about one hour at around eight knots, or for four days at two knots. But the air became foul after about a day submerged, despite oxygen supplies and CO^2 absorption equipment, which the Germans were the first to develop. When the batteries became too low to provide power, the submarine had to surface to start diesels and recharge. The surface range of large submarines motoring on diesels without refuelling was many times that of any destroyer. The big German Type VII C had a range of 23,300 kilometres (12,600 nautical miles), and 59,300 kilometres (32,000 nautical miles) for the even bigger IX D. The Germans used large Type XIV *Milchkuh* or "Milch Cow" submarines as tankers to extend the range of their boats in the South Atlantic and Mediterranean.

By mid-1942, the Allied development of centimetric airborne radar, carried in very-long-range aircraft covering large areas of the Atlantic, made surfacing at night very hazardous for all U-boats, including "Milch Cows". The Germans, searching for a solution, remembered that they had found the answer on Dutch submarines captured when they overran Holland in 1940. This consisted of a pipe that could reach the surface from a dived submarine at periscope depth. A valve at the top closed the pipe automatically when the submarine dived or an unexpectedly large wave covered the top, just as the ball in a recreational diver's snorkel does today. By mid-1944 about half the U-boat fleet had been fitted with these *Schnorchels*. But there were problems with *Schnorchel*-fitted boats: the boat could not exceed about six knots or the *Schnorchel* would break off; and sometimes the valve would stick in the closed position, so the diesels sucked air from inside the boat until the engine shut down for lack of oxygen, meanwhile causing a vacuum in the boat resulting in very painful eardrums and even deafness among the crew; and finally, the noise of the running diesels blanked out the boat's sound-detection that warned of approaching enemy escorts.

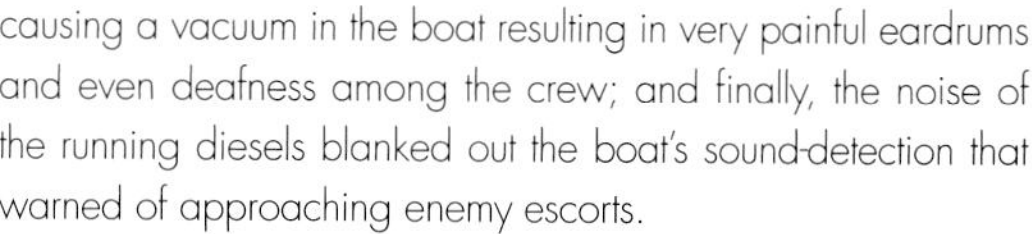

The Germans constantly sought improvements to their boats in order to frustrate the Allies' increasingly effective anti-submarine measures. The Type XXI Electro boat, with greatly increased battery capacity, had a top submerged speed of 17.2 knots, and a range at five knots of 676 kilometres (365 nautical miles) without using its *Schnorchel* except to refresh air in the boat. Luckily for the Allies, this type arrived too late to take part in active operations. Even more fortunately, so did another German invention: a boat with a turbine propulsion system supplied with oxygen and steam from the chemical reaction of hydrogen peroxide. It needed no air from outside the boat, and was the forerunner of the nuclear boats of today.

LEFT: A German U-boat captain tracking his target through the periscope.

ABOVE: The U-505 in the Atlantic west of Africa after its capture on 4 June 1944 by a US Navy Task Force consisting of the escort carrier USS *Guadalcanal* and escorts.

11 The Maginot Line

At the outbreak of the Second World War, the French relied heavily on the Maginot Line, either to deter Germany from invading or to frustrate any attempts to do so. It was named after the War Minister from 1929 to 1932, who as Sergeant Maginot had been wounded at Verdun during the First World War. Loss of some of the forts defending Verdun had nearly cost the French the battle. Their experiences there and during other battles in the First World War, and the terrible losses they suffered, persuaded the French that fortresses and artillery were the answer in any future war. They fell into the age-old trap of planning to fight the next war on the basis of the previous one.

Constructed between 1930 and 1935, and extending from Luxembourg to the Swiss border, the Maginot Line was not really a line but a string of concrete forts built about five kilometres (three miles) apart and interspersed with smaller casemates. Both types were well buried, with only observation cupolas and gun turrets visible, and even these in many cases could be lowered flush with the roof. Advanced-warning posts, anti-tank obstacles, wire and mines screened the forts. The garrisons varied from about 12 to 30 men in each casemate, and from 200 to 1,200 in the forts. The latter were like underground villages, with barracks, kitchens, generators, magazines and even electric railways to transport men and ammunition from barrack and magazine to the gun positions. Casemates contained machine guns and one 47-mm (1.85-in) anti-tank gun, with heavy artillery in the forts.

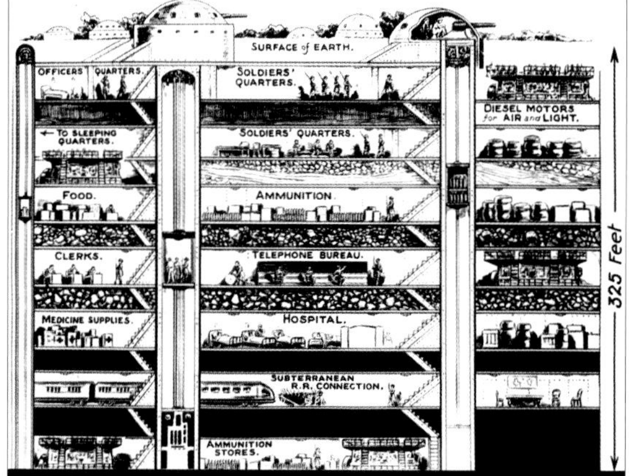

Belgium was still an ally of France when the Maginot Line was being built, and so extending the line to cover the 400 kilometres (250 miles) of the Franco–Belgian border was considered tactless, as it would send a signal of no confidence in Belgium's capability to resist invasion and would isolate her on the "wrong side" of the line. An added disincentive to extending the line was cost. The 139 kilometres (87 miles) completed by 1935 had cost 4,000 million francs, an overspend of 3,000 million francs. Finally, an extension of the line would run through the heavily industrialized region of Lille-Valenciennes, causing major disruption to French industry. To avoid losing this region, as they had in the First World War, the French decided that they would have to stop the invader before he crossed the French frontier. So when Belgium naively decided to opt for a policy of strict neutrality, the French planned to enter Belgian territory from the west the moment the Germans invaded from the east, with or without Belgian permission. When Belgian neutrality did not spare them from invasion in May 1940, the French were allowed in, but instead of fighting from behind the concrete and steel of the Maginot line on which so much treasure had been spent, they were forced to engage in a mobile battle of encounter in open country, a contest for which they were neither mentally prepared nor organized.

This would have been unsettling enough, but the German armoured advance through the supposedly "impassable to armoured vehicles" Ardennes, which sliced the French armies in half, was the final straw that broke the French. They had deployed their best formations into Belgium, and thus deprived themselves of the means to form a reserve. When Winston Churchill flew to Paris to find out what was happening, he asked General Maurice Gamelin, commander of all French land forces, "*Où est la masse de manoeuvre?*" (Where is your strategic reserve?), to which Gamelin replied, "*Aucune*" (There isn't one). The soldiers who might have formed a reserve were sitting uselessly on the Maginot Line. Although at the last minute some troops were pulled out of the line, they possessed neither the training nor the equipment in the shape of amour or mobile artillery to fight as a strategic reserve against a highly mobile enemy.

LEFT: A drawing of the Maginot Line that appeared in a British illustrated magazine in January 1940. It was a piece of propaganda aimed at reassuring the British public by depicitng the impregnable Maginot Line with its stocks of food, medical supplies and underground hospital. The internal railway was actually of a much more modest size.

ABOVE: In the foreground, a steel gun or observation cupola, which could be lowered flush with the ground during a heavy artillery bombardment. In the background a concrete casemate housing heavier artillery.

BELOW: French officers show visiting British officers the Maginot Line.

12 Civilian Gas Masks

Both well before and during the first two years of the Second World War, it was believed that any attack on the United Kingdom would include gas. This was because it had been used frequently during the fighting in the First World War against troops in the field, although never against civilians. Furthermore, proponents of air power, such as the Italian General Giulio Douhet, had forecast the use of gas against cities. He and others were responsible for most of the predictions that aerial bombing would cause the rapid collapse of any populations subjected to it. In the event, these predictions proved wildly exaggerated, but among those who believed them were Britain's political leaders. Their fears were fed by the RAF's insistence that the bomber would always get through, a claim that helped in the battle with the other services for funding. Along with Douhet, they proved to be wrong.

In September 1939, the only power to have an offensive gas capability was the Soviet Union. The Germans had about 2,900 tons of gas but no means of delivering it, as Hitler had banned its use. As the war progressed, they also developed a variety of lethal nerve gases, but never used them. Despite these facts, the British believed that such weapons would be used against their civilian population, and perception was everything. British gas protection, detection and decontamination equipment were rated the best in the world. By 1938, gas masks for the civilian population were being manufactured in such quantities that by September 1939 some 38 million gas masks had been issued to households all over the country.

Everyone was required to carry their gas mask in its cardboard container with them at all times. Posters exhorting them to do so were widespread, as were instructions on how to don the mask. There were special masks for children and for babies. Wardens carried wooden gas rattles that would warn of an impending gas attack. A bell would signal the All Clear.

Civilians were not issued with protective clothing of any kind, so had mustard gas, for example, been used, their exposed skin would have been badly blistered. Thus, despite the universal issue of masks, and penalties for not carrying them, the protection measures instituted in Britain were not as effective as they might at first sight seem.

As the war progressed, people stopped carrying their gas masks, and soldiers, who in 1940 were never seen without them, stopped carrying them too. Paradoxically, this was just as the Germans were starting to develop the nerve agent Tabun, and by the end of the war an even more deadly gas, Sarin, was ready for production, with the deadliest of them all, Soman, under development. Neither the civilian population nor the armed forces of any Allied nation had clothing capable of giving protection against nerve gas.

In the event, the gas masks issued to the civilian population of Britain were never needed, and fear of retaliation prevented the Germans from using nerve gas.

ABOVE: An air raid warden gives directions to a mother and two children during a gas drill in Southend.

LEFT: A poster reminding people to carry their gas masks at all times and showing the correct way to hold it before pulling it on.

BELOW: A gas mask of the type issued to the civilian population of Britain.

Hitler will send
no warning –
so always carry
your gas mask
ISSUED BY THE MINISTRY OF HOME

13 The Mitsubishi A6M Zero

The Mitsubishi Zero, the most famous of all Japanese aircraft of the Second World War, was the first carrier-based aircraft to outperform contemporary land-based fighters. Its appearance when Japan attacked Pearl Harbor, and during the next year of the war, came as a great shock to the Americans and British, who had failed to note its performance in China in late 1940 and ignored reports by the US General Claire Lee Chennault, commander of the Flying Tigers operating in support of Chinese forces, a year before America came into the war.

The A6M Zero was built by Mitsubishi in response to the Japanese navy's demand for a fighter with a top speed of 500 kph (311 mph) and fitted with two cannon and two machine guns. It was put into production in 1940, the Japanese year 2600, so it became popularly known as the Zero-Sen (Type 0 fighter), and to its enemies it was the "Zero", although its official Allied codename was "Zeke". It first flew operationally in China in mid-1940 and in the first year of the war the Zero swept away Allied fighter opposition so completely that the Japanese began to believe it was invincible.

The Zero was light, manoeuvrable and had exceptionally long range. Its maximum speed at 563 kph (350 mph) exceeded the original specification and it had a range of 3.060 kilometres (1,900 miles) with a drop tank. The American equivalent carrier fighter had a range of 2,820 kilometres (1,750 miles). The Zero was able to operate from island bases if a carrier was not available; for example, during the Guadalcanal Campaign (7 August 1942–February 1943), Zeros were able to fly from islands 1,050 kilometres (650 miles) away from the combat area. At low speeds, the lightly built Zero could easily out-turn its heavier American opponents. At the beginning of the war it could climb twice as fast as its

LEFT: Deck handlers on the flight deck of the Imperial Japanese navy carrier *Hiryu* prepare Zero fighters just before launching for the raid on Pearl Harbor on 7 December 1941.

ABOVE: A Zero as seen in the World War II gallery at the National Museum of the United States Air Force.

rivals. It was one of the most agile fighters ever built and in the hands of its well-trained navy pilots it was deadly, able to match any fighter in the world. This led the Americans to adopt the saying, "Never get into a dogfight with a Zero."

It had one drawback: in order to achieve this performance, and carry heavier guns than its rival US and British fighters, it sacrificed protection. The Zero pilot was not protected by armour, nor did the aircraft have self-sealing fuel tanks. By the end of 1943, when the Zero was starting to lose its edge over American fighters, notably the Grumman F6F Hellcat, the Japanese produced the A6M5c Zero. Improvements included a large canvas flotation bag in the rear end of the fuselage in case the aircraft ditched, mainly for use on take-off or landing in the vicinity of the carrier. It had a 20-mm (0.8-in) cannon and 13.2-mm (0.5-in) heavy machine gun on each wing, as well as a heavy machine gun over the engine, which fired through the propeller. But other than armoured glass in the cockpit, it still had no armour or self-sealing fuel tanks. The improvements made to the Zero were not enough to enable it to take on the Hellcat with any great chance of success.

As the tide turned against Japan, this great fighter aircraft was mainly used in the suicide Kamikaze role.

14 The 88-mm Gun

The German 88-mm gun, the anti-tank weapon most feared by the Allies in the Second World War, was originally produced as an anti-aircraft, or *flak* gun – *flak* being German slang for *Fliegerabwehrkanone* or anti-aircraft gun. In its anti-aircraft version, thousands of 88s were produced during the war. It had a very high muzzle velocity and ceiling (the distance up in the sky to which it could shoot). Although not as powerful as the nearest British equivalent, the 3.7-in (94-mm) heavy anti-aircraft gun, the 88's high muzzle velocity and hence flat trajectory was what made it such a formidable anti-tank gun.

The Germans first realized the potential of the 88 as an anti-tank weapon during the Spanish Civil War (1936–39) when the German Condor Legion employed it against armoured vehicles. During the 1940 Battle for France, the British and French faced this weapon for the first time, as the German army order of battle in France and Flanders included *flak* battalions. The Germans found that their 37-mm anti-tank guns could not penetrate the frontal armour of the British Matilda MkII and French Char B tanks, whereas the 88-mm shell could. Perhaps the most dramatic demonstration of this occurred during the British counter-stroke at Arras on 21 May 1940, where the British met Erwin Rommel for the first time in the war, when he was a major-general commanding the 7th Panzer Division. Rommel personally ordered his anti-aircraft guns to fire on the British tanks attacking Wailly, southwest of Arras, bringing the British advance to a dead stop.

The British were slow to learn. The Germans repeatedly used the 88 in North Africa to devastating effect, a favourite ploy being to pull their armour back through a shield of well-concealed 88s, which then shattered the British tanks following as if they were hunting a fox. By now the anti-tank version of the 88 had been officially designated *Panzerabwehrkanone* or PAK for short, meaning anti-armour gun.

In Russia, the 88 proved to be the only anti-tank gun able to penetrate armour of the Soviet T34; except at very close range, shells from German 37-mm and 50-mm anti-tank guns bounced off. The flat terrain of Russia suited the characteristics of the 88 perfectly, as did the desert. It was less effective in the *bocage* in Normandy or the mountains of Italy, although still greatly feared.

The versatility of the 88 was never better demonstrated than during the battle codenamed Goodwood, 18–20 July 1944, during the Normandy campaign. This operation was an attempt by three British armoured divisions to break out into open country east of Caen. The rolling country, interspersed with small woods and villages, was very different to the *bocage* further west. After making good progress, the British 11th Armoured Division was approaching the village of Cagny, when mayhem ensued. Cagny was occupied by four 88-mm *flak* guns of the 16th Luftwaffe Field Division. Also in the village was Colonel Hans von Luck, a battle group commander of 21st Panzer Division. He ordered the Luftwaffe officer in command to engage the approaching British armour. When the Luftwaffe officer demurred, von Luck prodded him in the stomach with his pistol, saying, "You can either die now, or later winning a medal." The 88s were duly switched from pointing at the sky and re-laid on the approaching tanks. The 11th Armoured Division lost a total of 126 tanks that day, many of them to the 88s.

The 88-mm was arguably the best anti-tank gun on either side in the Second World War. It was also mounted in several types of armoured fighting vehicle, notably the Nashorn, Ferdinand and Jagdpanther tank destroyers and the Tiger tank.

LEFT: An 88 on an anti-aircraft mount, a *flak* 36 cruciform, engages armour in Russia.

ABOVE: An 88 gun on wheeled mount, easy to tow and quicker to deploy than on anti-aircraft mount; especially useful in the anti-tank role.

15 The Little Ships

The role of the "little ships" in the evacuation of the British Expeditionary Force (BEF) from Dunkirk between 26 May and 4 June 1940 is perhaps the thing that most people remember about the event.

In 1940, Dunkirk was the biggest harbour on the Channel coast. It had seven deep-water basins, four dry docks and eight kilometres (five miles) of quays. When the decision was made to evacuate the BEF, the port was under almost continuous attack by the Luftwaffe and fires and extensive damage made the quays unusable. A plan was therefore put forward to take the troops off the 16 kilometres (ten miles) of beach east of Dunkirk. These shelved gently, so even small craft could get no nearer to the waterline than about a hundred metres/yards, and soldiers had to wade out to them. There were no jetties, fishing harbours or piers. Large vessels had to anchor well offshore, and craft ferrying troops to them had a long turnaround time. Clearly the more small craft, the quicker the job would be done.

The officer responsible for organizing the evacuation (Operation Dynamo) was Vice Admiral Bertram Ramsay, the Flag Officer Dover. He arranged for the Admiralty Small Boat Pool to gather at Ramsgate as many small craft as could be found: tugs, trawlers, dredgers, fishing boats (some still under sail), cockle boats, yachts and small motor cruisers whose owners loved "messing about in boats". Here their skippers, mostly their owners, were issued with charts, many of them with the course to Dunkirk already laid out for them. Many skippers had never crossed the Channel before and their knowledge of navigation was sparse; some had never even left the Thames. Navigation was made more challenging by the fact that the direct course for Dunkirk ran near Calais, which was occupied by the Germans who shelled any vessel that came within range, making an alternative "dog leg" course necessary. British minefields laid in the Channel were an additional hazard, and it was necessary to keep to the swept route.

Admiral Ramsay's representative ashore at Dunkirk was Captain W G Tennant, with a beach party of 12 officers and 150 ratings. His arrival on 27 May coincided with repeated German air raids. By the end of that day it was apparent that evacuation from the beaches was desperately slow. By midnight on 27/28 May, only 7,669 men had arrived in England, and about two-thirds of these had loaded in Dunkirk harbour before its use was suspended. But Tennant spotted that the 1,600-metre/yard-long East Mole protecting Dunkirk harbour was connected to the beaches by a narrow causeway, and that evening he ordered a destroyer to come alongside the Mole, followed by six more. The gamble succeeded, and this became the principal means of evacuation. Late on the afternoon of 28 May, the first "little ships" appeared off the beaches. The evacuation gained momentum. Nevertheless, 30 May was the only day on which more men were lifted from the beaches (29,512) than from the harbour (24,311), and the day's total was the largest so far. The job of the "little ships" was to ferry troops out to waiting ships offshore. The courage displayed by civilian crews ploughing back and forth hour after hour, day after day, in the face of bombing was unquestionable.

At 14.23 hours on 4 June, the Admiralty gave the signal ending Operation Dynamo. Originally it was thought that some 45,000 soldiers might be rescued; in the end a total of 338,226 was reached. That the contribution of the "little ships" to the successful evacuation from the Dunkirk beaches was significant is without doubt, but their role has become the enduring myth of the operation to the extent of obliterating the contribution of the Royal and Merchant Navies. This can be understood in the context of the time – to boost national morale and cohesion, the story of the "little ships" was milked as hard as possible. The facts are that over two and a half times as many troops were taken from Dunkirk harbour than from the beaches, and of those taken off the beaches, the majority were transported in destroyers or other ships, albeit in many cases ferried out to these larger vessels, either by "little ships" or ships' boats. The actual number of men taken directly from the beaches to England by the "little ships" was small.

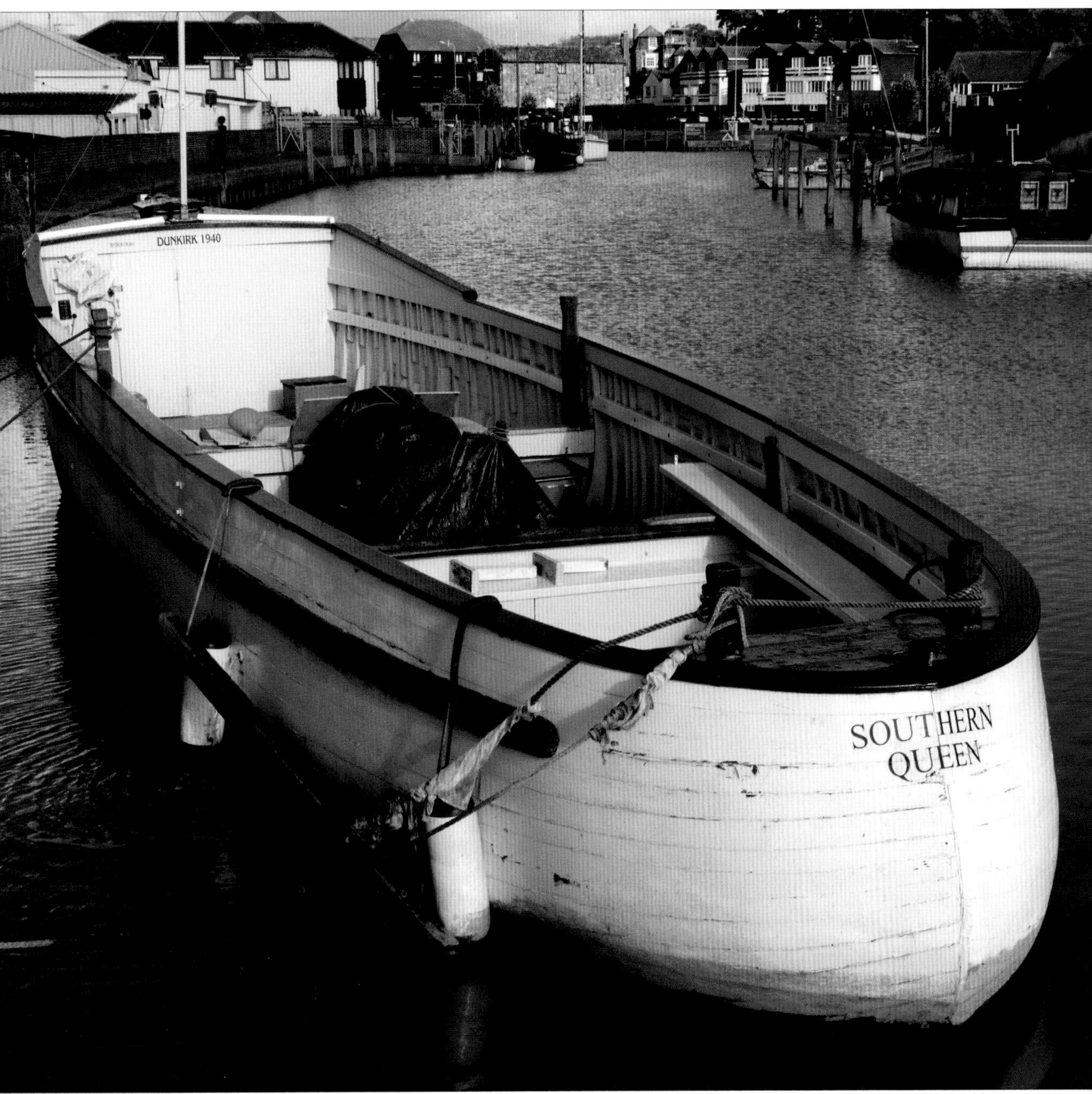

LEFT: Low tide on the beaches between Dunkirk and La Panne; British troops await evacuation.

ABOVE: One of the Dunkirk "little ships", moored in Rye harbour.

OVERLEAF: A river motor cruiser gets a tow from a trawler, both laden with troops from the Dunkirk beaches.

16 The Airborne Smock

Among the specialized items of equipment issued to British airborne troops in the Second World War, perhaps the most popular with the troops themselves was the airborne smock. The first pattern was modelled on the German parachutist's jump jacket, which was made to be stepped into and pulled up like a pair of overalls, except that the legs were cut off just above the knee. This was replaced by the "Smock Denison Airborne" (listed as such in the quartermaster's stores), designed by Major Denison. This was a camouflage-pattern, cotton, semi-waterproof garment that was put on and removed over the head like a jersey. It had a zipped collar, which opened as far down as the lower chest, knitted woollen cuffs and four external pockets, two on the chest and two below the waist. The inside of the collar was lined with khaki flannel.

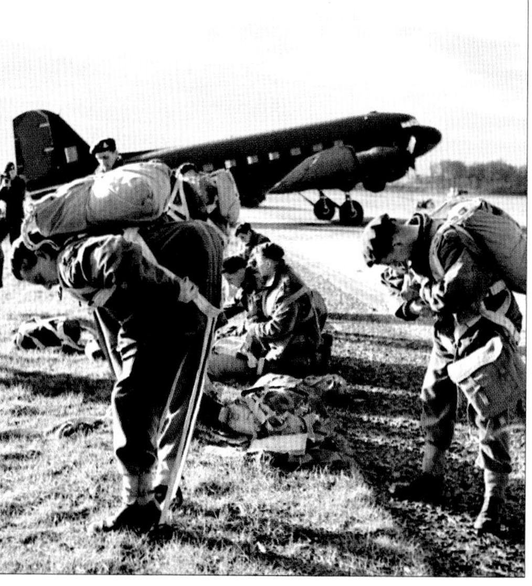

It had a tail on the back, which could be taken up between the legs and fastened by press-studs inside the front skirt of the smock, to prevent the skirt riding up. The tail sometimes rubbed uncomfortably when the wearer was running about in the field, and soldiers left it unfastened, hanging down. Arabs in North Africa referred to the soldiers of the 1st Parachute Brigade as "the men with tails". A later version of the smock had press-studs on the back of the skirt so that the tail could be folded back and fastened to the back.

The Denison Smock was worn over the standard issue battledress. It was an excellent garment and highly prized not only by airborne soldiers but also by commandos, who were issued with it in late 1944. Its outside pockets, and the fact that it covered the wearer's nether regions, made it a considerable improvement on battledress, which had been introduced in 1939. This had been modelled on fashionable ski outfits of the late 1930s and was not a clever design for a fighting soldier. The blouse had insufficient pockets, provided no cover for the nether regions, and after a few minutes crawling about often detached from the trousers. The map pocket on the front of the trousers, instead of the side, made extracting maps difficult while lying down taking cover. Many parachute soldiers modified their battledress trousers by sewing a capacious pocket on the side.

The Denison smock was worn under webbing equipment, small pack and ammunition pouches. However, it was found that parachute rigging lines occasionally snagged on equipment after the parachutist had left the aircraft, causing accidents and even fatalities. This led to the introduction of a sleeveless canvas over-smock, with full-length zip, and tail, which was worn over the equipment and Denison Smock. The over-smock had big elasticated pockets on the skirt for grenades, safer than descending with them clipped on the braces of the webbing – and gave the wearer a "pregnant" appearance. It was discarded after landing, and frequently the long zip was cut off and used to convert the Denison Smock to a full-length zip garment.

The Denison Smock was popular among senior officers, including those who had no connection with airborne forces but could use their influence to obtain an item of clothing that was supposed to be confined to parachute and commando troops. Montgomery frequently wore a full-zip version with a fur collar, as did General Miles Dempsey commanding the British Second Army.

The Airborne or Denison Smock was an example of a really good piece of kit, and was worn by airborne soldiers and commandos until the late 1970s.

LEFT: Soldiers of the British 6th Airborne Division fitting parachute harnesses on top of over-smocks and Denison Smocks before emplaning in Dakotas for Exercise Mush, 21–25 April 1944, a rehearsal for the Division's forthcoming task on 6 June 1944.

ABOVE: The second version of Denison Smock, with zip collar opening to the lower chest, flap and button closing at the wrists instead of knitted woollen cuffs.

17 The Cross of Lorraine

The double-barred French Cross of Lorraine dates back to the days of the Crusades. It was worn as a heraldic device by the Knights Templar, an order of warrior monks who played a prominent part in the Crusades. At that time the two crossbars were of equal length and placed equidistant down the shaft of the cross. Later, another version came into use, on which the two crossbars were placed near the top of the shaft, the top bar being shorter than the lower bar. The Cross of Lorraine was part of the coat of arms of the province of Lorraine. Following the French defeat in the Franco–Prussian War (1870–71), the northern part of Lorraine, along with Alsace, was annexed to Germany between 1871 and 1918. To many Frenchmen, the Cross of Lorraine became a symbol of the provinces lost to France and their determination to regain them. This they achieved following the First World War, only to lose them again in 1940.

Just before the fall of France in June 1940, the hitherto little-known French colonel, Charles de Gaulle, was promoted to brigadier general and appointed under-secretary for national defence. He was the most junior general in the French army. In this capacity he met Churchill twice at conferences between British and French ministers. He made a strong impression on the British Prime Minister, which was to bear fruit when France asked Germany for an armistice on 16 June. De Gaulle was flown to England in an RAF aircraft, and authorized to broadcast an appeal on BBC radio to Frenchmen to continue the fight. A few days later, the British government recognized de Gaulle as the leader of all Free Frenchmen, "wherever they may be", and agreed to finance the Free French forces. At this juncture, a French naval officer, Capitaine de Corvette (Lieutenant Commander) Thierry d'Argenlieu, suggested to General Charles de Gaulle that the Free French adopt the Cross of Lorraine as a symbol of resistance against the Germans with their Nazi Swastika. The Cross was borne on the tricolour flags of Free French warships, on their aircraft and on their uniforms.

To begin with, the most significant response to De Gaulle's appeal to join the Free French was a death sentence from the French government, now situated in the town of Vichy, whence it administered the rump of France left unoccupied by the Germans. In mid-August 1940 the Free French Army consisted of a mere 2,240 officers and soldiers. The first gleam of hope came when the colonies of French Equatorial Africa declared for de Gaulle in early 1941, partially sparked off by a British Long Range Desert Group patrol. This gave de Gaulle a base in Africa, and from there General Philippe Leclerc marched to join hands with the British in the Western Desert.

Despite this success, the years leading up to the complete liberation of France in autumn 1944 saw relations between de Gaulle and the British, and later the Americans, follow a roller-coaster pattern: up one day and down the next. In truth, the British never really trusted de Gaulle; and he did not improve matters by being aloof and exceedingly difficult at times. He was kept in the dark about the forthcoming invasion of French North Africa in November 1942. The Allies dealt exclusively with former Vichy French senior officers; and for a time it seemed that he would be shunted off into a siding. But clever political footwork led de Gaulle to regain command of all French armed forces in liberated parts of the world, including North Africa, by March 1944. Despite this, he was told neither the date nor the place for the invasion of Europe in June 1944. However, following a visit to Washington in July 1944, his Committee for National Liberation (CLFN) was recognized by the British and Americans as the authority in liberated France. He entered Paris on 26 August 1944 and was acclaimed by the people of Paris.

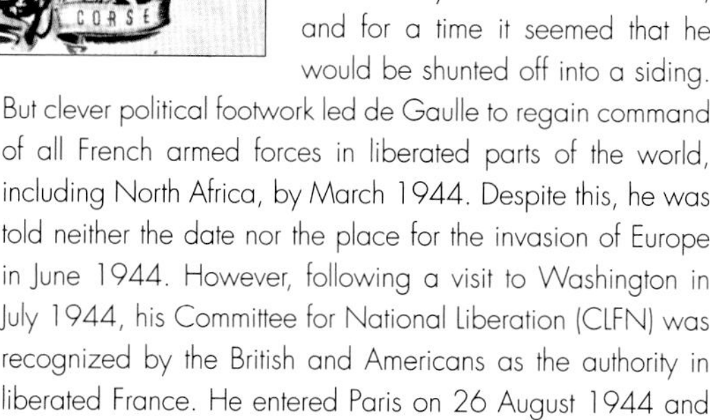

His relationship with Churchill in particular, and his British allies in general, is encapsulated in the remark made by a friend of Churchill's, Louis Spears, after de Gaulle had been especially obdurate at the Allied conference at Marrakech on 12 January 1944: "The hardest cross that Britain had to bear was the Cross of Lorraine."

LEFT: Free French propaganda poster with "France never gave up the fight" superimposed on the Cross of Lorraine and, anti-clockwise from top left, engagements and campaigns in which Free French forces took part: Bir Hacheim during the Gazala battle in the Western Desert, Fezzan in southern Libya, Tunisia, Corsica, Italy and the liberation of France. **ABOVE:** The Cross of Lorraine.

ABOVE: General Charles de Gaulle wearing a Cross of Lorraine badge above his left breast pocket.

RIGHT: The cover of a booklet issued by the French Ministry of War celebrating the liberation of Alsace and Lorraine between November 1944 and February 1945 by the French First Army under General Jean de Lattre de Tassigny.

DÉLIVRANCE

METZ NOVEMBRE 1944
MULHOUSE NOV. 1944
STRASBOURG NOV. 1944
COLMAR FÉVRIER 1945

8 PAGES

12 FRANCS

NUMÉRO ★ SPÉCIAL
SUR LA DÉLIVRANCE DE L'ALSACE ET DE LA LORRAINE
ÉDITÉ PAR LA DIRECTION DES SERVICES DE PRESSE DU MINISTÈRE DE LA GUERRE

18 The Spitfire

The Supermarine Spitfire is the most famous British aircraft ever built. It was among the fastest and most manoeuvrable fighters of the Second World War and served in every theatre of that war. One of the most beautiful aircraft ever produced, it was designed by R J Mitchell, the chief designer at Supermarine Aviation Works (part of Vickers Armstrong Aviation) in response to a British Air Ministry specification to produce a fighter capable of 404 kph (251 mph). He was not satisfied with his initial designs, and it was not until March 1936 that the first successful prototype took off from Eastleigh Airport (now Southampton Airport) piloted by Joseph "Mutt" Summers, Chief Test Pilot for Vickers. In June 1936, the Air Ministry placed the first order for 310 Spitfires. Although Mitchell died the following year as a result of cancer, he lived long enough to see his prototype fly.

Mitchell's design, the Spitfire MK1A, the first all-metal stressed-skin fighter to go into production in Britain, was an eight-gunned aircraft with elliptical wings powered by a Rolls Royce Merlin engine. Spitfires were hand-built and took three times as long to assemble as their main rival, the German Messerschmitt Bf 109E. But it was produced in sufficient numbers to play a key role in the Battle of Britain (July–October 1940). With a top speed in level flight of 570 kph (360 mph), it was comparable to the Messerschmitt BF109E (569 kph/354 mph), but more manoeuvrable in a tight turn, provided the pilot could withstand the G forces on his body. The bulged canopy gave the pilot a better all-round view than the Bf 109E, but the latter was faster

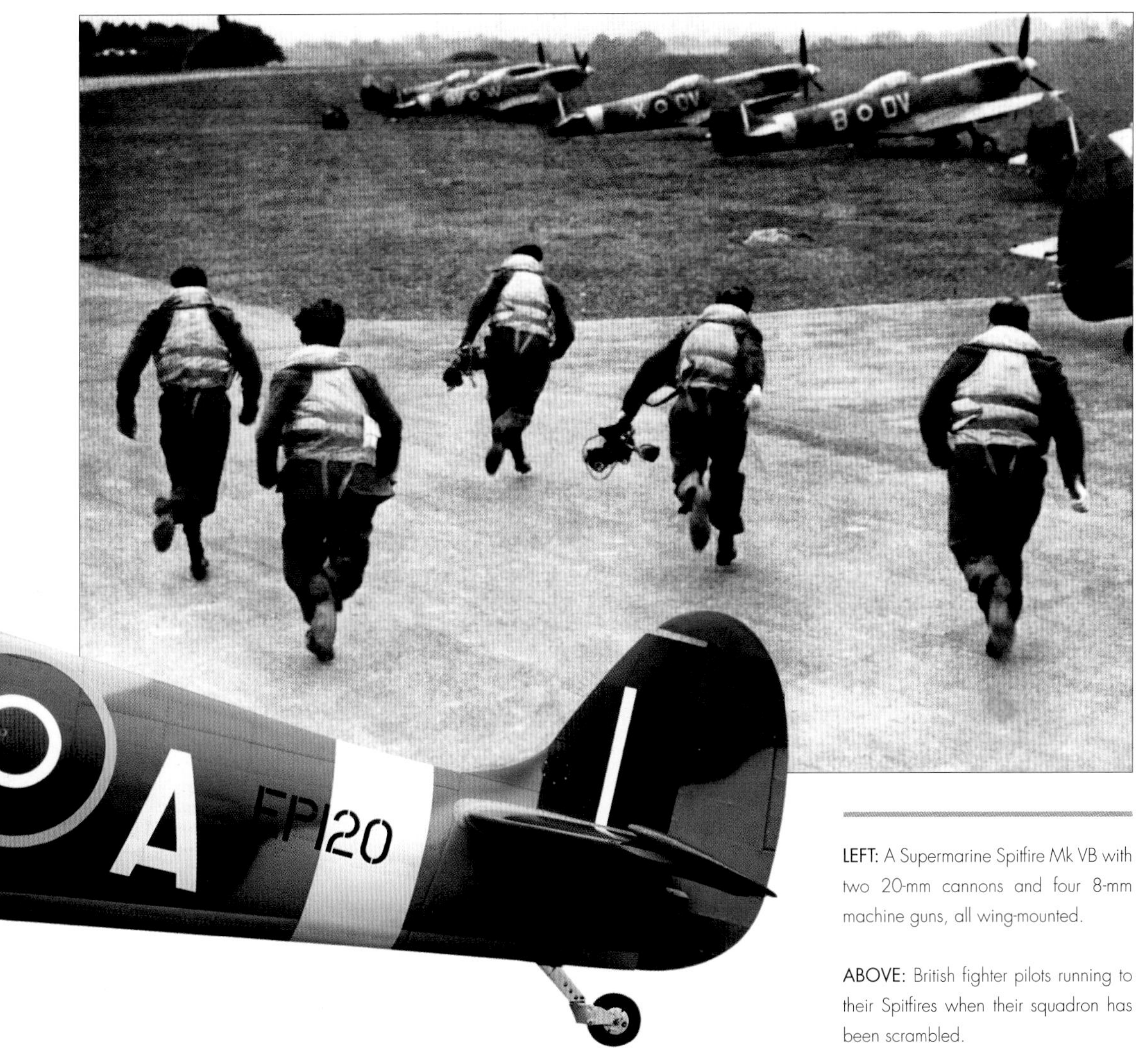

LEFT: A Supermarine Spitfire Mk VB with two 20-mm cannons and four 8-mm machine guns, all wing-mounted.

ABOVE: British fighter pilots running to their Spitfires when their squadron has been scrambled.

in a dive than the Spitfire MK1A, and had a higher ceiling, thanks to its fuel-injected engine. The Bf 109E's 20-mm cannon gave it a significant range and hitting power advantage over the Spitfire MK1A. In 1941, Spitfires came into service with two similar-sized cannon and four machine guns. The engine was constantly modified during the war, and in the later versions the Rolls Royce Griffon had twice the power of the original Merlin.

Eventually, 22,890 Spitfires of 19 different marks were built between 1936 and 1947. Although used as a fighter until the end of the war, its main role became high-level photo-reconnaissance. The United States Army Air Force flew more than 600 Spitfires during the Second World War. The Spitfire was modified to operate off carriers, and the Seafire, as it was called, played a significant part in air battles fought by the Royal Navy's Fleet Air Arm, especially in the Mediterranean during the North African campaign in 1942–43. The last of the 2,556 Seafires produced flew in the Korean War (1950–53) with considerable success.

The last mark of Spitfire produced during the Second World War was the MkXIX reconnaissance version, with a pressurized cockpit and wing tanks to give it a 2,896-kilometre (1,800 mile) range compared with the Mk1A's range of 635 kilometres (395 miles). In April 1954 the MkXIX flew the last-ever RAF Spitfire sortie over Malaya.

19 The Messerschmitt Bf 109

First produced in January 1937, long before any production Hurricanes or Spitfires, and thanks to its participation in the Spanish Civil War (1936–39), the Messerschmitt Bf 109 was a thoroughly combat-proven aircraft by the time of the Munich crisis in September 1938. Earlier versions were the 109 B, C and D (the original prototype being Type A), but by the outbreak of the Second World War the 109E was available in ever increasing numbers. Nicknamed the "Emil" by its pilots, the 109E outclassed all other fighters except the Spitfire during the first couple of years of the war.

It was a small aircraft, cheap to produce and very manoeuvrable, with a fast rate of climb and dive, and high acceleration. It was normally fitted with two, or sometimes three, 20-mm cannon as well as two machine guns, which gave the 109 greater range and hitting power than fighters carrying eight machine guns, notably the earlier Marks of Spitfires and Hurricanes. As the war progressed, the 109E and succeeding models were fitted with a variety of weapons including rockets and bombs. It had very narrow landing gear, specifically designed to allow wings to be removed for repair or replacement without having to place the fuselage on jacks; and to allow maintenance to be carried out on forward airstrips with minimal facilities. The narrow landing gear resulted in a pronounced swing on take-off and landing, which in the hands of an inexperienced pilot sometimes ended in a crash.

The cockpit was narrow with a poor forward view through armoured glass, and some pilots complained about the cramped conditions. One 109 ace, Adolf Galland, designed a higher cockpit hood named after him and fitted in the K series 109s.

The 109E, with a top speed of 569 kph (354 mph), was marginally slower than the Spitfire Mk 1A (570 kph/360

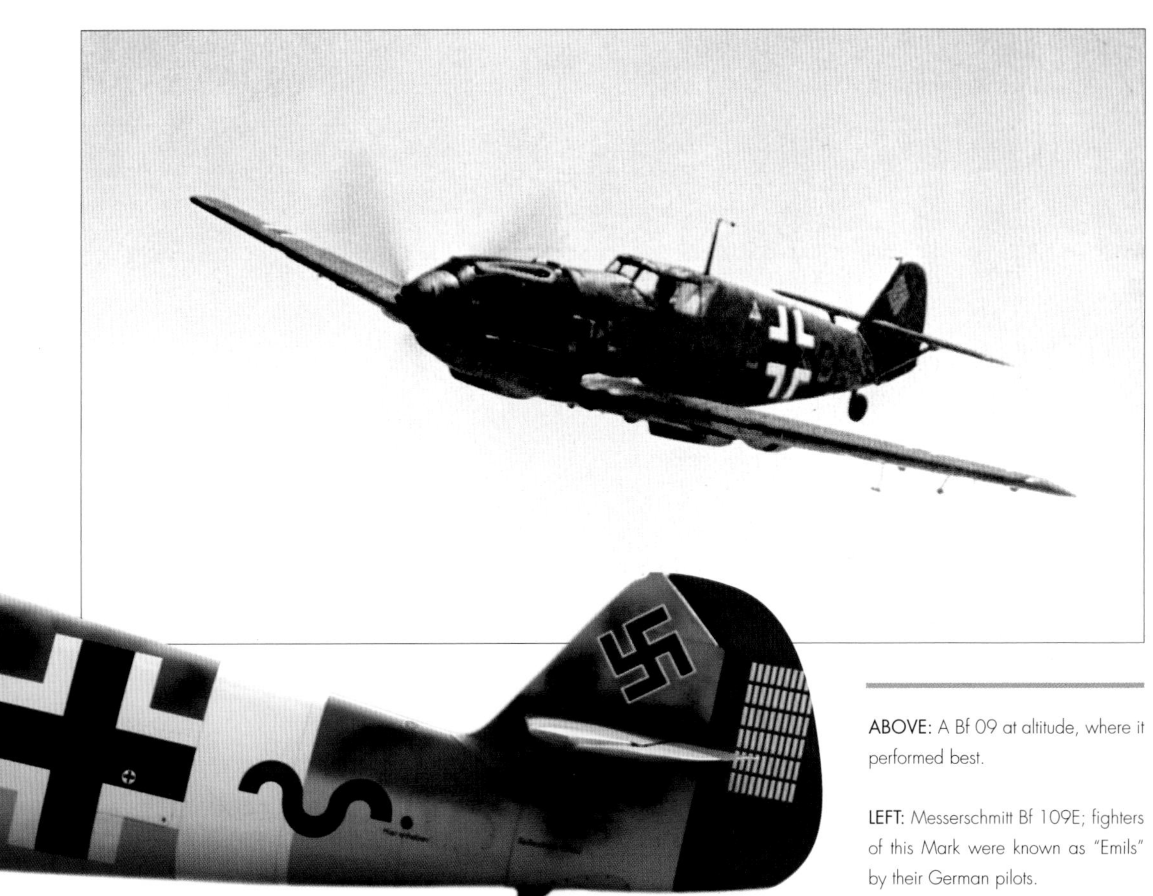

ABOVE: A Bf 09 at altitude, where it performed best.

LEFT: Messerschmitt Bf 109E; fighters of this Mark were known as "Emils" by their German pilots.

OVERLEAF: A Messerschmitt Bf 109E on the ground in 1941.

mph) at some altitudes, but faster in a dive and at very high altitude thanks to its two-stage engine supercharger. The Spitfire could turn more tightly than the 109E. The climb rate of the 109E was impressive: 1,005 metres (3,300 feet) per minute, compared with the Spitfire Mk 1A at 771 mpm (2,530 fpm) and Hurricane at 668 mpm (2,260 fpm). The 109-E outclassed the Hurricane (518 kph/322 mph) under all conditions.

Although it had control of the skies over Poland and France in the first year of the war, certain aspects of the Battle of Britain combined to limit the 109's effectiveness. If allowed to cross the Channel at around 9,100 metres (30,000 feet) and engage the Spitfires and Hurricanes on their own, the 109s proved superior. But the RAF turned the Hurricanes on the German bombers, dealing death and destruction at small loss to themselves. This forced the Luftwaffe to change tactics and order the 109s to escort the bomber stream if they were not to take unacceptable losses in their bomber force. Tied to the bombers, the 109s, without drop tanks (which were introduced later), could spend only 30 minutes over England, and were unable to fly high and use their superior diving and climbing speed to advantage. Their two-stage supercharger made the 109 far more effective at high altitude than their rivals. It is possible that had the Battle of Britain been fought at 9,100 metres (30,000 feet) the RAF would have lost.

Radar also gave the British an overpowering advantage by giving ample warning of the approach of raids, which the Germans had totally discounted in their strategic calculations. To engage the RAF, the German aircrew had long flights over water and a similar return trip. All these factors limited the effectiveness of the ME 109. The happy days of almost uncontested skies over Poland and France were gone.

20 The Fairey Swordfish

The Swordfish was obsolete before it entered service. It was an open cockpit, fabric and wire-braced bi-plane, looking like a survivor from the First World War rather than an aircraft of the Second. But it served throughout the Second World War in a variety of roles, and did magnificent work. It was designed as a torpedo attacking aircraft and carried one 18-in torpedo. Its maximum speed was a mere 222 kph (138 mph), but it had a respectable range of 1,694 kilometres (1,028 miles) and could carry as good a weapon load as the Japanese carrier-borne bomber, the B5N Kate, and a far better one than the American Douglas Devastator. The latter was more advanced, but far less effective than the Swordfish, which was the most successful British torpedo bomber of the war, sinking more ships than all the Royal Navy's battleships added together.

The Swordfish usually had a crew of three: pilot, observer (navigator in RAF parlance), and a radio operator/air gunner. His single Vickers K .303-in machine gun was no match for a modern fighter. The pilot communicated with his crew through a voice pipe, known as a Gosport tube. The Swordfish was nicknamed the "Stringbag" because, like the household shopping bag of the time, it seemed to be able to carry anything and was infinitely flexible and indestructible. It could be patched up much more quickly than more sophisticated aircraft.

On 11 November 1940, 21 Swordfish were launched from the carrier *Illustrious* 285 kilometres (180 miles) from the Italian fleet main base at Taranto. They attacked in two waves, an hour apart. Surprise was complete; one new and two old battleships were torpedoed, a cruiser was hit, and the dockyard damaged. Two Swordfish were lost, but the balance of maritime power in the Mediterranean tilted in favour of the Royal Navy. The Commander-in-Chief Mediterranean Fleet, Admiral Andrew Cunningham wrote:

> *The 11th and 12th November 1940 will be remembered for ever as having shown once and for all that in the Fleet Air Arm the Navy has a devastating weapon. In a total flying time of about six and a half hours carrier to carrier, twenty aircraft inflicted more damage upon the Italian Fleet than was inflicted on the German High Seas Fleet in the daylight action of Jutland.* (*Engage the Enemy More Closely: The Royal Navy in the Second World War*, by Correlli Barnett, Hodder & Stoughton, 1991, page 249)

One outcome of the attack was not so welcome. The Japanese took note that battleships could be attacked in harbour by torpedo-carrying aircraft, and duly put this into effect a year later at Pearl Harbor.

Six months after Taranto, the Swordfish struck another devastating blow. The German battleship *Bismarck*, having sunk the British battle cruiser *Hood* in the Denmark Strait on 24 May 1941, was heading for Brest to repair damage inflicted in the battle. A Swordfish strike launched from the *Victorious* early on 25 May failed to damage the *Bismarck* further. As the *Bismarck* neared Brest, and Luftwaffe fighter cover, the Home Fleet battleships pursuing her in heavy seas were running short of fuel and lagging 210 kilometres (130 miles) behind. But the *Ark Royal* in Admiral James Somerville's Force H was about 65 kilometres (40 miles) north-east of the *Bismarck*. A Swordfish strike was launched and one torpedo hit the *Bismarck's* rudder, crippling her. The Home Fleet battleships caught up and sank her.

Swordfish were also extensively employed in the anti-submarine role carrying a radar set and rockets. The aircraft could carry depth charges, mines and bombs, and its long endurance enabled it to remain on patrol over convoys for hours. A total of 2,391 Swordfishes were built between 1934 and 1944. The last front-line Swordfish squadron was disbanded on 21 May 1945, two weeks after VE Day. The "Stringbag" had outlasted many of its more modern rivals.

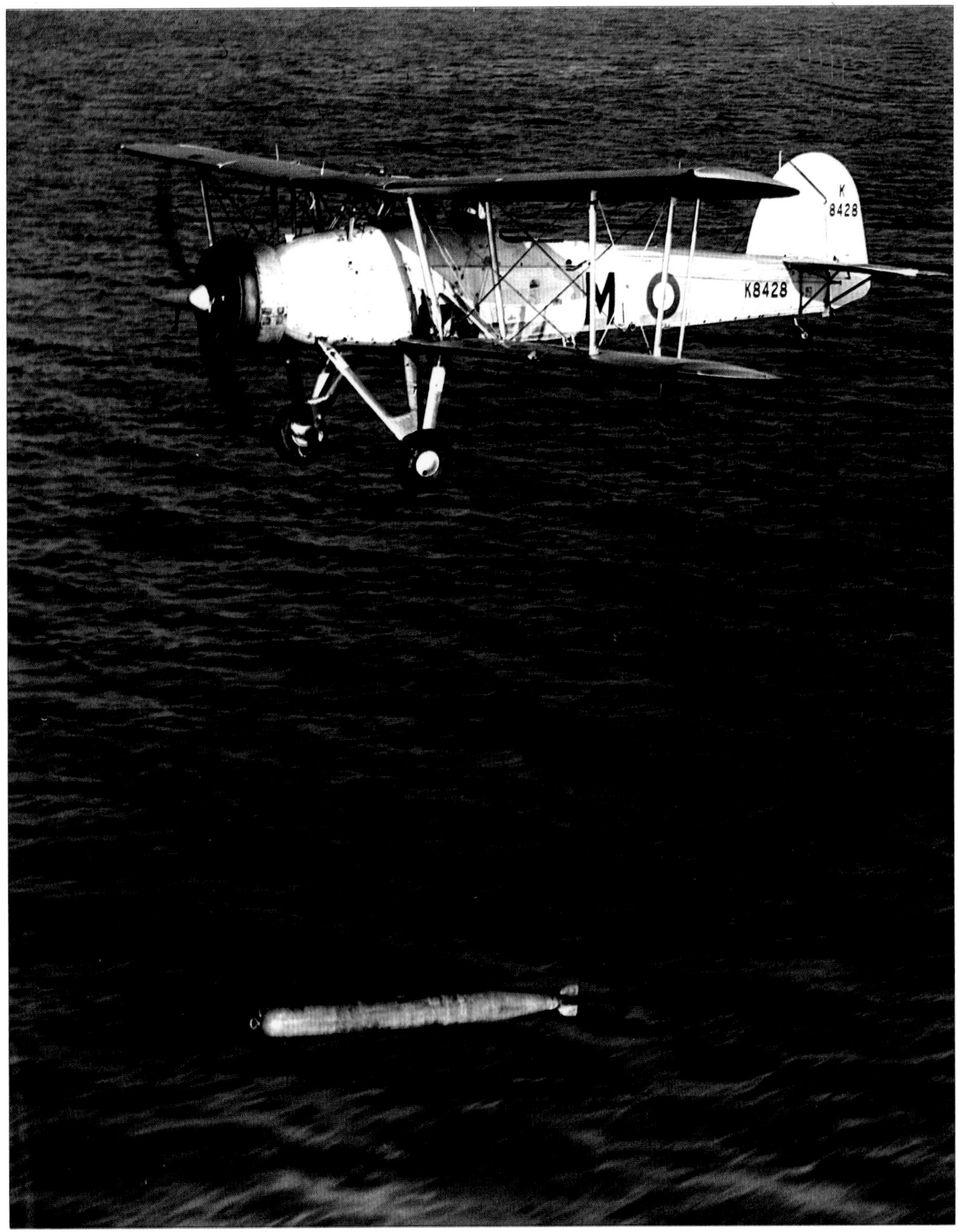

LEFT: Royal Navy Fleet Air Arm Swordfish in formation.

ABOVE: Despite its antiquated appearance, the Swordfish could deliver a torpedo to devastating effect, as it could bombs or depth charges.

21 An Air Raid Shelter

In 1937, government officials predicted that in any future war with Germany, bombing raids on the civilian population would cause massive casualties. The German air raids on the United Kingdom in the 1914–18 war had killed 1,413 people; next time, it was estimated, Germany would bomb the United Kingdom immediately war broke out and continue the assault for 60 days. Each ton of explosive dropped would kill or wound 50 people, a total of almost two million casualties. The fact that these statistics flew in the face of reason, not least because the Germans would be incapable of mounting an air assault of these proportions, was not material: they galvanized the government into taking a number of precautions.

In 1938, the Munich crisis led to the digging of trenches in public parks and by the outbreak of war, enough covered trenches were available to shelter half a million people. At the same time, Anderson shelters were issued. This was intended to be erected in a town or suburban back garden and to accommodate six people. It was designed by William Paterson, and named after the Lord Privy Seal, John Anderson, who was responsible for British civil defence. The Anderson shelter consisted of 14 panels of corrugated galvanized steel: six curved panels formed the roof, six straight ones the walls and two straight panels were erected at each end, one fitted with a door. The resulting upside-down U-shaped structure was 1.8 metres (6 feet) high, 1.37 metres (4 feet 6 inches) wide, and 1.8 metres (6 feet 6 inches) long, and internal fitting out was left to individual householders. It was buried 1.2 metres (4 feet) deep and the roof was covered with about 0.4 metres (15 inches) of soil; the earth roof and walls were often planted as gardens.

Anderson shelters were issued free to householders who earned less than £250 a year; anyone with a higher income had to pay £7. Up to the outbreak of war, some 1.5 million shelters were distributed, and a further 2 million after that. The Anderson shelter did provid good protection except against a direct hit by a bomb, but as the war progressed and all-night alerts became more frequent, it was found that, particularly in winter, many people were reluctant to go to a damp, cold hole in the ground which often flooded.

Because many houses lacked cellars, Herbert Morrison, the Minister of Home Security, decided that there was a need for an effective indoor shelter. The result was the Morrison shelter, devised by John Baker. It was issued in kit form to be bolted together inside the house, and consisted of a cage 1.8 metres (6 feet 6 inches) long, 1.2 metres (4 feet) wide, and 0.75 metres (2 feet 6 inches) high, with a steel top, wire mesh sides and a steel floor. The shelter was designed to protect people against the upper floor of a typical two-storey house falling on them if the house collapsed through blast, but it was unlikely to save their lives if the house received a direct hit. A family could sleep in the cage at night, and use it as a dining table on other occasions. Over half a million

LEFT: Damage caused by the first night raid on London on 24/25 August 1940; the house has been destroyed, along with the Anderson shelter in the garden.

ABOVE: A family uses its Morrison shelter as a dining table, as envisaged by its designer, John Baker.

RIGHT: A German photograph of two Dornier Do 217 bombers over the Silvertown area of London in 1940. Fires have started in the gasworks at Beckton. West Ham greyhound track is in the centre of the picture.

Morrison shelters were issued in the course of the war and they were highly effective, saving many lives.

Some householders built their own brick and concrete shelters in their gardens. In addition to the small shelters intended for household use, larger shelters of concrete were built in some communities to provide protection for local inhabitants who lacked alternative means of taking cover from bombing.

Before the outbreak of war, and until the night raids on London in September 1940, taking cover in Tube stations in London was banned on health grounds, the main justification for this being the spread of disease through lack of sanitary facilities. However, on the night 19/20 September thousands of Londoners took the matter into their own hands and went to the Tube stations for shelter. The government recognized defeat and took steps to make the use of Tube stations as efficient as possible, including closing off short spur sections of Underground and concreting over the tracks there, and fitting 79 stations with bunks and chemical toilets.

ABOVE: Londoners asleep on the platform at Piccadilly Tube station during an air raid.

RIGHT: A row of houses in Stepney, London gutted by bombs dropped in a night raid.

STEPNEY WAY, E.1

22 HMS *Hood*

At 46,680 tons deep load and 262 metres (860 feet) long, the battle cruiser HMS *Hood* was the largest ship ever built for the Royal Navy, and at the outbreak of the Second World War, the biggest warship in the world. Launched on 22 August 1918, she was not completed in time to take part in the First World War. Her design included modifications intended to compensate for some of the faults in battle cruiser construction exposed by the loss of three British battle cruisers in one afternoon at Jutland in 1916. Despite this, by the mid 1930s it was recognized that she still lacked armour protection in comparison with the newer capital ships being built by the Americans and Germans. But the outbreak of the Second World War in 1939 led to the cancellation of the planned reconstruction. Modifications were carried out in 1937 and 1938, but these were largely confined to anti-aircraft armament. The *Hood*'s high speed, impressive size and beautiful lines concealed grave weaknesses, none of which were rectified by her final refit from January to March 1941. They included a lack of armour and a much-reduced top speed thanks to machinery defects. When she emerged from refit, she could achieve only about 46 kph (25 knots) instead of the 59 kph (32 knots) she clocked up in sea trials in 1920.

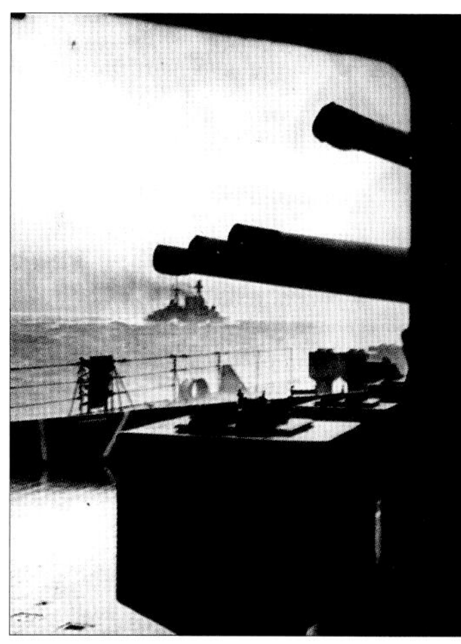

The outbreak of the Second World War found the *Hood* as flagship of the Home Fleet battle cruiser squadron. After the fall of France in June 1940, she became flagship of Force H in the Mediterranean, where she took part in the destruction of part of the French fleet in Oran on 3 July 1940. Returning to the Home Fleet in September, and after a refit in early 1941, she re-joined the Home Fleet based at Scapa Flow in the Orkneys. It was from here on 22 May 1941 that the *Hood*, flying the flag of Vice-Admiral Lancelot Holland, sortied in company with the brand-new battleship *Prince of Wales* to engage the German battleship *Bismarck*. On 18 May, Admiral Günter Lütjens in the newly commissioned *Bismarck* had sailed from Gydnia in the Baltic for the Atlantic, accompanied by the heavy cruiser *Prinz Eugen*, to attack British merchant shipping. The *Bismarck*, armed with eight 38-cm (15-in) and 12 15-cm (5.9-in) guns, displacing 42,500 tons and with a top speed of 54 kph (29 knots), was the most formidable ship then afloat. No single ship of the Royal Navy could both catch her and destroy her. At this stage in the war the potential of carrier-launched aircraft had not been fully appreciated by the British, and Holland's squadron did not include a carrier, although a follow-up force, under C-in-C Home Fleet Admiral Sir John Tovey, did.

At 5.35 hours on 24 May, the cruiser *Norfolk*, which had been shadowing the enemy through the Denmark Strait, reported Lütjens's position at the same time as Holland, coming up to the southwest of Greenland, spotted him. Holland steered at high speed to engage the enemy. Both the *Hood* and the *Prince of Wales* were taking waves of green water over the bows as they smashed into high seas. Spray blinded their main range-finders, and the *Prince of Wales*'s gunnery radar was jammed by her own high-power radio transmitting the enemy movement report to the Admiralty in London. The German and British ships opened fire at 5.53 am at a range of 23,000 metres (25,000 yards). Unfortunately, the *Hood* directed her fire at the *Prinz Eugen*, so the *Bismarck* received only half the weight of fire Holland had available. The loss of his squadron's most important advantage – its heavier broadsides – was exacerbated by the fact that neither the *Hood*'s nor the *Prince of Wales*'s initial salvoes were effective, whereas the *Bismarck* hit the *Hood* heavily with her second or third salvo, and at 6 am, just as Holland had ordered a turn to port to unmask the *Hood*'s after turrets, *Bismarck*'s fifth salvo found its mark. *Hood* blew up with a massive explosion, and only three of her crew of 1,419 officers and men survived. The precise cause of her destruction is still argued about to this day.

The *Prince of Wales* hauled off after taking seven hits, but had hit the *Bismarck* twice, damaging her fuel tanks. This was to have important repercussions because Lütjens decided that, as his flagship's endurance had been much diminished, he would abandon his Atlantic sortie and head for France.

LEFT: The last known picture of HMS *Hood*, taken from the *Prince of Wales* as both steamed into action to engage the *Bismarck*.

BELOW: The "mighty" *Hood*, as she was known in the Royal Navy, viewed from astern, showing her two twin after 38-cm (15-in) turrets. She had two forward turrets of the same design.

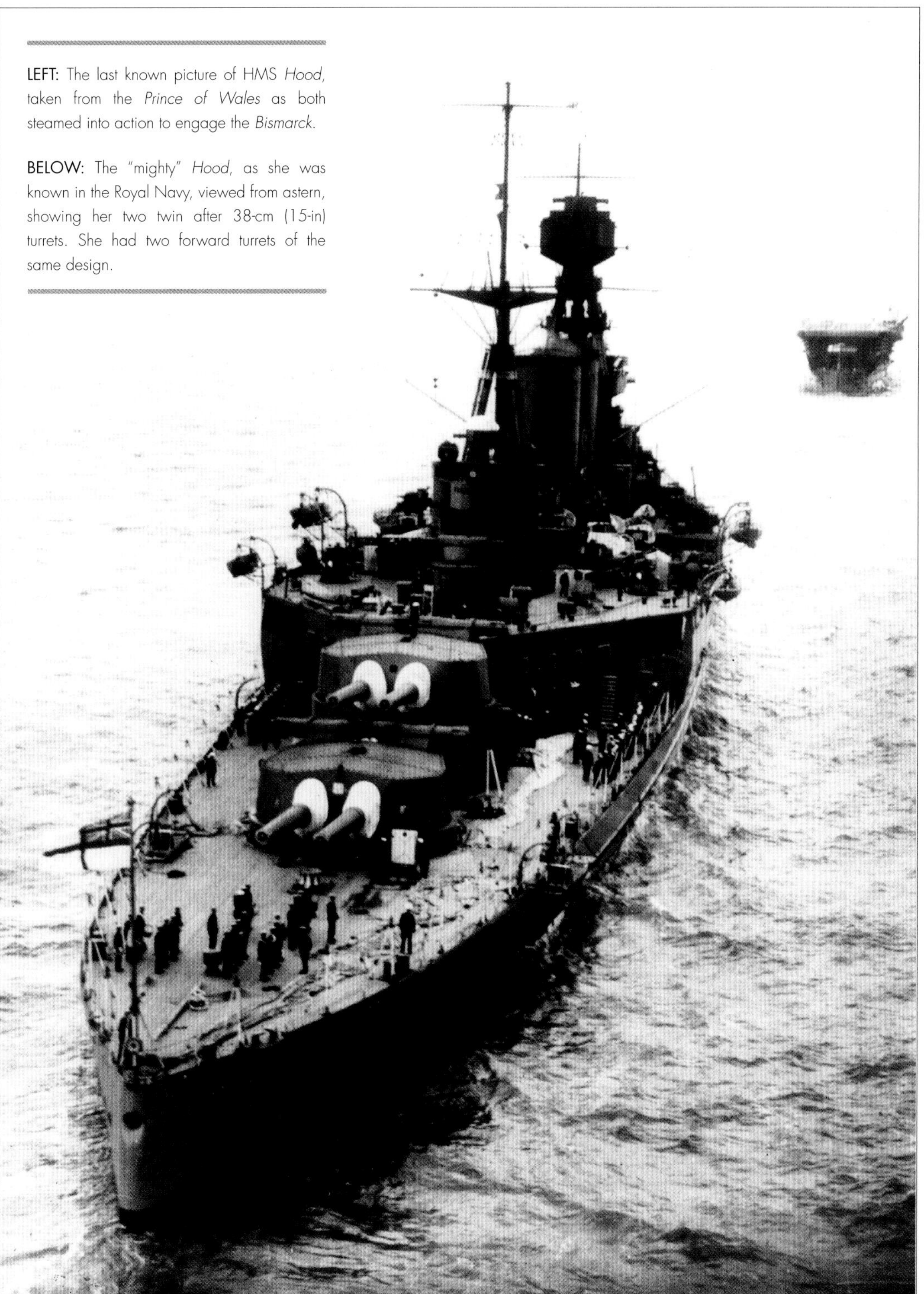

23 The Parachute X-Type

Britain's first parachute troops started training in the summer of 1940 in response to Winston Churchill's directive of 22 June, which asked for "a corps of at least five thousand parachute troops". To begin with, jumpers were trained using the RAF parachute designed for emergency use, operated by pulling a ripcord after leaving the aircraft. The person jumping had to estimate when to do so and have his hands free to operate it. This method was, however, soon found to be unsuitable for army parachute troops, who would be required to jump in groups from the lowest height consistent with safety while carrying heavy equipment. The parachute school at Ringway therefore changed to a parachute of American design, the statichute.

After 135 descents, one man was killed when he became entangled in the rigging lines of his parachute. The American statichute, which their airborne forces used in a modified form throughout the War, was designed so that as the parachutist jumped and fell, the static line connected to the aircraft pulled the canopy out of the bag on his back, followed by the rigging lines, the cords connecting the canopy to the harness. If the jumper made a bad exit, twisting and tumbling before the lazy cord – the final tie connecting the canopy to the static line – broke, he risked being entangled in his own rigging lines. At best, he would then descend hanging by one or both feet and would land on his back or his head. At worst he would get wrapped up so badly that the parachute would not deploy at all. British parachute soldiers did not jump with reserve 'chutes in the Second World War, so if this happened he would die. Even if all went well, the jumper always experienced a testicle-tweaking shock as he was brought up with a jerk at the end of his rigging lines.

Raymond Quilter of the GQ Parachute Company found the remedy. Working with Irvin's Parachute Company, he produced the combination of an Irvin parachute in a GQ packing bag. This X-type parachute, which was to be the standard parachute until the 1960s, worked using a different sequence of opening. As the man jumped, the parachute pack itself broke away from his back, remaining attached to the static line and the aircraft. As the man continued to fall, his weight pulled first his lift webs – the canvas straps attaching the rigging lines to the harness – and then the rigging lines out of the bag. Finally, at the end of the taut and extended rigging lines with the jumper 6 metres (20 feet) below the bag, the canopy pulled out of the bag, the final tie which held the apex of the canopy to the pack broke, and the parachute was fully extended, leaving pack and static line attached to the aircraft. The opening shock was negligible and the danger of becoming entangled greatly reduced. The next 24,000 drops were made without a single accident.

Despite the success of the X-type, as the number of parachute soldiers requiring training increased, a team from the Airborne Forces Experimental Establishment and the Royal Aircraft Establishment monitored the procedures followed at the Parachute Training School. As a result, it was decided that twisting and somersaulting in the slipstream could be reduced if a new design of pack was introduced, in which the strap which connected the parachutist to the static line in the aircraft pulled out of the pack at the level of his neck, rather than at waist level. Some accidents still occurred because canopies made of silk sometimes failed to open properly when the material adhered to itself through static electricity. This problem was solved by changing to canopies made of nylon.

The X-type parachute was the standard type used by British airborne forces throughout the Second World War. Of a total of more than half a million descents made in training at No 1 Parachute Training School with this statichute up to August 1948, only 42 fatal accidents occurred: a ratio of one in 12,000.

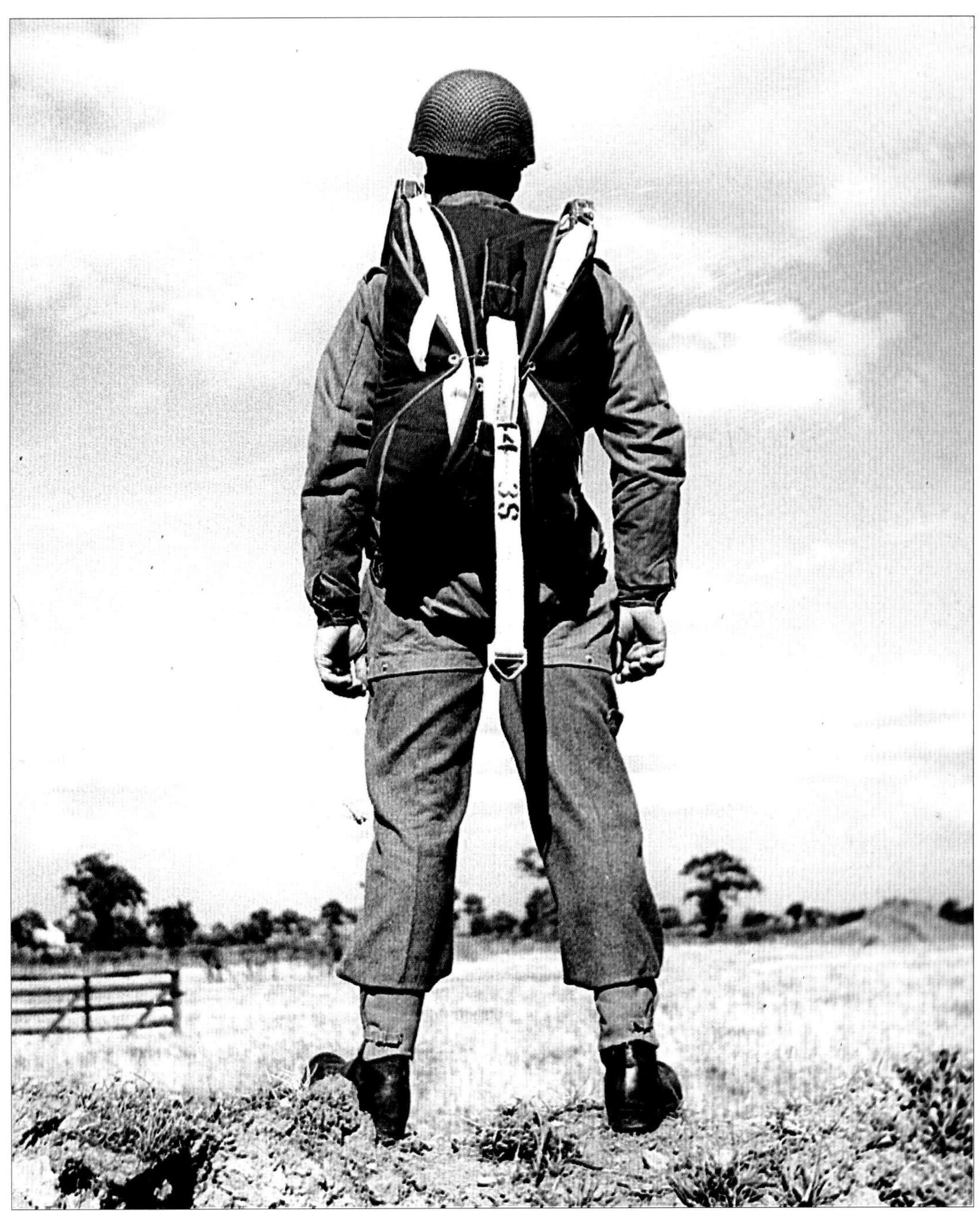

LEFT: A parachutist at the moment of landing. His feet are not together, risking a broken ankle and a reprimand.

ABOVE: Back view of a parachutist in a steel helmet, wearing an X-type parachute. The "D" ring at the end of the strap is to connect it to the static line in the aircraft.

24 The Sten Gun

During the 1940 campaign leading up to the fall of France, the British Expeditionary Force (BEF) encountered an enemy armed with sub-machine guns, principally the German MP28. A British soldier armed with a bolt-action rifle, especially at close quarters, was at a disadvantage against a German equipped with a sub-machine gun with automatic fire; officers and specialists such as despatch riders armed only with a revolver, even more so.

Following the evacuation of the BEF, there was a pressing need to manufacture small arms to make up losses incurred in the campaign, as well as to equip a rapidly enlarging army. The British bought as many Thompson sub-machine guns (Tommy guns) from the United States as could be spared from America's own programme to re-equip their expanding armed forces, but this made up only part of the shortfall. The Royal Small Arms Factory at Enfield was therefore charged with producing a British sub-machine gun. The design selected was the Sten, an acronym formed from the first letter of the surnames of the designers (Major Reginald V Shepherd and Mr Harold J Turpin) and the first two letters of Enfield.

The Sten was cheap and easy to manufacture and could be turned out in small workshops by relatively unskilled labour. Eventually there were eight marks, including models with suppressers or silencers. The Mark III, which was the cheapest and simplest, consisted of only 47 parts and took five man-hours to assemble.

The magazine was side-mounted, copying the German MP28, but this made the gun awkward to hold and fire, especially from the waist, as the firer had to either curve his left wrist under the magazine to grip the fore end or hold the magazine. The latter was discouraged as the vibration caused by automatic firing against the lever effect of the hand holding the magazine could distort the poorly manufactured magazine catch, altering the angle of the magazine and so causing the round to misfeed and jam. It was not unknown for the magazine to be wrenched out of its socket, leaving the firer holding the gun in one hand and the magazine in the other – embarrassing if not fatal. Despite this being well understood, there are numerous photographs of troops taken in the Second World War holding their Stens by the magazine.

The Sten worked on the blow-back principle: the explosion that sent the bullet up the barrel also blew back the bolt, so only half the energy of the explosion was used to send the round on its way. This, combined with the type of 9-mm ($^{1}/_{3}$-inch) ammunition used, meant that the Sten had poor penetrating power. Earlier marks had no safety catch and as a consequence the Sten was sometimes more dangerous to its owner and to friends standing around than to the enemy – wounds and fatalities from accidental discharges were commonplace. Even if the weapon was not cocked, banging it hard on the butt or dropping it butt-down could cause the bolt to drive back sufficiently far for it to pick up a round from the magazine when the spring reasserted itself and pushed the bolt forward. Once the round was seated in the breech, the fixed firing pin on the bolt fired the round, blowing back the bolt to repeat the process until the magazine was empty. To prevent this from happening, later marks had a hole drilled in the casing to take the cocking handle.

Despite these imperfections, millions of Stens were produced during the Second World War, and on the whole it was a successful weapon in the right circumstances. It was suitable for close-quarter battle, but ineffective at ranges above about 90 metres (100 yards), and therefore useless in open country.

LEFT: A posed photograph of British Paratroops at Oosterbeek, Holland, September 1944, in the battle for Arnhem. Shown here holding their Sten guns by the magazine.

ABOVE: A Mark III Sten with skeleton butt.

25 The T-34 Tank

The T-34 was the most significant Soviet tank of the Second World War. Its inventor, Mikhail Koshkin, named it the T-34 because he first conceived the basics of its design in 1934. Some 40,000 were built during the Second World War, and it was the most advanced design of its time anywhere in the world. Prototypes were completed in early 1940, and production started immediately, stimulated by the German invasion of France and the Low Countries, even though the Soviet Union was not at war at the time. The T-34 was fast and had fully sloped armour which was thicker than that of any contemporary German, British or American tanks, with a low silhouette. Its main armament as the vehicle developed was the formidable 76.2-mm L40 gun. Its wide tracks and Christie suspension (with wheels connected to springs) gave it a low ground pressure and hence good terrain-crossing ability, even in mud and snow. This was critical in Russia, and in this respect it was far superior to any German tank. Its V12 diesel engine was also less flammable than the petrol engines in German tanks.

Simple to maintain and operate, the T-34 looks more modern than any other tank of its day. Right up to the end of the Second World War, the Germans and the British, and to some extent the Americans, were building tanks with flat front glacis plates and front turret plates. A flat surface at 90 degrees to the trajectory of an incoming round is more easily penetrated by armour-piercing shot, which ricochets off fully sloped armour like that of the T-34.

As with any armoured vehicle, you only achieve a combination of thick armour, a big gun and high speed with a trade-off. In the case of the T-34, it was size and crew space – the tank was very cramped. Until the improved T-34-85 came into service in early 1944, there was room for only two men in the turret: the commander and the loader. Most tanks in other armies had a three-man turret crew: commander, gunner and loader. A T-34 commander had to aim and fire the gun while attempting to command his tank, and in the case of platoon commanders, command his sub-unit at the same time. The commander's problems were not made any easier by the fact that few Soviet tanks were fitted with radios. Only company commanders and upwards had radios, while the rest had flags. Therefore a company commander could speak only to fellow company commanders and his battalion commander; even he had to give orders to his company using flags.

The Germans remained ignorant about the T-34 in the first few months after they invaded Russia, as few T-34s were deployed when Operation Barbarossa was launched in June 1941. To begin with, the Germans had a field day destroying several thousand Soviet tanks, but in September 1941 they met the T-34 in large numbers, and it soon demonstrated that it could outshoot, outrun and outlast any German tank. The effect was to make all German tanks obsolete. The Panzer divisions that had hitherto swept all before them in Poland, France, the Low Countries and North Africa were no longer kings of the battlefield. Field Marshal Ewald von Kleist called the T-34 "the finest tank in the world". Major General Friedrich von Mellenthin wrote later, "We had nothing comparable." But the Germans continued to inflict defeats on the Red Army until late 1942, and occasionally beyond, because until that time Soviet tactics were faulty; their command and control and operational techniques were nothing like as good as the Germans' – lack of radios being a factor – and they deployed their armour badly. An additional contributor to German continued success for a while was the introduction of new tanks, notably the Tiger heavy gun tank and the medium Panther. The T-34 remained the backbone of Soviet tank divisions to the end of the Second World War.

LEFT: T-34s taking up firing positions on the Third Byelorussian Front in 1944. Their wide tracks enabled them to operate in mud.

ABOVE TOP: The T-34. Its sloped armour gave protection against armour-piercing ammunition.

ABOVE: T-34s entering Berlin in May 1945.

OVERLEAF: T-34s moving at speed, carrying infantry. The nearest tank has a radio aerial, and is probably a company commander's tank or even battalion commander's.

26 The Atlantic Charter

Even before the United States became an official belligerent in the Second World War, President Franklin D Roosevelt worried about the common war aims of the US, Great Britain and the Soviet Union. By covenant and inference Roosevelt, Churchill and Stalin had agreed to the defeat of Nazi Germany as a common war aim. For their nations to survive and prosper, Germany would be forced to disarm, reform and submit to an international treaty regime that would forever restrict its power for imperialistic expansion and political coercion through the threat of war.

In the face of domestic opposition to entering the war or forming an alliance with Great Britain and the Soviet Union, Roosevelt, a wiser and older Wilsonian (ie committed to the idea of collective international security), wanted a general statement of war aims that would appeal to idealistic, internationalist Americans, the sort of people who wrote and read magazine and newspaper articles on foreign policy. Since Churchill and Stalin had reputations as imperialists, Roosevelt knew they had few admirers in the United States beyond Anglophiles and dedicated Communists but. FDR could at least improve Churchill's image as a firm ally and internationalist.

Between 9 and 12 August 1941, Roosevelt and Churchill met aboard warships in Placentia Bay, Newfoundland to discuss their current strategic relationship and their future plans if and when the United States became a belligerent.They also wanted to reassure Stalin they would aid him in his defence of the Soviet Union, largely by threatening Japan and saving Stalin from a two-front war. Part of FDR's bargain in aiding Great Britain with surplus US Navy destroyers and Lend-Lease supplies was to convince Churchill to sign the Atlantic Charter. The document was a promissory pact between the United States and Great Britain that was supposed to reassure their own people and potential allies that they did not seek imperial gains in territory or economic advantage, that they believed in national self-determination and freedom of the seas.

The document also contained a hope for the future that embodied FDR's "Four Freedoms". They were: freedom from fear, freedom from want, freedom to worship and freedom of speech, announced by FDR in a speech in January 1941. Churchill, who at that point in the war would, by his own admission, have made a pact with the devil, agreed that these goals were admirable statements of principle. He did not comment on their likelihood of realization. Sharing Churchill's desperation, Stalin agreed to accept the Atlantic Charter later in the year.

Neither FDR nor Churchill actually signed an Atlantic Charter document; instead they made it a press release. However idealistic and expedient, the provisions of the Atlantic Charter eventually took on life in the Charter of the United Nations.

ABOVE: American president Franklin Delano Roosevelt with British prime minister Winston Churchill on board HMS *Prine of Wales* in Placentia Bay, Newfoundland in August 1941.

RIGHT: The final draft of the Atlantic Charter with Winston Churchill's corrections marked.

OVERLEAF: The declaration of the United Nations, signed by 26 nations, agreeing to the principles of the Atlantic Charter.

Prime Minister's meeting with President Roosevelt – Aug. 1941
Draft of Joint Declaration –

COPY NO: 1

MOST SECRET

NOTE: This document should not be left lying about and, if it is unnecessary to retain, should be returned to the Private Office.

PROPOSED DECLARATION

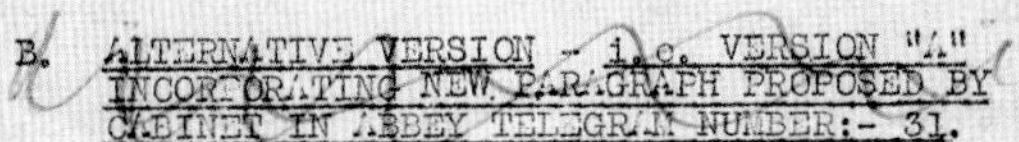
B. ALTERNATIVE VERSION - i.e. VERSION "A" INCORPORATING NEW PARAGRAPH PROPOSED BY CABINET IN ABBEY TELEGRAM NUMBER:- 31.

The President of the United States of America and the Prime Minister, Mr. Churchill, representing His Majesty's Government in the United Kingdom, being met together, deem it right to make known certain common principles in the national policies of their respective countries on which they base their hopes for a better future for the world.

First, their countries seek no aggrandisement, territorial or other;

Second, they desire to see no territorial changes that do not accord with the freely expressed wishes of the peoples concerned.

Third, they respect the right of all peoples to choose the form of government under which they will live; and they wish to see self-government restored to those from whom it has been forcibly removed.

Fourth, they will endeavour, with due respect to their existing obligations, to further the enjoyment by all peoples of access, on equal terms, to the trade and to the raw materials of the world which are needed for their economic prosperity.

Fifth, they support fullest collaboration between Nations in economic field with object of securing for all peoples freedom from want, improved labour standards, economic advancement and social security.

Sixth, they hope to see established a peace, after the final destruction of the Nazi tyranny, which will afford to all nations the means of dwelling in security within their own boundaries, and which will afford assurance to all peoples that they may live out their lives in freedom from fear.

Seventh, they desire such a peace to establish for all safety on the high seas andoceans.

Eighth, they believe that all of the nations of the world must be guided in spirit to the abandonment of the use of force. Because no future peace can be maintained if land, sea or air armaments continue to be employed by nations which threaten, or may threaten, aggression outside of their frontiers, they believe that the disarmament of such nations is essential pending the establishment of a wider and more permanent system of general security. They will further the adoption of all other practicable measures which will lighten for peace-loving peoples the crushing burden of armaments.

Private Office.
August 12, 1941

DECLARATION BY

DECLARATION BY UNITED NATIONS:

A JOINT DECLARATION BY THE UNITED STATES OF AMERICA, THE UNITED KINGDOM OF GREAT BRITAIN AND NORTHERN IRELAND, THE UNION OF SOVIET SOCIALIST REPUBLICS, CHINA, AUSTRALIA, BELGIUM, CANADA, COSTA RICA, CUBA, CZECHOSLOVAKIA, DOMINICAN REPUBLIC, EL SALVADOR, GREECE, GUATEMALA, HAITI, HONDURAS, INDIA, LUXEMBOURG, NETHERLANDS, NEW ZEALAND, NICARAGUA, NORWAY, PANAMA, POLAND, SOUTH AFRICA, YUGOSLAVIA.

The Governments signatory hereto,

Having subscribed to a common program of purposes and principles embodied in the Joint Declaration of the President of the United States of America and the Prime Minister of the United Kingdom of Great Britain and Northern Ireland dated August 14, 1941, known as the Atlantic Charter.

Being convinced that complete victory over thei· enemies is essential to defend life, liberty, independence and religious freedom, and to preserve human rights and justice in their own lands as well as in other lands, and that they are now engaged in a common struggle against savage and brutal forces seeking to subjugate the world, DECLARE:

(1) Each Government pledges itself to employ its full resources, military or economic, against those members of the Tripartite Pact and its adherents with which such government is at war.

(2) Each Government pledges
with the Governments signatory he
a separate armistice or peace wit

The foregoing declaration ma
other nations which are, or which
material assistance and contribu
for victory over Hitlerism.

Done at Washington
January First, 1942

The Unit
by F
The United K
& Northern
by

On behalf
of the Union
Republics

National Gover

The Commonw
by

The Kingdom
by
Canada
by

UNITED NATIONS

to cooperate
nd not to make
enemies.
ered to by
, rendering
the struggle

tes of America
Roosevelt
of Great Britain
Churchill
the Government
Secretary
Litvinoff
of the Republic of China
Minister for Foreign Affairs
of Australia
Belgium
McCarthy

The Republic of Costa Rica
by [illegible] Fernández

The Republic of Cuba
by Aurelio F. Concheso

Czechoslovak Republic
by V. S. Hurban

The Dominican Republic
by J. M. Troncoso

The Republic of El Salvador
by [illegible]

The Kingdom of Greece
by Cimon G. Diamantopoulos

The Republic of Guatemala
by Enrique Lopez-Herrarte

La République d'Haïti
par Fernand Dennis

The Republic of Honduras
by Julián R. Cáceres

India by
Girja Shankar Bajpai

The Grand Duchy of Luxembourg
by Hugues Le Gallais

The Kingdom of the Netherlands
A. Loudon

Signed on behalf of
the Govt of the Dominion
of New Zealand
by Frank Langstone

The Republic of Nicaragua
by Léon De Bayle

The Kingdom of Norway
by W. Munthe Morgenstierne

The Republic of Panamá
by Jaén Guardia

The Republic of Poland
by Jan Ciechanowski

The Union of South Africa
by Ralph W. Close

The Kingdom of Yugoslavia
by Constantin A. Fotitch

27 An Air Raid Warden's Helmet

In Second World War Britain, a man or woman wearing a helmet with a big W painted on it was instantly recognizable as an Air Raid Warden. Air Raid Precautions, or ARP for short, were a series of measures set up in 1935 by the British government in response to the prediction of massive casualties that would be caused by German bombing in the event of war. The Air Raid Wardens' Service was created in 1937 and, while by mid-1938 it had grown to 200,000 strong, the Munich crisis saw another 500,000 join the Service. Most of these part-time volunteers, sometimes called ARP Wardens, had other jobs which they carried out when not engaged on Warden duties. ARP Wardens wore overalls with an armband, and a black steel helmet with a W in white lettering. Chief Wardens wore white helmets with a black W. Later in the war, all ARP Wardens wore blue serge battledress.

Contrary to government and public expectation, there were no large air raids on the United Kingdom during the first 11 months of the Second World War. One of the reasons for this was the fact that the Luftwaffe was incapable of providing fighter escorts for its bomber force all the way from Germany to the United Kingdom and back; this became possible only after airfields in France became available in June 1940. Without air raids, there was little for Air Raid Wardens to do in those early months other than enforce the blackout regulations, which led to the image of the Warden as a self-important busybody of the kind portrayed by Chief Air Raid Warden Hodges in the popular UK TV series *Dad's Army*. However, they came into their own during the Blitz in 1940–41; along with other Civil Defence, Casualty Service and Fire Service men and women, the Air Raid Wardens performed devotedly, and often with heroism.

The Civil Defence Service included rescue and stretcher parties, control centre staff and messenger boys; the Casualty Service comprised emergency ambulance workers and first-aid-post staff. The Fire Service was made up of full-time and part-time regular firemen, and part-time auxiliaries. Full- and part-time police officers, and hundreds of thousands of members of the Women's Voluntary Service (WVS), were also part of Civil Defence.

In London, Air Raid Wardens were based at local posts placed at about ten to a square mile. They patrolled regularly, reporting the locations of bombs as they fell. If it was an incendiary bomb, they would attempt to smother it with sandbags. They supervised the public shelters and were in effect the "eyes and ears" of Civil Defence. Rescue teams summoned to bomb-damaged areas included stretcher-bearers and "heavy rescue men"; the majority of the latter were building workers familiar with house construction.

While patrolling the streets, Air Raid Wardens ensured that no light was visible from any of the buildings in their "patch". On seeing a light, they would call out, "Put out that light," and regular offenders were reported to the police. They helped to police bomb-damaged locations, and gave immediate assistance to bomb victims. They were trained in firefighting and first aid, and attempted to keep a situation under control until the rescue services arrived.

Two ARP Wardens were awarded the George Cross for gallantry during the Second World War. The first-ever recipient of the newly created George Cross was ARP Warden Thomas Alderson on 30 September 1940; ARP Warden Leonard Miles was awarded his posthumously, on 17 January 1941.

LEFT: A Chief Warden (left) and a Warden help an injured woman to a reception centre from a first-aid post after her home in Liverpool was bombed on 6 May 1941.

ABOVE: A warden's helmet.

28 The Mosin-Nagant Rifle

The Mosin-Nagant rifle was in service for over 100 years, first with the Imperial Russian Army, then the Red Army, and finally the Northern Alliance forces in Afghanistan in 2001. Experience in the Russo–Turkish war of 1877–78, where the Turks were using Winchester repeaters and the Russians single-shot rifles, persuaded the Imperial Army that modernization of their small arms was overdue. Captain Sergei Ivanovich Mosin submitted a design for a 7.62-mm ($^{1}/_{3}$-in) magazine-fed rifle, in competition with a rifle designed by a Belgian, Léon Nagant. After some deliberation, the commission formed to decide which rifle should be adopted by the Imperial Army chose Mosin's design, but as the final production model of 1891 incorporated some features of Nagant's design, the rifle was designated the Mosin-Nagant M1891. Production was started both in Russia and in France. By the outbreak of the Russo–Japanese War in 1904, about 3.8 million Mosin-Nagants had been delivered to the Imperial Army, but few were actually used, as scarcely any soldiers had been trained to use them.

Because of the poor state of Russian industry at the outbreak of the First World War, a shortage of Mosin-Nagants forced the government to place orders for M1891s with two companies in the USA: Remington and Westinghouse. The first consignment arrived just as the 1917 October Revolution broke out, followed by the Russians signing the Treaty of Brest-Litovsk with Germany and its allies, which took Russia out of the war for a while. To avoid the risk that the next consignment would fall into the hands of the Germans or Austrians, the US Army bought the remaining quarter of a million Mosin-Nagants. These rifles were used to equip the British and US forces sent to northern Russia in the anti-Bolshevik campaign of 1918–19.

The Mosin-Nagant was used by both sides in the Russian Civil War of 1918–24, and by the Finns in the "Winter War" of 1939–40 against the Red Army. The Mosin-Nagant was the standard-issue weapon for the Red Army when Hitler invaded Russia in 1941. By the end of the Second World War about 17.4 million M1891s had been produced. The Mosin-Nagant was highly popular, and easy to maintain; Russian soldiers called it just the Mosin, or "Mosinka". It was also modified as a sniper rifle and used by the famous Red Army snipers, notably at Stalingrad (1942–43) but in all other battles too. The Finns also used the sniper model against the Red Army: one Finnish sniper claimed over 500 kills with a Mosin-Nagant.

After the Second World War, the Soviet Union ceased producing Mosin-Nagants, progressively replacing them with the AK series of assault rifles. However, the M1891 was used in many of the campaigns that followed the Second World War: Korea (1950–53), Vietnam (1955–75) and Afghanistan (2001–present). Every country or insurgent group that received military aid from the Soviet Union used some Mosin-Nagants, including Egypt, Syria, Iraq and Palestinian terrorist groups.

Through its long service life, eight models of Mosin-Nagant were produced. In addition several countries, including Finland, Czechoslovakia, China, Hungary, Romania and Poland, manufactured variants.

ABOVE LEFT: The Mosin-Nagant rifle

ABOVE: Red Army infantry with Mosin-Nagant rifles jump down from a T-34 in December 1942.

29 The SAS Cap Insignia

In October 1941, Lieutenant David Stirling of the Scots Guards, attached to Number 8 Commando, part of Colonel Robert Laycock's Force Z, was lying in a Cairo hospital, temporarily paralysed from the waist down following a parachuting accident. The army commandos of Force Z were bored and frustrated. Raids had been cancelled, or had gone awry. Participation in the final stages of the battle for Crete, where they had not exactly covered themselves in glory, was the final straw. Force Z was disbanded at the end of July 1941.

Stirling pondered how best to improve the raiding operations in which Number 8 Commando had been engaged with so little success. He concluded that the numerous enemy bases, particularly airfields, strung out over hundreds of miles behind their lines were ideal targets. The way to get at them was by the two open flanks: the desert to the south, the sea to the north. The latter had been used as an approach by commandos, but their raids had been wasteful in resources, even scarcer now since the losses suffered by the Royal Navy in the Greece and Crete evacuations in 1941. Poor planning by amateurs in the amphibious art had led to failures. Perhaps a number of smaller parties, each of no more than four or five men inserted by parachute, submarine, fishing boat or vehicle, would have a greater chance of achieving surprise, and could attack a number of targets simultaneously.

He committed his idea to paper. When fit to walk, he bluffed his way in to GHQ Cairo, and was eventually summoned by General Claude Auchinleck, C-in-C Middle East, who promoted him to captain and told him to raise a force of 65 men who would be dropped behind enemy lines. The force was to be known as L Detachment Special Air Service Brigade, a totally imaginary formation that existed only in the fertile brain of Brigadier Dudley Clarke who was responsible for deception in the Middle East. He was trying to persuade the Germans that a fully equipped airborne brigade was stationed in Egypt. Real parachutists, albeit a mere 65 men and the only ones at that in the whole Middle East, were the icing on the bogus cake Clarke was baking.

The first raid, on 16–17 November 1941, was a disaster. High winds and sandstorms resulted in all the SAS men being dropped miles from the dropping zones (DZs). Eventually 22 men including Stirling, out of the 55 who had dropped, turned up at the rendezvous manned by Captain David Lloyd Owen of the Long Range Desert Group (LRDG). He argued that Stirling should in future let the LRDG take them to the target; eventually Stirling agreed. For the next year, until the SAS got their own jeeps, the LRDG, the desert experts, provided a "taxi" service.

The SAS now began to achieve some notable successes, mainly raiding airfields. Time after time they destroyed every aircraft on the airfields they hit. Captain "Paddy" Mayne's personal score was higher than any Allied air ace. When the desert campaign finished, they went on to operate in Italy, the Aegean and France. Although they sometimes parachuted into their operational areas, they used Jeeps to greater effect. Perhaps their most notable achievements were the long Jeep patrols behind enemy lines in France after the Allied invasion in June 1944.

The SAS winged dagger badge is worn to this day by the three Special Air Service Regiments (21, 22, 23), as are the distinctive straight-top SAS parachute wings. These were designed by two SAS officers: Lieutenant Jock Lewes, Welsh Guards, President of the Oxford University Boat Club, and Lieutenant Tom Langton, Irish Guards, a Cambridge rowing blue. They were modelled on the wings of the sacred ibis depicted in the décor of Shepheard's Hotel in Cairo. The light and dark blue feathers of the wings are based on the Cambridge and Oxford rowing colours, chosen by Langton and Lewes.

LEFT: An AS patrol wearing Arab headdress in the Western Desert. By 1943, the SAS was equipped with Jeeps, here mounting Vickers K guns.

ABOVE: The winged dagger SAS capbadge.

30 The Boeing B-17

At the heart of Allied strategy for the defeat of Nazi Germany, the Combined Bomber Offensive, code-named Pointblank, required the Royal Air Force and US Army Air Forces (USAAF) to destroy Germany's industrial heartland. The aircraft for this mission could not be developed overnight, and it was decisions made in the 1930s by the Ministry of Air and the US War Department that dictated the bomber types the RAF and USAAF used to strike Germany.

After underfunded, incremental bomber development following the First World War, in 1934 the US Army Air Corps asked Boeing Aircraft to develop a multi-engine bomber that could carry one ton of bombs a minimum of 1,600 kilometres (1,000 miles) and return to base. It gave Boeing no advance payment but the company would be paid if its bomber became the USAAC's choice. Boeing's Model 229 or XB-17 flew for the first time in July 1935, but crashed four months later. The accident, which happened at take-off, killed much of the design and testing team, but the USAAC ordered 13 more aircraft because this bomber had become its highest priority.

The development of the B-17 focused on over-water flight and the bombing of an enemy invasion fleet. While such a mission seemed far-fetched for the protection of the Atlantic Coast, it was relevant to the defence of the Commonwealth of the Philippines, the Territory of Hawaii and the Panama Canal Zone. Although USAAC planners in 1939 foresaw the need for bombers to reach Germany and Japan in the future, the coastal defence mission was the only one that convinced Congress to fund the XB-17 project.

As more models received testing between 1936 and 1941, the basic character of the wartime B-17 (E and F models) took shape. The four-engine bomber (four Pratt & Whitney 1,200hp supercharged radial piston engines)

ABOVE: A B-17 bomber circa 1941.

OVERLEAF: The "Flying Fortress" being built in a Boeing factory during the Second World War.

could drive a 29,000 kg (65,000 lb) aircraft almost 3,200 kilometres (2,000 miles) at speeds up to 462 kph (287 mph) and at altitudes up to 10,700 metres (35,000 feet). The aircraft would be a "Flying Fortress" with a crew of ten, eight of whom could man an assortment of 13 turret-mounted or swinging machine guns. The bomb load for missions might run as high as 7,700 kg (17,000 lbs). The bombsight, the Norden type developed by Sperry-Rand, allowed the bombardier to fly the plane for greater accuracy, and made automatic corrections for altitude, wind and drifting.

Although the USAAC (US Army Air Forces after June 1941) ordered B-17s for operational deployment, the number of B-17s (models B-E) numbered fewer than 600 by December 1941, and did little to slow the Japanese campaign of 1941–42. Some of these models had been sent to RAF Coastal Command to attack U-boat bases. The models E and F (almost 4,000 aircraft) went to British bases in 1942 to begin the daylight bombing of Germany, but German air defences brought long distance raids to a halt in December 1943. Actual combat experience brought changes to the models G and H, principally improvements to the engine and armouring, and the addition of a chin turret to meet head-on fighter attacks. By war's end, Boeing and two other contractors had built 12,677 B-17s. Enemy air defences destroyed about 5,000 of them across all theatres of war, and hundreds more crashed in operational accidents.

KEEP 'EM FLYING!

31 Oboe

During the Second World War the Germans, British and Americans introduced electronic navigation systems to assist their bombers in finding the correct target at night or in bad weather. Early in the war, both sides discovered that bombing a well-defended country by day in good weather without heavy fighter escort was extremely costly. The RAF was the first to learn that its doctrine that "the bomber will always get through", so assiduously proclaimed before the Second World War, was spurious. The losses sustained by the RAF in the first months of the war persuaded the Air Staff that the only way a strategic bombing campaign against Germany could be sustained was by bombing at night. The Americans in their turn discovered that daylight bombing without using fighter protection when over heavily-defended occupied Europe was unsustainable. Their solution was to provide plenty of long-range fighter escorts.

The main problem when night bombing was locating the target. The Germans, turning to night bombing of Britain after their defeat in the Battle of Britain, were the first to light on a solution. They used a system of radio beams, initially Knickebein, but superseded by X-Gerät (X-Apparatus), and Y-Gerät. Despite these the German results were mediocre, not least because the system could be jammed. Meanwhile, the RAF's performance, without any navigational aids, was abysmal. Only one in three RAF crews placed their bombs within eight kilometres (five miles) of the aiming point; some were tens of miles off target.

In early 1942, the RAF introduced a radio system called Gee. It was not so accurate as Knickebein, but it did improve bombing accuracy until the Germans started jamming it. The RAF's answer, in early 1943, was Oboe, so called because its radar pulses sounded like the woodwind instrument. The system used two ground stations in England. One tracked the aircraft as it flew along an arc of constant range running through the target, and passed correction signals if it deviated from the arc. The second station measured the range along the arc, and when the aircraft reached the previously computed bomb release point, a signal was broadcast. Mosquito pathfinder aircraft were fitted to receive the signals, and they marked the target with flares for the main force to bomb.

Oboe was very accurate and difficult to jam. Its one drawback was that the curvature of the earth reduced its range to about 450 kilometres (280 miles) from the ground stations. Pathfinder Mosquitoes flew as high as they could so that they were still "visible" to the radar beams as far out as possible. After sufficient French territory had been liberated in 1944, ground stations could be set up much nearer Germany and could thus cover more of the country east of the Ruhr, which had been only just within the range of Oboe stations based in England.

The installation in mid-1943 of H2S radar sets in RAF bombers, which gave a "picture" of the ground on a screen, enabled sorties to be carried out beyond the range of Oboe, although bombing accuracy depended on the quality of the radar echo. Coastal targets showed up clearly; targets inland, especially in broken terrain, were more difficult to find.

The Americans installed electronic navigation systems similar to Oboe in their bombers, to enable them to find and attack daylight targets through cloud and haze.

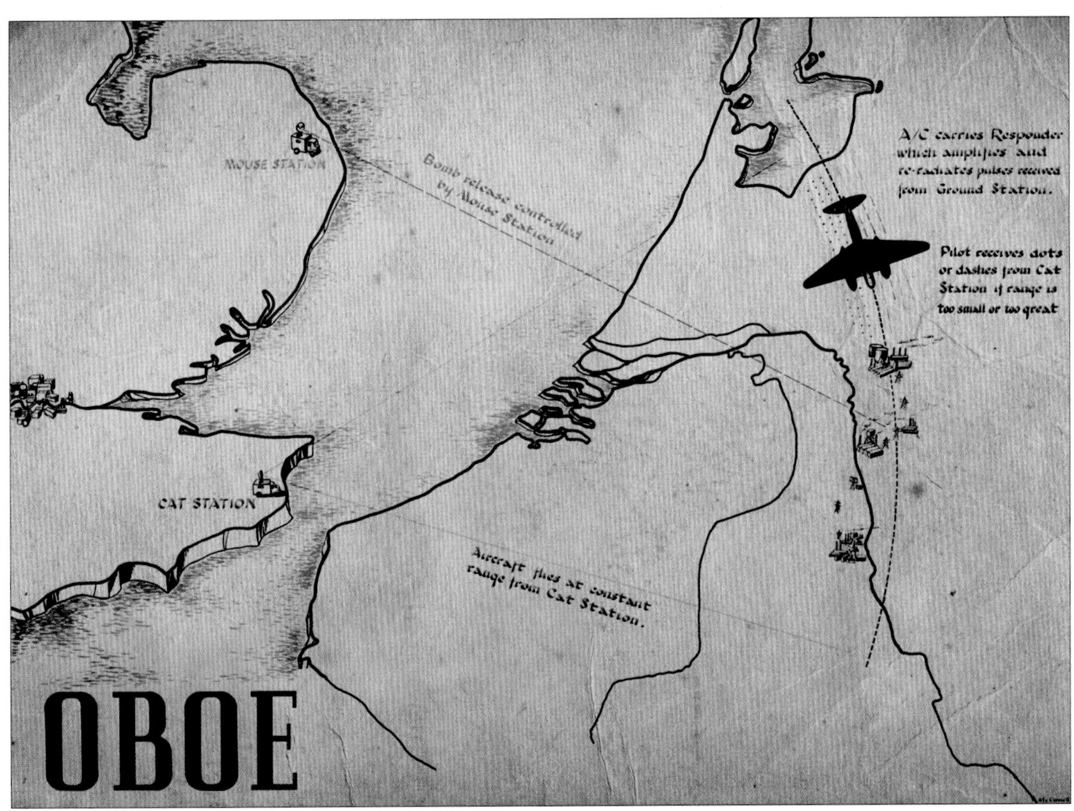

MOUSE STATION
Bomb release controlled
by Mouse Station
A/C carries Responder
which amplifies and
re-radiates pulses received
from Ground Station.
Pilot receives dots
or dashes from Cat
Station if range is
too small or too great
CAT STATION
Aircraft flies at constant
range from Cat Station.
OBOE

LEFT: A Mosquito B MkXVI fitted with a ventral raydome testing an H2S radar. This aircraft was also used to test Oboe.

ABOVE: A diagram showing the principle on which Oboe worked, with two ground stations in England tracking the Mosquito marker aircraft as it flies along the arc.

32 The Human Torpedo

The Italians were the first to use human torpedoes in the Second World War, and were swiftly copied by the British, Germans and Japanese. The Italian *Maiale* ("pig") was 6.7 metres (22 feet) long, with a detachable explosive nose. It had a two-man crew who sat astride the torpedo wearing rubber suits and oxygen cylinders and masks.

On 19 December 1941, two Italian frogmen were caught sitting on the bow buoy of the British battleship *Valiant* in Alexandria harbour. Under interrogation they said that they had got into difficulties outside the harbour and had had to abandon their equipment and swim. A few minutes later there was an explosion under the stern of the tanker *Sagonia*. The Italians told the captain of the *Valiant* to bring everyone on deck, as there would shortly be an explosion under his ship. He did so, and minutes later a massive explosion caused extensive damage to the *Valiant*. Soon after, another explosion severely damaged the battleship *Queen Elizabeth*. Three pairs of Italians on human torpedoes, brought to Alexandria by submarine, had immobilized the only two battleships in the Mediterranean Fleet and put them out of action for many months, though there were no casualties. The Italians also used human topedoes to attack Allied shipping in Gibraltar, Malta and Algiers Bay later in the war.

Copying the Italian example, the British developed the Chariot, based on a 7.6 metre (25 foot) torpedo, specifically to attack the German battleship *Tirpitz* at Trondheim in Norway. On the night of 30/31 October 1942, two Chariots were taken into the Trondheimfjord slung under a fishing boat, but on the approach while still about 15 kilometres (ten miles) from the *Tirpitz*, the Chariots broke loose and sank. The Chariot crews however made their way to Sweden as planned.

On 28 October 1944, a successful attack was made by a pair of Chariots on two ships at Phuket in Siam (Thailand). The crew were taken to the target area by the submarine *Trenchant*, motored in on their Chariots, and clamped the explosive heads to the bilges of the two target merchant ships, the *Sumatra* and the *Volpi*. Having returned to the *Trenchant*, two explosions were heard, and both ships were out of action for the rest of the war. It was the last and only completely successful Chariot operation, out of a total of eight, in the whole war.

The German one-man Neger, sometimes called the Mohr after its inventor Richard Mohr, consisted of two torpedoes clamped together on top of each other. The upper one had a small plexiglass-covered cockpit instead of a warhead. It was slow and could not dive, motoring with the cockpit above the water. It had to be released close to the target, and was easily seen in daylight, often with sunlight flashing off the cockpit. Negers were used against Allied shipping at Anzio in January 1944 and again in Normandy in June. They damaged two minesweepers and a light cruiser off the Normandy beaches, but large numbers of Negers were lost. The successor to the Neger, the Marder ("pine marten") was no more successful.

The Japanese Kalten was a converted Long Lance torpedo, which included a compartment for the crewman and a conning tower. The Long Lance was a huge torpedo, 9 metres (30 feet) long, with half a ton of explosive in the warhead, and capable of 91 kmp (49 knots). It was usually driven straight at the target as a suicide weapon. They were first used at Ulithi atoll, the US fleet anchorage, in November 1944, sinking a tanker for the loss of eight Kalten pilots. At Iwo Jima, Okinawa and at other beachheads in the Pacific, they sank four US vessels (the largest being the destroyer USS *Underhill*). The Japanese loss rate was huge. Of the 18 submarines converted to carry Kaltens, eight were sunk either before or after launching the human torpedoes; others were forced to abort their missions. About 80 Kaltens were also lost.

The Italian human torpedo attacks were the most successful in terms of "return on investment" – the result balanced against the cost in the lives of extremely brave men, the time, expense, and effort in developing the weapon, and taking it to the target. The return on investment by the British, Germans and Japanese on human torpedoes was negligible; but this is not in any way to denigrate the courage of the men who rode the torpedoes.

ABOVE: The Italian human torpedo, known as the Maiale (pig).

RIGHT: The controls of the "pig".

OVERLEAF: A damaged Italian human torpedo captured with the mother ship *Otterra*, a converted merchant ship was used to mount attacks against Allied shipping in Gibraltar in 1942 and 1943. After the ship was surrendered to the British in 1943, the torpedo was found in a secret compartment.

1
2
3
4
5
6
7
8
FEET

9
10
11
12
B

33 Japanese Headgear

The two most familiar forms of headgear worn by the Japanese armed forces were the pot-shaped steel helmet, and the cloth field cap with its short, cloth, occasionally leather, peak. A star for the Imperial Japanese Army (IJA) and an anchor for the Imperial Japanese Navy (IJN) was welded onto the front of the helmet, and sewn on to the front of the cap.

The comfortable and practical field cap was worn with more formal uniforms, as shown in the photograph of Japanese officers attending the surrender ceremony aboard the USS *Missouri*, and as worn by General Tomoyuki Yamashita at his trial by the War Crimes Commission in Manila in October 1945. The cap was the same pattern for all ranks.

The steel helmet was often covered in a net into which foliage and grass camouflage could be inserted. Even in the equivalent of service dress, Japanese officers of all ranks often wore a tunic open at the neck, over a white shirt without a tie.

The ubiquitous field cap was symptomatic of the practical approach to kit and equipment on the part of the Japanese, especially in the IJA. For example, their soldiers were equipped with a very efficient grenade launcher which threw a 0.8 kg (1 lb 12 oz) shell out to around 640 metres (700) yards, accurately and effectively – far better than anything possessed by the Allies.

The Japanese were trained to fight with their 38-cm (15-in) bayonet fixed to a 6.5 mm (.256 inch) calibre rifle at all times to instil fear into their enemy. Their infantry especially was recruited from the rural population, whose tough farmers made excellent soldiers. It would be wrong to imagine them as uneducated peasants, for the standard of schooling in Japan was high. They were indoctrinated to believe that they were the toughest race in the world, and that death was to be expected, not feared.

In addition to the field cap in blue cloth, Japanese seamen wore a round white hat, like those issued in the British Navy, when in white uniform, and a blue one with their blue, winter uniform. Both types of round hat had what the Royal Navy called a cap "tally" round the brow part of the cap with the name of the wearer's ship in Japanese characters. Officers and petty officers of the IJN wore blue or white peaked caps, according to the time of year. These caps were similar to those worn in most navies. Japanese sailors in working dress wore either the field cap or, when working with aircraft on carrier flight decks, a cotton flying helmet.

ABOVE: A Japanese soldier in Bataan in the Philippines after it fell.

RIGHT: An example of the typical Japanese cloth field cap.

34 The Secret Radio

Inserting spies, agents and saboteurs into enemy territory was usually only the first phase of a clandestine operation. If they could not communicate they were probably useless. Among other things, they needed to receive instructions from base and likewise pass information back; ask for airdrops of equipment; request extraction, either for themselves or others; and vector and talk to the dropping or pick-up aircraft. The only efficient and speedy way to achieve this was by radio, or wireless as the British called it, so special radio sets had to be devised for use by agents which had to meet several important criteria.

First, the set had to be rugged and able to stand up to rough treatment. It also needed to be as small as possible in order to be easily portable, and if possible fit into a suitcase or some other innocuous container for concealment. It had to be capable of transmitting and receiving over long ranges. Ideally it needed to be able to work on batteries, mains power or a hand or pedal generator.

Some of these requirements conflicted. The technology of the time usually demanded a big radio set with plenty of power to transmit over long ranges. The transistor had not been invented at that time and all radios worked using valves, which were easily broken. Meanwhile, long-range communications normally required big antennae, which was out of the question for clandestine operations.

These problems were addressed mainly by the Special Operations Executive (SOE) in Britain, and the Office for Strategic Services (OSS) in the US, and by early 1942 sets that fulfilled the key criteria were being produced. The smallest radio for agents was the Paraset Clandestine Radio designed for SOE and the Secret Intelligence Service (MI6), weighing about 2.3 kg (5 lbs). But more reliable, and seen in many a film, was the SOE Type A, Mk III suitcase radio weighing about 6 kg (13 lbs), which had a range of 800 kilometres (500 miles). The US equivalent was the AN/PRC-1 suitcase design, weighing about 13.5 kg (30 lbs).

The radios in existence at the time were insecure; they could not automatically "scramble" their messages to prevent anyone listening in from deciphering the text. Today clandestine radios use burst transmission to send a long text message over the air in micro-seconds, giving an enemy direction-finding station too little time to fix the transmitting radio's location. The sets in the 1940s could not do this.

The high-frequency radios used by agents were unable to send and receive voice messages over long distances, so Morse code was the communicating method. Messages were enciphered using one-time pads: the sender and receiver had identical pads of tear-off sheets containing the information for enciphering and deciphering a signal, the sender transmitting the sheet number. Once the message had been sent and deciphered at the other end, both operators destroyed their copy. No other copies existed. This method was unbreakable but slow, and tapping out a long message exposed the sender to the danger of being picked up by hostile direction-finding equipment, of which the Germans had numerous high-quality sets. Many operators were caught this way.

The agent communicated with supply aircraft over an S-phone using voice transmission – radio telephone in the jargon of the day. The aircraft carried the master set while the agent carried the "ground set" which weighed around 7 kg (15 lbs), fitted in a suitcase or pack on the agent's back. The theoretical range when used as a radio telephone to an aircraft at 3,000 metres (10,000 feet) was about 65 kilometres (40 miles), down to 10 kilometres (6 miles) at 150 metres (500 feet). Ground detectors more than a mile away could not pick up transmissions to an aircraft. The signal from the set could also be used to aid in vectoring the aircraft to the dropping zone from about 130 kilometres (80 miles) away.

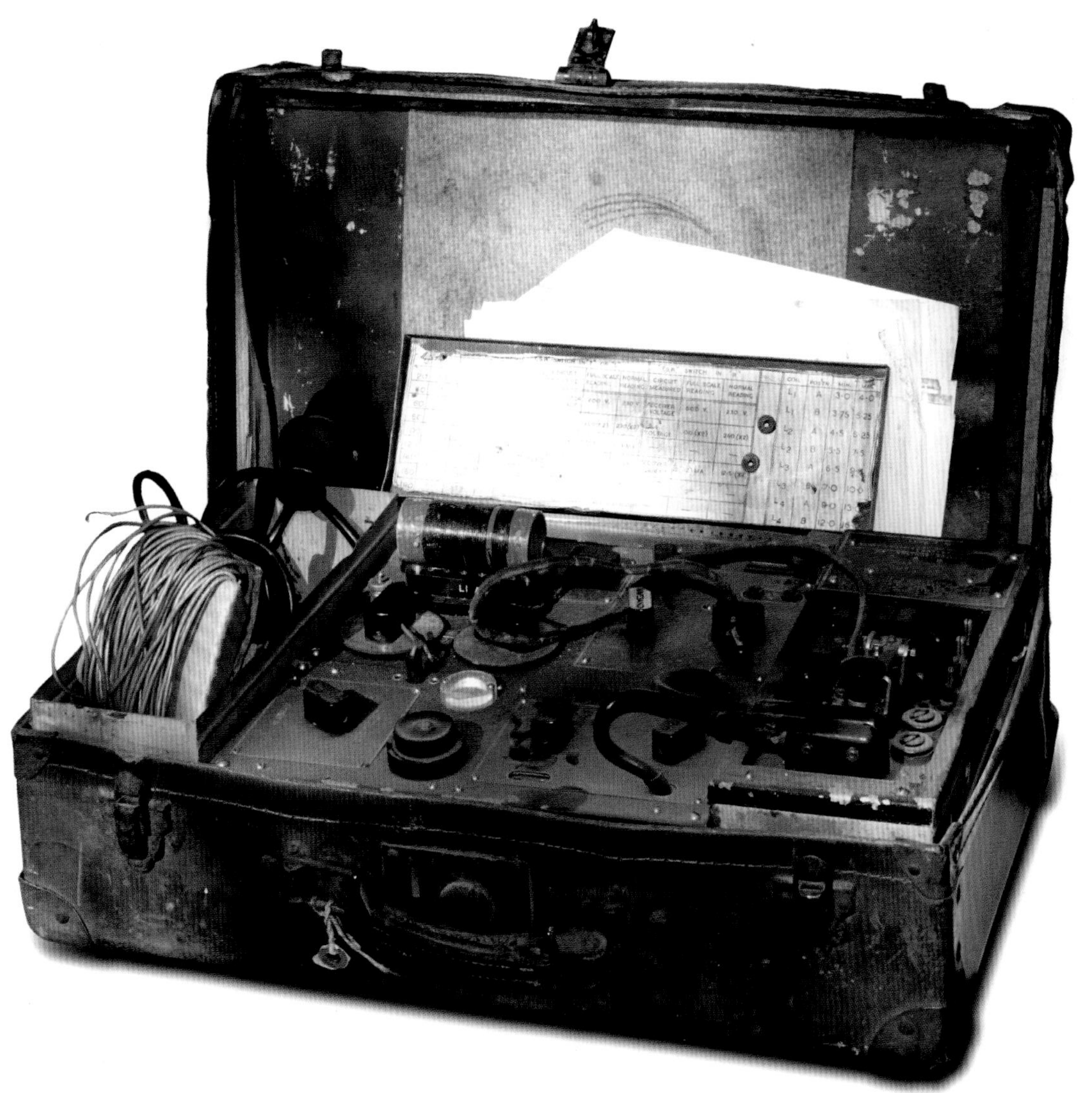

LEFT: Members of the French Resistance operating a radio.

ABOVE: The radio set used in training by Yvonne Baseden an F Section SOE radio operator. Aged 22, she was parachuted into France to join the SCHOLAR circuit operating near Dijon. Following participation in the largest daylight drop of supplies to the Resistance up to that time, she was captured on 26 June 1944, interrogated by the Gestapo, sent to Ravensbruck Concentration Camp, and liberated in April 1945. She was awarded the MBE (Military), Legion d'Honneur and the Croix de Guerre with Palm.

35 A Silk Escape Map

Silk escape maps were produced by MI9, the secret British escape service, and by MIS-X, its US equivalent. A branch of the military intelligence directorate in the War Office formed in December 1939, MI9 had several tasks: to garner intelligence about the enemy from repatriated prisoners of war (POWs) and through coded correspondence with those still in POW camps; to assist prisoners to escape, through advice given beforehand and by smuggling escape kit to them; to train the armed forces in methods of escape and evasion; and to organize groups of helpers abroad to assist escapees on their way home.

MI9 provided aircrew going on operational flights or commandos embarking on raids with wallets containing about £10-worth of local currency, a small hacksaw and a small compass. They also carried maps printed on silk, which was hardwearing and easy to conceal. A company well known for producing playing cards and board games including Monopoly, Waddington Limited, printed British escape maps. These were copied from those produced by the map publisher Bartholomew, who waived all copyright and royalties for the duration of the war.

A silk map could be concealed in a cigarette packet or the heel of a shoe, and could survive hard treatment, even immersion in water. The maps were small scale and covered a large area, and some were double sided. The range of British maps was extensive: for example, the 1943 series for the European theatre of operations consisted of ten maps, which in various combinations gave coverage of France, Belgium, Holland, Germany, Czechoslovakia, Poland, Hungary, Romania, Serbia, Bulgaria, Spain, Switzerland, Greece, Albania, Turkey, Crete and Portugal. Other series covered Norway, Italy, Cyrenaica, the Asia-Pacific theatre, in short almost everywhere in the world where British service people and agents might find themselves.

Issuing silk maps to aircrew or commandos before embarking on a mission was one thing; smuggling them to POWs was another. No maps or other escape gear were included in Red Cross food parcels in case these were banned – most POWs relied on them for survival as the rations, especially towards the end of the war, were meagre. Nor could parcels from families be used as a means of smuggling in such kit, for it was known that they were always thoroughly searched. Fictitious charity associations were therefore set up to send parcels of games and clothing to POWs and some of these included board games, which the Germans permitted on the grounds that POWs might be less troublesome if they had something to do. There were clues as to which map was concealed so that the right maps went to the right POWs: in a Monopoly board, for example, this would be a full stop after the name of a place on the board: Mayfair, Marylebone and so forth.

The POWs had escape organizations which as well as making civilian clothes, false papers and other items of escape kit, printed maps using the silk maps as masters. These "re-prints" were drawn by hand, and reproduced using jelly from Red Cross parcels, ink from pitch and rollers from window bars. We shall never know how many maps were successfully smuggled into POW camps, but we do know that more than 33,000 British, Commonwealth and US servicemen reached Allied lines from enemy territory, either as escapers or evaders (those who had never been captured in the first place).

RIGHT: The silk escape map carried by Squadron Leader Hugh Beresford Verity RAFVR while serving in Number 161 Squadron RAF in support of the SOE.

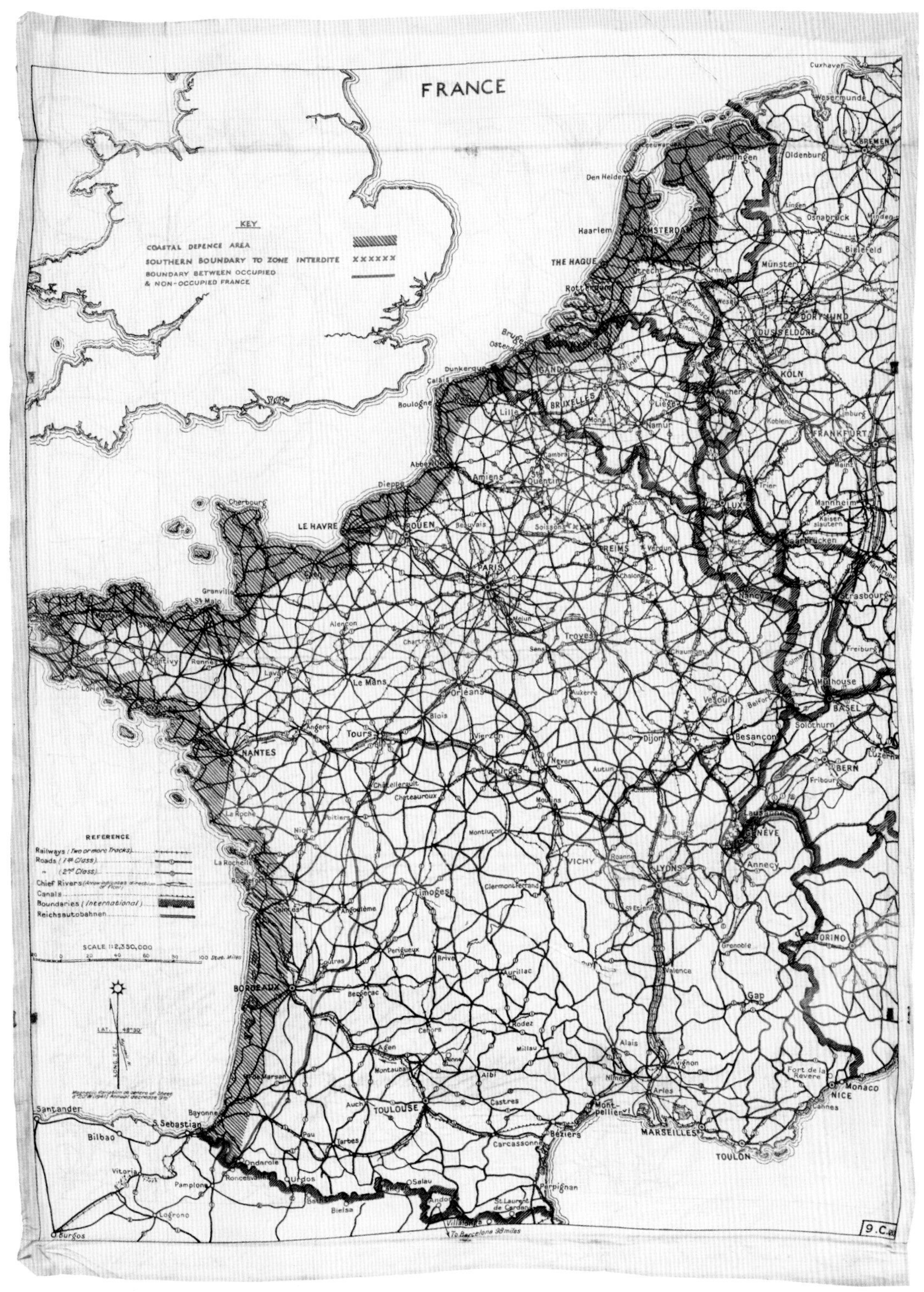

FRANCE
KEY
COASTAL DEFENCE AREA
SOUTHERN BOUNDARY TO ZONE INTERDITE XXXXXX
BOUNDARY BETWEEN OCCUPIED & NON-OCCUPIED FRANCE
REFERENCE
Railways (Two or more Tracks)
Roads (1st Class)
" (2nd Class)
Chief Rivers
Canals
Boundaries (International)
Reichsautobahnen
SCALE 1:2,350,000
100 Stat. Miles
LAT. 48°30'
LONG. 2°E.
AMSTERDAM
THE HAGUE
Rotterdam
Utrecht
Haarlem
Den Helder
Groningen
Oldenburg
BREMEN
Wesermunde
Cuxhaven
Osnabrück
Münster
Bielefeld
DORTMUND
DUSSELDORF
KÖLN
Aachen
Koblenz
FRANKFURT
Mannheim
Saarbrucken
Strasbourg
Freiburg
Mulhouse
BASEL
Solothurn
BERN
Fribourg
Lausanne
GENEVE
Annecy
TORINO
Brugge
Ostende
Dunkerque
Calais
Boulogne
GAND
BRUXELLES
Liege
Namur
Mons
Lille
Cambrai
Amiens
Dieppe
LE HAVRE
Cherbourg
ROUEN
Beauvais
Soissons
REIMS
Verdun
LUX
Metz
Nancy
PARIS
Chalons
Troyes
Chaumont
Granville
St Malo
Rennes
Pontivy
Quimper
Lorient
Alençon
Chartres
Melun
Sens
Auxerre
Le Mans
Laval
Orleans
Blois
Angers
Tours
NANTES
Vierzon
Bourges
Nevers
Dijon
Besançon
Belfort
Autun
Chatellerault
Chateauroux
Poitiers
Niort
La Roche
La Rochelle
Montlucon
Moulins
VICHY
Roanne
LYONS
Bourg
Limoges
Angoulême
Clermont Ferrand
St Etienne
Grenoble
Perigueux
Brive
Aurillac
Valence
Gap
BORDEAUX
Bergerac
Cahors
Rodez
Millau
Alais
Agen
Montauban
Albi
Castres
Mont-pellier
Nimes
Arles
Avignon
Fort de la Revere
NICE
Monaco
Cannes
Bayonne
Auch
TOULOUSE
Pau
Tarbes
Carcassonne
Beziers
MARSEILLES
TOULON
Perpignan
Santander
S. Sebastian
Bilbao
Vitoria
Pamplona
Logrono
Burgos
Roncesvalles
Urdos
Salau
Andorra
Bielsa
St. Laurent de Cerdans
To Barcelona 98 miles
9.C.

36 The Bombe and Colossus

The Bombe, spelt with an "e", was precursor to the first ever computer, Colossus. It was an electro-mechanical machine invented to break coded messages transmitted by the Germans. These messages were usually enciphered on an Enigma machine before being transmitted. Invented in 1923, the Enigma was used by the German Army and Navy, the Luftwaffe, the SS, the Military Intelligence Service (Abwehr) and the German State Railways (Reichsbahn). Originally it consisted of three rotors and a keyboard linked by an electric circuit, arranged in such a way that pressing a lettered key would light up a different letter on a display on the machine. Having been given the text of a message in clear, the operator would rewrite it substituting the original letters for those displayed by Enigma. The rotor settings were changed daily. Even in its simplest form, for every letter there were hundreds of millions of possible solutions. As the war progressed, an additional rotor was added, hugely increasing the number of steps that anyone deciphering the message had to get right before the message made sense. Throughout the war the Germans believed that Enigma was unbreakable.

Although a number of Enigma machines fell into British hands during the war, knowing how it worked was only the beginning; and anyway the British already possessed a similar machine known as Typex. The trick was to know the daily rotor settings. The British, recognizing that Enigma could be "broken", installed a group of university mathematicians at the Government Code and Cypher School at Bletchley Park, north of London. To begin with, the deciphering of messages was partly achieved by the application of mathematical formulae based on the fact that a) there are only 26 letters in the alphabet, b) no letter could stand for itself, and c) without number keys, figures had to be spelt out. To assist in this process, a type of machine devised by Polish code breakers, and greatly improved by a brilliant mathematician, Alan Turing, was installed at Bletchley. Nicknamed the Bombe, these machines were continually upgraded throughout the war, and eventually there were five types in use, not all at Bletchley. However it was there that the first Enigma codes were broken mechanically by the Bombe on 1 August 1940.

The Colossus, the world's first ever true computer which was devised to break the Lorenz enciphering machine code, was installed at Bletchley in December 1943. The Lorenz had 12 rotors instead of the improved Enigma's four. Eventually five Colossus machines were installed at Bletchley, some of which were used to decipher Japanese codes. The breaking of these codes provided an unexpected bonus in the form of intelligence for Allied planning for the landings in Normandy in June 1944. Early in 1944, the Japanese Military Attaché in Berlin was given a comprehensive tour of the part of the Atlantic Wall defending among other places, the beaches selected for the Allied assault. On return to his embassy, he sent a series of long messages back to Army HQ in Tokyo giving a highly detailed description of what he had seen in the minutest detail. His messages were intercepted by one of the British listening stations in England, and deciphered. The information they contained proved invaluable when read in conjunction with air photographic reconnaissance in establishing the number and calibre of guns, down to machine gun nests, defending the beaches.

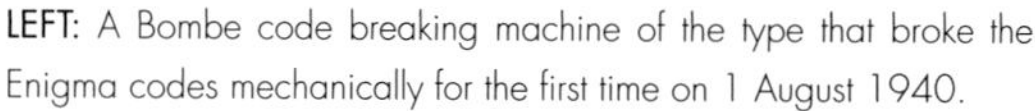

LEFT: A Bombe code breaking machine of the type that broke the Enigma codes mechanically for the first time on 1 August 1940.

TOP: A rare picture of the Colossus with its Wren operators. The Mark I was powered by 1,500 valves, the Mark II by 2,500.

ABOVE LEFT: One of the priority teams at work at Bletchley Park, handling the high priority coded radio traffic, such as signals that affected key operations including the Normandy landings.

ABOVE RIGHT: A Bombe unit room at Eastcote in Middlesex. This was similar to the Bombe room at Bletchley. As the workload on the Bombe machines increased during the war, units were established at more than eight other locations in addition to Bletchley Park. By 1944, there were at least 200 machines in operation at their various sites.

37 The *Stars and Stripes*

Published as a newspaper for the soldiers of the American Expeditionary Forces in 1917–19, *Stars and Stripes* came to life again in 1942 in order to provide news of the Home Front and the global war effort to deployed GIs. The newspaper had the War Department's endorsement and financial support, but editorial control swung back and forth between on the one hand, the Army's commanders and senior public affairs officers, and on the other, the newspaper's editorial staff, most of whom were established journalists who wore uniforms but remained more loyal to the First Amendment than to the Articles of War.

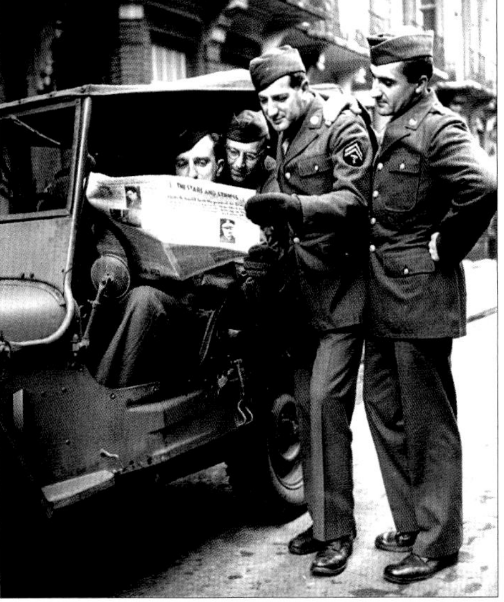

Reporting news from the Home Front presented no special "freedom of speech" problems since *Stars and Stripes* relied on US news services and national newspapers for domestic news. Sound coverage of government policies and domestic events, even unpleasant ones, offset rumours, the biased views of families and enemy propaganda. *Stars and Stripes* could also give GIs a sense of the conduct of the war in other theatres, the contributions of the other services and the Allies, and the reasoning behind the Army's strategic and operational decisions as seen from the War Department. There were few revelations about operations that violated security. *Stars and Stripes* reporters followed the censorship rules on security which applied to all newsmen.

Where *Stars and Stripes* ran into trouble was among senior commanders who saw the newspaper as a subversive influence that undermined their authority and encouraged indiscipline. The *Stars and Stripes* editorial staff, however, did not regard senior officers as infallible, or all Army policies as wise. Popular cartoonist Sergeant Bill Mauldin created his characters Willy and Joe, the iconic GIs of the Second World War, as a vehicle to criticize what he saw as the Army's tactical sophistry, and to expose the unjustified privileges for officers and rear area personnel. *Stars and Stripes* sought examples of commanders violating Army policies that advantaged enlisted men. This investigative reporting ferreted out examples of black-marketeering and misallocation of scarce supplies meant for combat units.

General Mark W Clark continually hectored military reporters. General Douglas MacArthur, as senior military commander in the Pacific, banned *Stars and Stripes* in the area until 1945. However, *Stars and Stripes* reporters could attack command influence by leaking stories to their civilian war correspondent colleagues. General George S Patton wanted Mauldin court-martialled; instead he received a Pulitzer Prize in 1945.

Stars and Stripes reached more than a million readers during the Second World War, and its reporting on the war with Germany remains an invaluable source of information about the war as fought by American enlisted men.

ABOVE: US soldiers reading an issue of *Stars and Stripes.*

RIGHT: The special edition of *Stars and Stripes* published to mark VE Day on 9 May 1945.

NICE-MARSEILLE EDITION

V-E Day | THE STARS AND STRIPES | D+336

Daily Newspaper of U.S. Armed Forces in the European Theater of Operations

Vol. 1—No. 57 | Wednesday, May 9, 1945 | ONE FRANC

Allies Proclaim:

IT'S OVER

Surrender Is Signed At Rheims

By CHARLES F. KILEY
Stars and Stripes Staff Writer

RHEIMS, May 8 — The Third Reich surrendered unconditionally to the Allies here at Gen. Dwight D. Eisenhower's forward headquarters at 2:41 AM Monday.

The surrender terms, calling for cessations of hostilities on all fronts at one minute past midnight (Double British Summer Time) Wednesday, May 9, were signed on behalf of the German government by Col. Gen. Gustaf Jodl, Wehrmacht chief and Chief of Staff to Fuehrer Karl Doenitz.

Under Jodl's signature were those of Lt. Gen. Walter Bedell Smith, Chief of Staff to the Supreme Allied Commander; Gen. Ivan Susloparoff, head of the Russian mission to France who was authorized by Moscow to sign on behalf of Soviet forces, and Gen. Suvez of France.

The surrender was signed in five minutes in the SHAEF war room here, 55 miles east of Compiegne forest where Germany surrendered in the last war on Nov. 11, 1918, and the scene of the capitulation of France to the Third Reich in this war June 21, 1940.

Flew from Germany

The terms were signed in less than ten hours after the arrival of Jodl by plane from Germany, and 34 hours after final negotiations first begun with the arrival Saturday of Gen. Adm. Hans Georg von Friedeburg, commander in chief of German navy, who on Thursday headed the Nazi delegation which surrendered German forces in Denmark, Holland and Northwestern Germany to the 21st Army Gp.

Gen. Eisenhower did not take

(Continued on Page 8)

Announce the Victory

GEN. EISENHOWER

PRESIDENT TRUMAN

"The crusade . . . has reached its glorious conclusion."

3rd Told Big News After Taking Prague

On the day of official announcement of the European war's end Third U.S. Army troops drove into Prague, and Marshal Joseph Stalin announced the fall of Breslau, Germany's ninth city, after an 80-day siege.

The Czech radio announced yesterday that the Czechoslovak commander of Prague defenses had welcomed the commander of the First Div. to Prague. The Germans, who fought a four-day patriot uprising, surrendered effective the afternoon of May 9—today.

A Soviet correspondent reported that the German commander raised the surrender flag at Breslau at 1800 hours Monday. German defense efforts ended in almost complete destruction of the city.

SWEDES BREAK WITH GERMANY

Sweden yesterday severed diplomatic relations with Germany on the ground that there is no central government to be recognized. The Swedish radio said all German buildings in Sweden had been taken over

Doughs Watch 'Final' Battle

ON THE ELBE RIVER, May 8—One of the last battles of the European war was fought on the east bank of the Elbe today—between the Russians and the Germans with Americans as spectators.

Everybody knew the end of hostilities was only a few hours away.

For the last week the German 12th Army was pushed back on the Elbe, and began surrendering to U.S. troops. The Germans built bridges while Americans on the west bank of the Elbe watched and accepted their surrender.

Peace came to Europe at one minute past midnight this morning (Nice-Marseille time) when the cease-fire order to which Germany had agreed went into effect.

Formal announcement of Germany's unconditional surrender came nine hours earlier in radio proclamations by President Truman and Prime Minister Churchill.

As they spoke the last "all-clear" sirens sounded in London and Paris, and the streets in both cities were the scenes of frenzied celebrations. America took the announcement calmly and quietly, having staged its celebration Monday when the German announcement of the surrender was flashed.

All hostilities had not ceased yet, however. Some German pockets still were resisting the Russians in Czechoslovakia and on islands in the Baltic Sea. Moreover, up to a late hour last night Moscow had not proclaimed victory.

The surrender agreement, it was disclosed, was signed at 0241 hours Monday in Gen. Eisenhower's headquarters at Rheims, France. To the last the Germans attempted to split the Western Allies and Soviet Russia, offering surrender at first only to the Western Allies. This was rejected flatly by Gen. Eisenhower.

Defeat of Germany—concluded in the bomb-burned and

(Continued on Page 8)

Allied Soldiers Praised In Ike's Victory Order

The text of Gen. Eisenhower's victory order of the day follows:—

Men and women of the Allied Expeditionary Force:

The crusade on which we embarked in the early summer of 1944 has reached its glorious conclusion. It is my especial privilege, in the name of all nations represented in this theater of war, to commend each of you for valiant performance of duty. Though these words are feeble they come from the bottom of a heart overflowing with pride in your loyal service and admiration for you as warriors.

"... Astonished the World ..."

Our accomplishments at sea, in the air, on the ground and in the field of supply have astonished the world. Even before the final week of the conflict you had put 5,000,000 of the enemy permanently out of the war. You have taken in stride military tasks so difficult as to be classed as impossible. You have confused and destroyed your savagely fighting foe.

On the road to victory you have endured every discomfort and privation and have surmounted every obstacle ingenuity and desperation could throw in your path. You did not pause until our front was firmly joined up with the great Red Army coming from the east, and other Allied forces coming from the south.

Full victory in Europe has been

(Continued on Page 8)

38 The Auster Light Aircraft

The Auster light aircraft was arguably the best airborne artillery spotter in the Second World War. It was designed by Taylorcraft in the USA for the expanding light private aircraft market, and in 1938 Taylorcraft Aeroplanes (England) was formed to build the aircraft under licence. Several variants were produced and on the outbreak of the Second World War these were evaluated for use as airborne spotters for artillery. The Taylorcraft Plus C two seater was selected for military production and designated the Auster Mk I.

The design was so successful that it was developed into the Mk III version. It was fitted with a Gipsy Major I engine, and 470 of this type were built. The next progression was to the Mk IV, with an American Lycoming engine and a larger cabin to accommodate a third seat. The fully glazed cockpit of the Mk IV and subsequent models were a great improvement on the earlier variants, which did not afford good visibility to the side and rear. But the most common Auster found with British forces was the Mk V, which included blind-flying instruments. Around 800 of these were built.

The Auster could operate off short, rough strips, and could land on roads and tracks provided obstructions on either side were removed. It had a high mounted wing, which gave excellent lift, and provided an unobstructed view of the ground. Thanks to its large trailing edge wing flaps, the Auster could fly at very low speed without stalling, which was invaluable when observation over the ground was needed. This, combined with its large rudder giving it exceptional turning ability especially at low speed, made it surprisingly difficult for a fighter to shoot down. By twisting and turning in flight and suddenly applying full flap, a skilled Auster pilot could bring his aircraft almost to a stop momentarily, and a pursuing fighter would often overshoot. The Lysander developed by the RAF for air spotting was shot out of the sky when used in this role.

The Auster Mk V with a top speed of 209 kph (130 mph) was faster than the German equivalent, the Fieseler Fi 156C Storch whose top speed was 174 kph (108 mph), and the American O-49 Vigilant (196 kph [122 mph]). The Auster also had a greater range (204 kilometres [250 miles]) than the Storch (286 kilometres [240 miles]), although it was less than the Vigilant (450 kilometres [280 miles]). Thanks to its low take-off weight (837 kg [1,846 lbs]) the Auster could operate from smaller strips, forest clearings and the like, than either the Storch (1,322 kg [2,915 lbs]) or the Vigilant (1.539 kg [3,392 lbs]). This enabled the Auster to be deployed much closer to the front line and hence its reaction time to calls for support was usually quick.

The Auster was used for reconnaissance, often by senior commanders who wanted to see the terrain over which they were going to deploy their troops, in the way that a helicopter is used today. But by far the most common use of the aircraft was to put an artillery observer up in the air from where he could correct the fall of shot. Artillery officers were taught to fly and, together with RAF pilots, were formed into joint air observation post squadrons (Air OP for short). They were able to detect and engage targets out of sight of friendly artillery observers on the ground. As an added bonus it was found that the presence of an artillery spotter aircraft often caused the opposing side's artillery to cease firing for fear of being spotted and having counter-battery fire brought down on it.

The Air OP did not fly directly over the target, but usually remained on his own side of the battlefield, while remaining high enough to see dead ground out of sight of OPs on the ground.

To begin with, the formation of the Air OP was resisted by the RAF, who were paranoid, as they are to this day, about any suggestion that the Army was forming a private air force and about any threat to the notion that only the RAF should fly every type of aircraft.

RIGHT: An Auster Mk III with a 130-hp Gipsy engine, the most widely produced of the early Auster variants.

39 The MG 42 German Machine Gun

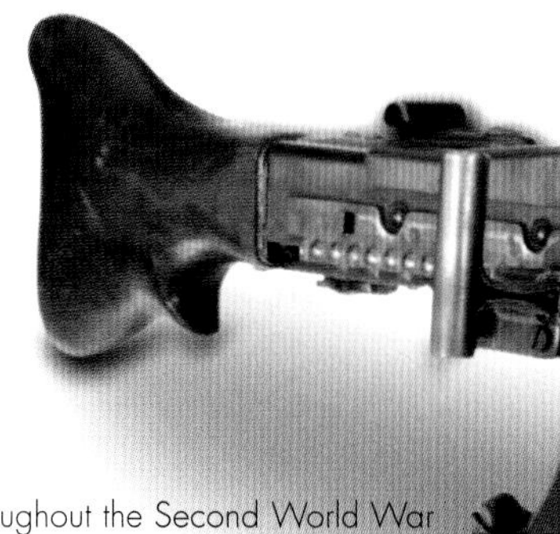

By the end of the First World War, machine guns consisted of two types: light and heavy. The latter, such as the Vickers, Maxim and Browning, were almost all water-cooled. Although the .50-calibre Browning was invented towards the end of the war, it did not come into service with the US army until 1922. The heavy machine gun, in some armies designated "medium", was designed to be used for long-range suppressive fire in support of attacks, and to be fired at all ranges in defence from fixed positions. It fired from a heavy tripod, or in some armies, an even heavier sled, and sometimes had a shield. The condenser can for the water-cooling system was cumbersome, and if all the water evaporated and no more was available, someone might have to urinate on the gun to cool it down. The ammunition was carried in a bulky box known in the British army as a "liner", containing one 250-round belt. The whole system – condenser can, ammunition liner, tripod and gun – could not be carried by one man. Because of its bulk, such a machine gun was difficult to conceal; to have a good chance of surviving, it had to be sited in a pit dug for it, or in a fold in the ground.

Before the First World War, the American Colonel Isaac Lewis designed a light machine gun, initially manufactured by the British Birmingham Small Arms Company. It saw much service with the British and US armies in the First World War, and was still used extensively in the Second. The Lewis, able to be carried by one man (although others carried extra ammunition for it) could be fired from a prone position, or, at a pinch, while standing; it was also easily concealed. The inter-war years saw the introduction of improved light machine guns into armies: the US Browning Automatic Rifle (BAR); the British Bren (actually a Czech design); and the French-designed Vickers-Berthier – all magazine-fed weapons. Light machine guns were all air-cooled, so that when the barrel became too hot from prolonged firing, it could be replaced with a cool spare barrel.

Most armies fought throughout the Second World War with at least two types of machine-gun: light, medium, and in some cases heavy as well. The German Army however believed that having two varieties of machine gun for different tactical roles often resulted in the correct weapon not being available. They therefore designed the first general purpose machine gun or GPMG. The basic weapon was the same, a belt-fed gun with an easily changed barrel, capable of being mounted on a tripod, and provided with long-range sights, but also with a bipod and shoulder butt. For long-range tasks the butt could be removed, the bipod unclipped, the gun quickly mounted on a tripod, and sights fitted that allowed indirect fire and night shooting on fixed lines. The advantage was that only one type of gun had to be manufactured.

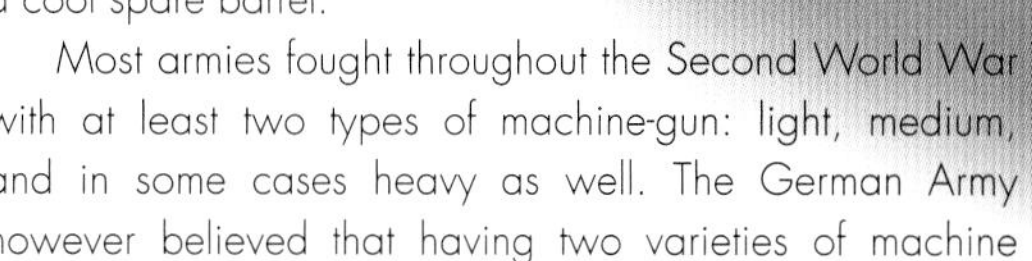

The first of the type was the MG 34, designed in the early 1930s and adopted for service in 1934. It weighed 12.1 kg (26 lbs 11 oz), fired 7.92mm ammunition, and was belt- or magazine-fed, with a cyclic rate of 650 rounds per minute. It remained the German army's GPMG until 1942, when it was replaced by the more reliable and cheaper MG-42. This gun at 11.6 kg (25 lb 8 oz) weighed marginally less than the MG 34 and was belt-fed only, but had a cyclic rate of 1,200 rounds per minute, twice that of the 34. Incorrectly called the Spandau, because the original pre-First World War Maxim had been modified for use by the Imperial German Army at the Spandau arsenal, it was actually made by Mauser. The MG 42 was a greatly respected and feared weapon; its rate of fire was so fast, it sounded like a buzz saw. By contrast British and US medium and light machine guns had cyclic rates of between 450 and 550 rounds per minute. A British infantry platoon commander remembered: "When it came to a firefight between a German platoon and a British platoon, their MG 42 won hands down. I remember my first reaction to actual infantry warfare in July 1944 was one of amazement at the crushing fire-power of this very rapid-firing gun." (*18 Platoon* by Sydney Jary, published by Sydney Jary Ltd, 1987.)

Now most armies have a GPMG in their inventory.

ABOVE: An MG 42 German machine gun.

LEFT: German paratroopers fire MG 42s across the River Arno in Florence in mid-1944 during the Italian campaign.

40 PLUTO

The acronym PLUTO stands for Pipeline Under The Ocean. As early as 1942, the problem was being considered of how to supply the huge quantities of fuel required by Allied forces invading and operating in Europe. Eventually there would be around two million soldiers and airmen ashore, with thousands of tanks, trucks and aircraft all requiring fuel. Following successful trials of a pipeline laid across the floor of the Bristol Channel, the development of a system to be laid in the English Channel went ahead. The final design was a 75-mm (3-in) diameter steel pipe welded into continuous lengths each of 48 kilometres (30 miles), and rolled onto big floating drums – Conundrums – from which the pipe would be laid. The Conundrums looked like giant cotton reels, 27.5 metres (90 feet) long and 15 metres (50 feet) in diameter, and when carrying a full length of pipe, weighed as much as a destroyer.

Starting at the Isle of Wight, the Conundrums were towed across the Channel, laying four lengths of pipe to Cherbourg after its capture by the Americans. Pipes were also laid from Liverpool to the Isle of Wight, over land except for the section in the Solent. These allowed fuel to be landed at Liverpool and pumped to Cherbourg.

PLUTO was unable to provide fuel for the Battle of Normandy in 1944 and the breakout operations, a period of over three months, because the first four pipelines, codename Bambi, could not be deployed until enemy minefields around the port and in the Cotentin Peninsula had been cleared. Pumping operations began on 18 September, by which time the Allied armies were hundreds of miles away on a line stretching from Holland and Belgium to the borders of Germany, and the Vosges.

Meanwhile fuel for the fighting was provided by Operation Tombola. This involved petrol being pumped ashore from small tankers off the Normandy coast along buoyed pipelines, direct to storage tanks at the British pipehead at Port-en-Bessin and the American one at Ste Honorine. These pipelines had a daily capacity of 8,000 tons. Fuel packed in jerry cans was also shipped in huge quantities to the Normandy beachhead – by the end of August 181,000 tons of fuel had been delivered to the British alone by this means.

From Normandy, petrol pipelines were linked up and extended to provide a through route from Cherbourg and Port-en-Bessin to Rouen. After 3 October, piped petrol was pumped into storage tanks at Darnetal, north of the Seine just outside Rouen.

With Ostend in Belgium in Allied hands, by 20 September tankers could dock there and discharge fuel directly ashore. In November 1944, three PLUTO pipes were laid from Dungeness to Boulogne, which had been captured by the Canadians on 23 September. Another three were laid by 1 December. These were set up just in time, as the Tombola pipes were put out of action by a storm that month. Pipeheads with a good storage capacity were established at Ghent and Boulogne for the British and near Paris and Lyons for the Americans. Pipelines for the southern group of US armies were extended towards Metz and Dijon, while in the north separate pipelines for the British and Americans were laid from Antwerp to the east and south-east.

The appetite for fuel of mechanized armies supported by air forces is brought home when one considers that of the three and a half million tons of supplies discharged at ports in France and Belgium in April 1945 alone, including ammunition, replacement tanks and vehicles of all kinds, railway engines and trucks, some 900,000 tons was bulk petrol. There were eventually 11 PLUTO pipes operating, pumping an average of 3,100 tons of fuel a day during March and April 1945; on the last day of the campaign 3,500 tons were delivered. PLUTO had played a major part in supplying what the French called *"le sang rouge de la guerre"* ("the red blood of war").

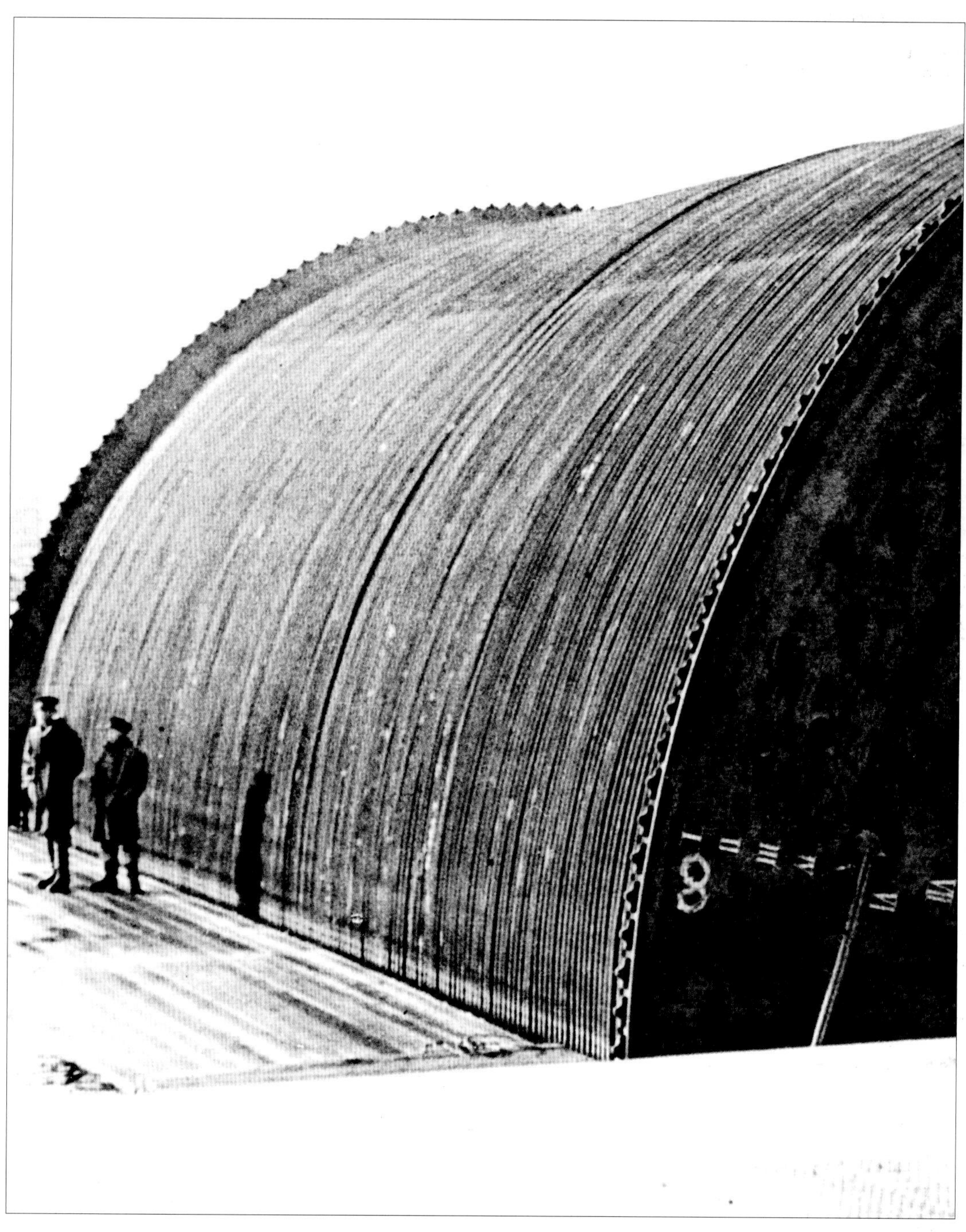

LEFT: The Pipeline Under the Ocean being reeled out over stern rollers from HMS *Sancroft* in June 1944.

ABOVE: A Conundrum ready to be towed across the Channel.

41 The Jeep

The vehicle's official title was the MB 4x4 Truck, but everyone called it a Jeep, and everyone wanted one. Before the Second World War ended, American automobile manufacturers, primarily the Ford Motor Company and Willys-Overland, had made 640,000 Jeeps.

Although the US Army had tried to standardize its family of motor vehicles into six different size classes in 1939, the field exercises of 1940 revealed a requirement for a small dual-drive wheeled vehicle that could carry a driver and three passengers in all sorts of terrain. The final model was powered by a four-cylinder inline engine of 60 hp and was capable of carrying 550 kg (1,200 lbs). Pulling a trailer added to its cargo capacity. It also had to have a removable canvas roof and side panels on a metal frame to deal with bad weather.

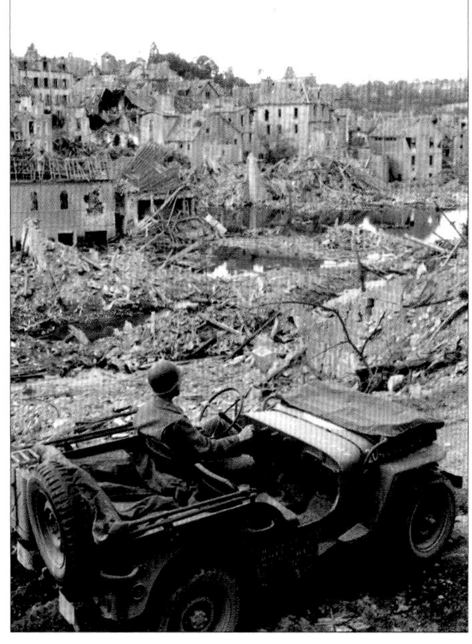

The War Department's request for a prototype went to 135 companies with a requirement to propose a design in 49 days. Only the American Bantam Car Company responded, submitting a design by Karl Probst, who drew up plans for the vehicle in two days. It was earlier design work by two Army officers for Bantam that made this response possible.

Because the American Bantam Car Company did not have the plant capacity or workforce to make the new vehicle, the Jeep contract went to Ford and Willys using the Probst-American Bantam Car design under a royalties agreement. The unloaded vehicle weighed 1,090 kg (2,400 lbs), which meant it could be pushed and pulled by soldiers if necessary. Its four-cylinder engine, 60 hp motor allowed it to creep up steep inclines, yet it could speed along good roads at 89 kph (55 mph). Its range was 450 kilometres (280 miles). It could be adapted to carry radios and stretchers, as well as a mount for a .30-calibre or a .50-calibre machine gun for combat zone missions. It could even pull light anti-tank guns and small howitzers.

Stuck with the name "Jeep" – whose origin is uncertain, but popular theories are that it came from "GP" meaning "general purpose", or was derived from the go-anywhere character Eugene the Jeep in *Popeye* cartoons – in various models and modes the vehicle became common in every Allied army, or was duplicated in some variant, as in the Red Army. American divisions normally rated around 1,350 service support motor vehicles, and of these, 612 would have been Jeeps. Every infantry company had one Jeep and trailer; enterprising units found more than one. Since seven out of every ten GIs came from families that had a car, a truck or a tractor, maintenance and minor repairs could be performed at the unit level. The simplicity of the Jeep's motor made this possible. It's utility in rough terrain made it popular in the Second World War, a popularity that explains the presence of Jeeps in a variety of models all over the world, even today.

ABOVE: A US solider looks over the destroyed city of Saint-Lô from his Jeep.

RIGHT: Finished Jeeps stand in rows having been mass-produced for the Allied invasion of Nazi-Europe.

42 The Green Beret

On the evening of 4 June 1940, Lieutenant Colonel Dudley Clarke, a military assistant to Sir John Dill, Chief of the Imperial General Staff (CIGS), was walking back from the War Office to his flat. At 14.23 hours that afternoon the Admiralty had signalled the end of Operation Dynamo, the evacuation from Dunkirk. The great bulk of the British Expeditionary Force (BEF) had been extracted from France and Flanders, but the outlook was grim.

In 49 days the Germans had occupied Denmark, Norway, Holland and Belgium. France was on the verge of collapse and the Channel ports were in the hands of the enemy. Clarke asked himself if there was any way the British army could strike back, and recalled how, some 40 years earlier, Boer commandos in South Africa, defeated in conventional battles, had harried huge numbers of British troops. He committed his ideas to paper and gave this to his boss, who presented it to the Prime Minister, Winston Churchill. Two days later, Dill told Clarke that his Commando scheme was approved and he was to mount a raid across the Channel at the earliest possible moment.

Even before the first raid, the question arose of what this force should be called. Someone in the War Office had already started calling them Special Service Battalions, either forgetting or ignoring the fact that the initials SS stood for the infamous Nazi *Schutzstaffel*. The CIGS decreed that the new force would be known as Commandos, although the brigades retained the name Special Service until late in 1944.

To begin with all Commandos wore their own regimental head-dress and badge, but in May 1942, Admiral Mountbatten, then Chief of Combined Operations, under whose command the Commandos came, wrote to the Under Secretary of State for War:

> *I have received a request from the Commander of the Special Service Brigade that the Brigade should be allowed to wear a distinctive form of head-dress.*
>
> *2. Approval is therefore requested for them to wear a green beret similar in design to the maroon beret worn by the Airborne Division and on which officers and men would wear the badge of their own regiment.*
>
> *3. I have been much struck by the intense desire on the part of all officers and men with whom I have spoken to have a distinctive form of head-dress and consider that it would make the greatest difference to esprit-de-corps.*
>
> *4. I have discussed this matter personally with the Adjutant General before forwarding this official request.*

The new beret was not issued until October 1942, and not all men were as keen to wear it as Mountbatten had implied: the colour was thought effeminate. But "feelings soon changed and it was not long before the practical and prestigious value of the green beret outweighed any colour prejudice" (*The Light Blue Lanyard: 50 Years with 40 Commando Royal Marines*, Major J C Beadle, Square One Publication, 1992). The green beret was worn with pride in action and on parade, in preference to any other head-dress. Royal Marines and Army Commandos wear it to this day.

FAR LEFT: A Commando with a silenced Sten and wearing a Denison Smock.

ABOVE & LEFT A British Royal Marines Commando beret featuring a metal Royal Marines cap insignia.

43 The Panzerfaust

The Panzerfaust ("armour fist") was a German shoulder-launched anti-tank weapon. It was the second generation of its type, the first being the Panzerschreck. The Americans had been first to produce a shoulder-launched anti-tank rocket fired from a 60-mm (2.36-in) tube: the Bazooka. Although a pre-war idea, it was not effective until the invention of the shaped or hollow charge, which could defeat armour. The principle was to mould the explosive round a cone, which increased its power by up to 15 times.

Until then, armour-piercing weapons relied solely on firing a projectile made of very hard steel, which "drilled" its way through the armour by virtue of its kinetic energy; some anti-armour weapons rely on this characteristic to this day. To produce the necessary muzzle velocity requires a large and powerful gun, which cannot be carried around by an infantry soldier. As the war progressed and tanks with heavier armour appeared on the battlefield, anti-tank guns became correspondingly bigger. The British army, for example, developed from the useless Boyes anti-tank rifle and 25-mm Hotchkiss in 1939 to the very effective 17-pounder in 1943. Anti-tank guns had to be towed or fitted in vehicles, and were difficult to conceal because of the dust and flame of their muzzle blast.

The hollow charge changed this. It works by projecting a stream of super-hot molten metal through the armour, which sprays the interior of the vehicle, killing the crew and setting fire to ammunition and fuel. This often causes a massive explosion, on occasions big enough to blow the turret off a tank. A hollow charge does not have to be especially large to achieve a "kill" against an armoured vehicle. With the addition of an aerodynamic nose cone, it can be fixed to a rocket, and this, with the launcher, is light enough to be carried by an infantry soldier.

The American Bazooka was sent in considerable numbers to Russia, where several fell into German hands. The Germans copied it and produced the Panzerschreck, which fired an electrically-ignited 88-mm rocket grenade. It was operated by two men, one to carry and fire it, the other to carry spare rockets and load the tube. It had a range of 135 metres (150 yards), and could penetrate 21cm (8.25in) of armour. The tube could be reloaded, and, like a Bazooka, fired as often as there were rockets available.

The Panzerfaust also fired a hollow-charge bomb, but from a disposable tube. It was light, and could be carried and fired by one man. It first appeared in late 1942, had a range of up to 90 metres (100 yards), and could penetrate 19.8 cm (7.8 in) of armour. It was cheap, and over six million were manufactured during the war. It was widely used by the German army, and, towards the end of the war, by the *Volkssturm*.

In built-up areas and thick country such as the Normandy Bocage, it was extremely effective. Small bodies of infantry could hide in ambush and, having allowed a tank to pass them, could fire a Panzerfaust into the side or rear of the tank, where the armour was usually thinner. For this reason the Panzerfaust was feared by Allied tank crews, especially when fighting in towns or villages, around agricultural buildings, and in terrain consisting of woods and thick hedgerows.

LEFT: A soldier of the Waffen SS with a Panzerfaust in the Ukraine on the Eastern Front in January 1944.

ABOVE: The Panzerfaust.

OVERLEAF: German infantry carrying Panzerschreck rocket launchers with blast shields. This weapon preceded the Panzerfaust.

44 Montgomery's Beret and Tank

When Bernard Montgomery took command of the Eighth Army in the Western Desert on 13 August 1942 he wore a standard issue general officer's service dress khaki cap with a red band. There are photographs of him wearing this as late as September. However, on his first morning in command, among the first troops he visited were the Australians, where he acquired the first of his distinctive hats: an Australian bush hat. As he went round his army over the succeeding days, he began to pin badges of many of the units he visited on to the hat. In his own words, "First of all because it was an exceedingly good hat for the desert, but soon because I came to be recognized by it: outside the Australian lines anyway!" (*The Memoirs of Field Marshal the Viscount Montgomery of Alamein KG*, Collins, 1958.) As the days passed he was given more and more badges and soon the bush hat was loaded with them. He wore this hat through the battle of Alam Halfa (20 August–5 September 1942), and there is a photograph of him wearing it on 6 September 1942 while he showed President Roosevelt's emissary Wendell Wilkie a German tank that had been burned out in the battle.

After the battle of Alam Halfa, Montgomery decided that he needed a command tank to enable him to get well forward in the next battle, El Alamein, and subsequent engagements. In the desert, provided one picked the right piece of ground, it was often possible to get an excellent view of a battle. But the approaches might not be suitable for a wheeled vehicle, and once there, if spotted by the enemy, one might well be shelled. Accordingly, a Grant tank was provided for his use, complete with a Royal Tank Regiment (RTR) crew. The good radio communications and armoured protection of the Grant were also desirable assets for a commander – attributes lacking in a staff car. However, when scrambling in and out of the hatch of a tank turret, Montgomery found that the brim of his bush hat kept catching on the rim of the hatch, and on projections inside the tank itself.

His RTR crew soon noticed this and suggested he wore a beret, lending him one of theirs – a black RTR beret complete with regimental cap badge. The RTR had been the first regiment in the British Army to wear a beret, approved by King George V in 1923, for the very reason that Montgomery discovered: it was eminently sensible headgear for a tank. Montgomery had a general officer's cap badge added to the RTR badge on his beret. In his *Memoirs* he wrote:

> *The twin badges in the beret were, in origin, accidental; but I quickly saw their functional result, and what started as a private joke with the tank regiment which gave it to me, became in the end the means by which I could be recognized throughout the desert. I soon learnt that the arrival of the double-badged beret on the battlefield was a help – they knew that I was about, that I was taking an intense and personal interest in their doings… It became, if you like, my signature. It was also very comfortable.*

Eventually the Grant tank was modified inside to provide space for his Aide-de-Camp, Captain John Poston,

LEFT: Montgomery with his RTR Beret with two cap badges. This photograph was taken in 1943.

ABOVE: Montgomery's command tank, pictured here in the Imperial War Museum in London.

or another staff officer to work, use the radio, spread out maps and so on. Montgomery used his command tank throughout the campaign in the North African Desert up to May 1943. It was not so suitable for the campaigns in Sicily and Italy; the narrow roads and the terrain made travelling by car or jeep, and walking to an observation point, more practicable. As an army group commander in northwest Europe, Montgomery did not need to go as far forward as he had as an army commander, and after becoming a Field Marshal on 31 August 1944, he travelled by staff car with a prominent flag on the bonnet: the Union Flag. However, he continued to wear his RTR beret with two badges whenever he appeared in khaki battle dress for the rest of his life.

45 The Midget Submarine

The British, Germans, Italians and Japanese all built midget submarines in the Second World War. They were usually used to attack warships in harbours which conventional submarines would find difficult to penetrate. British midget submarines, X-craft, carried two one-ton high explosive charges on either side of the hull which could be dropped on the seabed below the target, or fixed to the enemy ship's hull by magnetic clamps – the latter required a diver to exit from the X-craft. Axis midget submarines, on the other hand, fired torpedoes.

British X-craft carried out one of the most successful attacks of the Second World War on 22 September 1943, the target being the German battleship *Tirpitz* in Kaafjord, Norway. Of the six X-craft, each with a crew of four, that were towed across the North Sea by six submarines, four actually entered Kaafjord as two were lost en route, though the crew of one of them survived. X7, under Lieutenant Godfrey Place, was for a time caught in anti-submarine nets, but after freeing his boat Place went on to drop his two charges under the *Tirpitz*. X6 (Lieutenant Commander Donald Cameron) was sighted by the *Tirpitz* and engaged by small-arms fire, but Cameron surfaced alongside the battleship, dropped his charges and scuttled his boat. He and his crew were, however, taken prisoner.

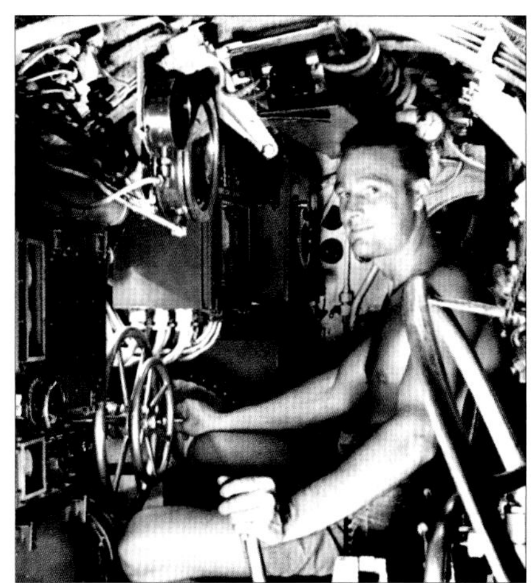

When all four charges detonated, X7 was temporarily trapped in another net on her way out, and with her controls damaged by the explosions, she shot to the surface, where she was sunk by enemy gunfire. Place and another officer survived, and were taken prisoner. One of X7's charges exploded right under the *Tirpitz's* engine room, putting the battleship out of action for six months and thereby altering the balance of sea power in the North Atlantic in the Allies' favour.

X5 was never seen again, and X10, which had been sent to attack the *Scharnhorst*, thought to be nearby but actually at sea, returned to her parent submarine, only to sink on the homeward trip. Cameron and Place were both awarded the Victoria Cross.

The following April, Lieutenant Commander Max Shean in X24 went in to attack a large floating dock in Bergen, Norway. A mistake in identifying the target resulted in the mines being placed under a large German merchantman, sinking it. Shean and his crew managed to return to the parent submarine.

Two X-craft were used to mark the approaches to the British beaches for the Normandy landings of 6 June 1944. Two of the later types, XE-class vessels, sank the Japanese heavy cruiser *Takao* off Singapore and both captains were awarded the VC. On the same day, two other XE-craft managed to cut the telegraph cables off Saigon and Hong Kong.

The Germans developed a number of types of midget submarine late in the war to counter Allied amphibious operations, and these were used in open waters off beaches rather than in harbours, though for little gain. The most successful class was the Seehund (Seal) operating against Allied sea lines of communication in the English Channel. In 142 sorties, eight ships were sunk for the loss of 35 *Seehunds*.

The Japanese built 50 midget submarines, but most attacks were unsuccessful. Five were used and lost at Pearl Harbor on 7 December 1941. An attack on Sydney harbour on 31 May 1942 by three midget submarines resulted in the sinking of the depot ship HMAS *Kuttabul*, killing 21 sailors for the loss of all the submarines. The day before, on 30 May 1942, two midget submarines entered Diego Suarez harbour in Madagascar: one of them damaged the old British battleship *Ramillies* while the other sank a tanker. One submarine was subsequently lost at sea; the crew of the other landed to find food and were killed in an encounter with Allied troops. Japanese midget submarine attacks around Guadalcanal , Okinawa and the Philippines were largely failures.

The Italians completed only four midget submarines in the Second World War. They deployed to the Black Sea during the German siege and blockade of Sevastopol in 1942, but without success.

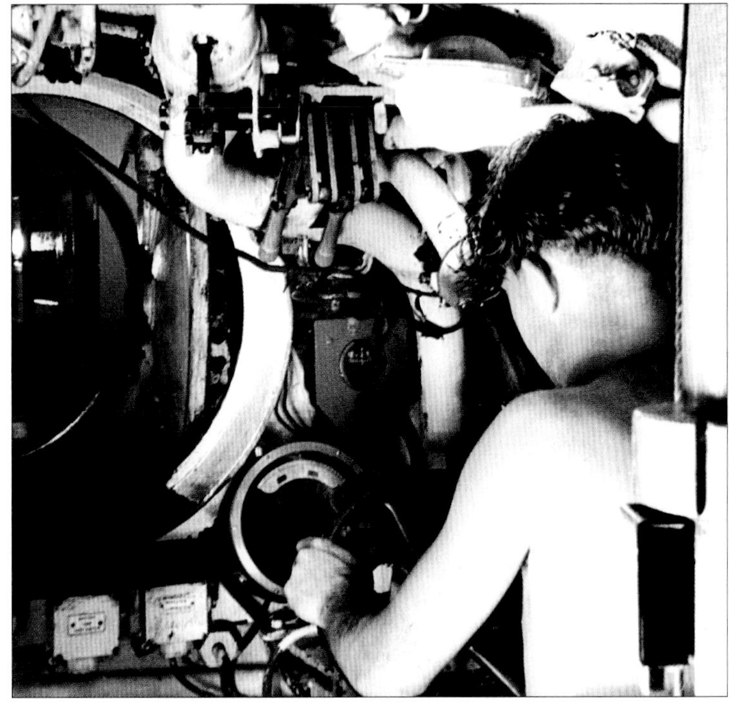

ABOVE: A German *Seehund* (Seal) midget submarine in a U-boat shelter.

LEFT: Leading Seaman Rhodes at the diving controls of a British XE4, the same type of midget submarine that sank the Japanese heavy cruiser *Takao*.

RIGHT: Another shot clearly showing the controls of the XE4.

OVERLEAF: A damaged Japanese dry dock at Kure with Japanese midget submarines. Taken after the Japanese surrender.

46 The Avro Lancaster Bomber

One of the greatest aircraft in the history of air warfare, the Avro Lancaster was produced because of a design flaw in its immediate predecessor, the Manchester. The RAF specification in 1939 was for a twin-engined bomber of an exceptional – for those days – size. The first Manchester flew on 26 July 1939, and 209 were delivered to operational squadrons. But its poor performance and unreliable engines resulted in its being withdrawn from service and all surviving aircraft were scrapped. It was decided to base its replacement on the Manchester design, but to build it with a longer span and four Rolls-Royce Merlin engines. The first Lancaster, called the Manchester III, flew at the beginning of 1941. It was so successful that the type went into immediate full-scale production. It was one of the few warplanes in history that was spot on from the start, and only minor changes were made to the design throughout its production history. In early 1942 the first operational squadron, number 44, received its Lancasters. From then until the end of the Second World War, 59 RAF squadrons flew Lancasters on 150,000 sorties in Europe, dropping 606,612 tons of bombs.

The Lancaster carried a heavier load and bigger bombs than any other aircraft in the European theatre, over twice that of the B-17 Flying Fortress. The normal bomb load for a Lancaster was 6336 kg (13,970 lbs) which gave it a range of 2,694 kilometres (1,674 miles), but it could carry the

ABOVE: An RAF Lancaster bomber.

FAR LEFT: Ground crews load anti-ship mines on to a Lancaster Bomber. Mining operations, codename Gardening, attracted little publicity but were flown on almost every night of the war by RAF Bomber Command, inflicting heavy losses on German shipping and submarines. It was highly dangerous, the dropping height was around 3,352 metres (11,000 feet) over the relatively few deep-water channels off the North Sea and Baltic coasts: obvious targets. The mining aircraft flew in small groups, and were easily detected by German radar and attacked often by fighters.

massive "Grand Slam" at 9,958 kg (21,954 lbs) over a shorter range – 450 kg (1,000 lbs), more than even a B-29 Super Fortress's capability. The B-17 Flying Fortress had the potential to carry almost as big a bomb load as the Lancaster, but the USAAF preferred to carry more and heavier guns together with much more armour, in line with their tactic of the self-defending bomber force attacking in daylight. The Lancaster's six 7mm (.303-in) machine guns were far less effective than the B-17's 13 12.7-mm (.5-in) heavy machine guns. Unlike the B-17, the Lancaster did not have a ball turret in the belly of the fuselage, and had no waist gunners. This made the Lancaster very vulnerable from below, the favourite attack position of the German night fighters. One Lancaster was built with a belly ball turret, but no more were produced thereafter.

The sortie that made the Lancaster famous to the British public was the Dams Raid on 17 May 1943, but the Lancaster was the "workhorse" of the RAF's bombing offensive over Germany and took part in every major night attack. They dropped 132 tons of bombs for every Lancaster lost, compared with 86 for the Halifax and 41 for the Stirling (the other two British four-engined bombers flown by the RAF). The German battleship *Tirpitz* was eventually sunk by a Lancaster dropping a 5,450-kg (12,000-lb) bomb on 12 November 1944. Lancasters were also used in support of ground offensives in Europe, perhaps most notably and controversially several times in and around Caen in Normandy, and most famously before Operation Goodwood in July 1944. After which the abrasive Commander of Bomber Command, Air Chief Marshal Sir Arthur Harris remarked, "Unfortunately the army did not exploit its opportunities."

The Lancaster remains the symbol of the RAF's strategic bombing effort and, although it was not yet in use at the time, one still flies today with the Battle of Britain Memorial Flight.

47 US Airborne Divisional Insignia

Of the 89 divisions the US Army organized in the Second World War, five were designated airborne divisions. This title meant that their soldiers had been trained to go into action by parachuting from a transport plane or riding to the ground in a piloted glider that had been towed to the landing zone by a transport plane. Three US airborne divisions fought the Germans: the 17th, 82nd and 101st. One, the 11th Airborne Division, fought the Japanese in the Philippines. The fifth, the 13th Airborne Division, went to Europe but did not see combat. During the course of the war, independent parachute infantry regiments also entered combat. One such unit, the First Special Service Force, was an American-Canadian parachute regiment that fought in Italy and southern France. The Army also organized an African-American airborne unit, the 555th Parachute Infantry Battalion, but it did not deploy overseas.

It was German use of airborne troops that encouraged the US Army to convert a parachute-training battalion to a fully-fledged 501st Parachute Infantry Regiment in early 1942, followed three months later by the re-designation of the 82nd Infantry Division to airborne status, and the creation of the 101st Airborne Division in August 1942. The three most famous members of the Army's "Airborne mafia", Matthew B Ridgway, Maxwell D Taylor, and James M Gavin, were part of these organizational creations.

During the formation of the two pioneer airborne divisions, Army planners debated their mission. One potential use was to land deep behind enemy lines by parachute and glider, and seize an airfield for follow-on forces delivered by transports. This "strategic" use looked too vulnerable to enemy air and armoured counterattacks. Instead, the "operational" mission won approval: using parachute and glider forces to give depth to an amphibious operation in which conventional forces of infantry, artillery and armour would join up with the airborne forces in 24–28 hours and thus spare them annihilation. This concept, tested in North Africa in November 1942 and Sicily in July 1943, led to larger operations in Italy (September 1943), France (June and August 1944), Holland (September 1944) and Germany (March 1945), with mixed results.

The basic problem was that unreinforced airborne units were left in combat too long to function because of mounting casualties, especially to troop leaders. The lack of adequate numbers and types of transports and gliders also shaped planning. Close air support in airborne operations never reached its potential.

By 1944, the organization of airborne divisions reflected the planners' assumption that they would fight violent but short-lived battles with a confused enemy. A division had three parachute infantry regiments: a glider infantry regiment, a four-battalion artillery regiment (75 mm and short 105 mm howitzers) and airborne engineer, anti-air and anti-tank battalions. Division strength climbed from 8,400 to 13,000 in an effort to increase firepower and infantry sustainability.

To the GI with physical confidence and an adventurous spirit, joining an airborne division became irresistible. A paratrooper received extra pay, wore jump wings and a special cap patch, and walked about in glistening jump boots below bloused trousers. He also wore a distinctive jump suit in combat and carried special infantry weapons designed for parachuting. A paratrooper could count on elite infantry comrades in his "band of brothers". High casualties also ensured rapid promotion for the survivors. The US Army never lacked for airborne volunteers.

LEFT: American paratroopers of either the 82nd or 101st Division preparing to jump during the invasion of Normandy, 6 June 1944.

ABOVE: (Top) The insignia for the 82nd Airborne Division. (Below) The insignia for the 101st Airborne Division.

OVERLEAF: Paratroopers of the 17th Airborne Division jump into Germany on 24 March 1945 as part of Operation Varsity. The Division was part of XVIII Airborne Corps, First Allied Airborne Army, and secured bridges over the Essel River for the US 12th Army Group's ground divisions in the final offensive on Germany.

48 The Desert Rats Insignia

The term "Desert Rats" is often incorrectly used to include everyone who fought on the British side in the North African desert in the Second World War. It is sometimes confused with the name bestowed by the traitor Lord Haw Haw, when broadcasting on German radio, on the Australian defenders of Tobruk – "the rats of Tobruk". In fact the Desert Rats was the name given to the British 7th Armoured Division from 1940 to 1945.

In March 1938, the British formed a Mobile Force on the coast of Egypt at Mersa Matruh, 195 kilometres (120 miles) west of Alexandria. Its aim was to protect the Egyptian frontier should the Italians, garrisoned in their colony of Libya, attack the British base in Egypt and the Suez Canal. The Mobile Force consisted of four armoured regiments: the 7th, 8th and 11th Hussars, and 1st Royal Tank Regiment supported by the 3rd Regiment Royal Horse Artillery (RHA). Their equipment was obsolescent: Rolls Royce armoured cars of First World War vintage, old light tanks, 15-cwt trucks and 3.7-inch howitzers.

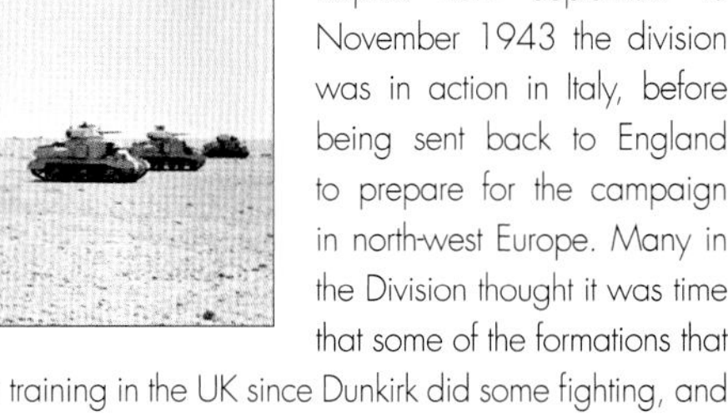

These units were soon joined by 1st Battalion the King's Royal Rifle Corps (KRRC), commanded by a man who was to become a legend in the Western Desert, Lieutenant Colonel William "Strafer" Gott. Many soldiers in Egypt regarded the Mobile Force as a joke, calling it the "Mobile Farce". Fortunately, in September 1938 it was taken over by Major General Percy Hobart. He took it out into the desert for weeks of vigorous, realistic training, and welded it into a first-class formation comprising a mobile division of three brigades. On the outbreak of war, this Mobile Division moved to the Egyptian/Libyan frontier but soon afterwards Hobart, who fell out with the British Commander in Egypt, was sacked, much to his soldiers' dismay. He returned to England and became a corporal in the Home Guard, and eventually formed and commanded the 79th Armoured Division.

On 16 February 1940, the Mobile Division became the 7th Armoured Division. The wife of the divisional commander, Major General Michael O'Moore Creagh, visited the Cairo Zoo, where she sketched a jerboa, and this became the basis for the divisional sign.

The 7th Armoured Division began its long years of fighting by defeating the Italians at the Battle of Sidi Barrani on 9 December 1940. After the British took Tobruk on 22 January 1941, the Desert Rats were sent in a daring cross-desert thrust to Beda Fomm where they inflicted a crushing defeat on the Italian 10th Army. Thereafter, the Division took part in most of the major engagements of the Desert War, including Operations Battleaxe (15–17 June 1941) and Crusader (18 November–30 December 1941), and the Battles of Gazala (26 May–21 June 1942) and the Cauldron (27 May–13 June 1942), Alam Halfa (30 August–5 Septemeber 1942) and the Second Battle of El Alamein (23 October–4 November 1942). From Alamein they participated in the fighting advance to Tripoli, ending the North African campaign in Tunis in May 1943.

By now they had been on the go for two and a half years. But there would be no respite: from September to November 1943 the division was in action in Italy, before being sent back to England to prepare for the campaign in north-west Europe. Many in the Division thought it was time that some of the formations that had been training in the UK since Dunkirk did some fighting, and there was considerable unhappiness. A senior officer, watching units of the Division on their way to embark for France in June 1944, remarked in shock, "They were arsing about… they were the Desert Rats, the most famous division in the British Army, and they were fed up and irresponsible." (Brigadier later General Sir Otway Herbert, quoted in *Monty: Master of the Battlefield 1942–1944* by Nigel Hamilton, Hamish Hamilton, 1984.)

Following some early setbacks in Normandy and a change of divisional commander, the Division regained its confidence and style. On 3 May 1945, the 11th Hussars led the 7th Armoured Division into Hamburg; except for taking part in the Victory Parade in Berlin on 21 July 1945, the long march of the Division was over. A sign on the outskirts of Berlin erected by the Division records the route from Alamein to the heart of Germany, omitting the first two and a half years in the life of one of the most famous divisions in the history of the British Army.

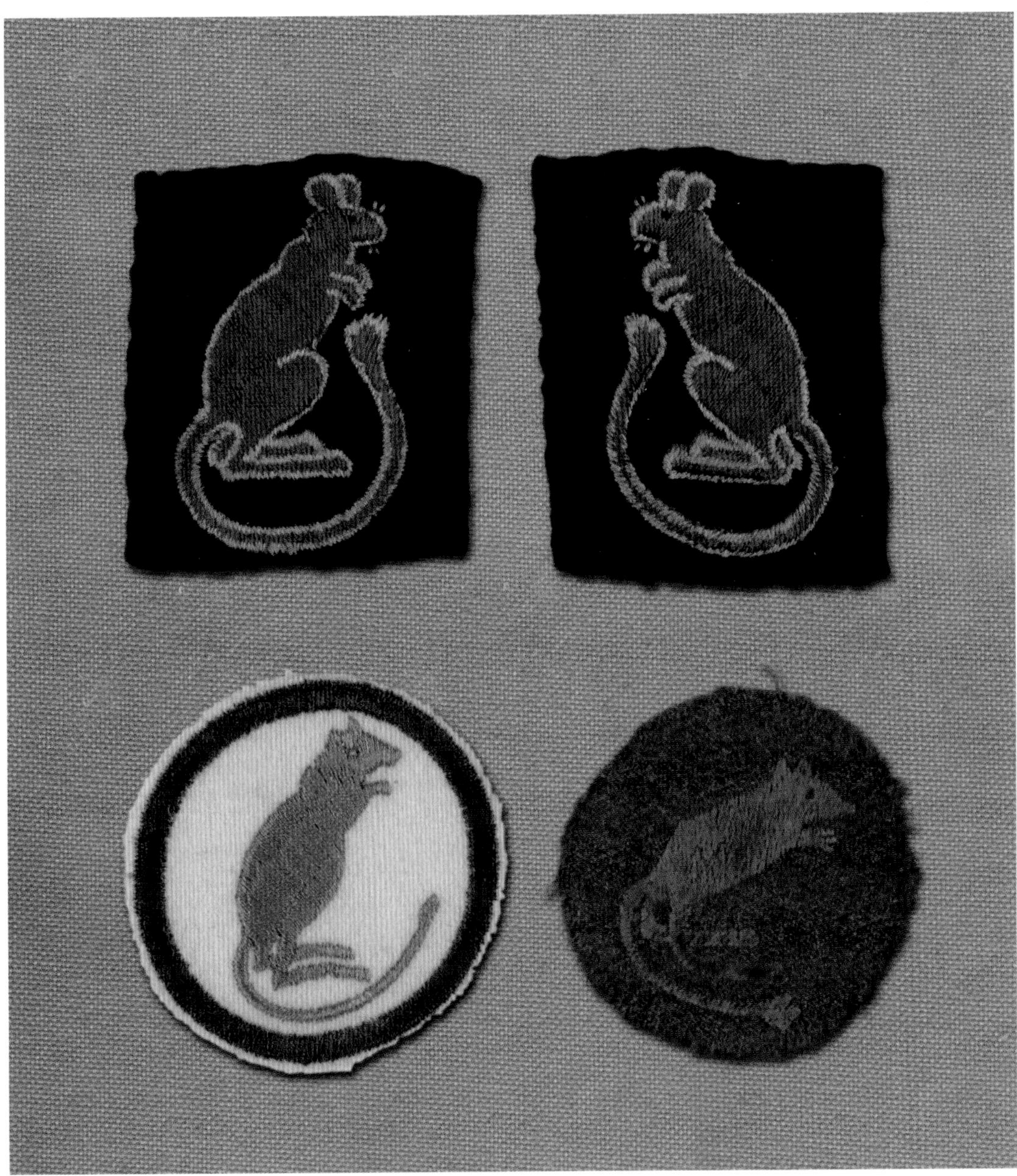

LEFT: Lee Grant tanks of 22nd Armoured Brigade of the 7th Armoured Division in the Western Desert in July 1942.

TOP: The Desert Rat insignia based on the design by the wife of the first commander of the division, Major General Creagh, after a visit to Cairo Zoo where she sketched a Jerboa. This is the modified version worn by 7th Armoured Brigade.

ABOVE, BOTTOM LEFT: After being sent to Burma in early 1942, the 7th Armoured Brigade returned to its parent formation, the 7th Armoured Division, but modified its badge to a green "jungle" rat.

ABOVE, BOTTOM RIGHT: An early-pattern desert version of the Desert Rat insignia.

49 Australian Divisional Badges

When the Second Australian Imperial Force (AIF) was formed at the start of the Second World War, the newly raised divisions chose typically Australian animals to appear on their identifying badges. The 7th Division had a kookaburra, and the 9th Division a platypus, while the 6th Division's badge featured a kangaroo and that of the 8th Division was an emu. All of the animals were generally shown on top of another Australian icon, a boomerang. A variant of the badges was used in white on black as a unit vehicle identifier. The 6th, 7th, 8th and 9th Divisions were the only ones to experience active service as complete divisions in the Second World War.

The 6th Division was the first to see action, in January 1941 at the Battle of Bardia, a stronghold held by the Italians just inside Libya which was then an Italian colony. After two days' fighting, the division captured 44,400 prisoners, 260 guns and 130 tanks for the loss of 130 Australian dead and 320 wounded. During the second night of the battle, some Italians came in to surrender and were told by an Australian officer that they had not got time to deal with them, and to come back in the morning. The division went on to capture Tobruk on 22 January 1941 and to participate in the crushing defeat of the Italian 10th Army at Beda Fomm. Further service in Greece and Crete was followed by fighting against the Japanese in New Guinea.

One brigade of the 7th Division took part in the defence of Tobruk with the 9th Division, while the remainder of the 7th took part in the invasion of Vichy French Syria in June–July 1941. After this, the division fought in New Guinea and Borneo between August 1942 and August 1945.

The 8th Division fought in Malaya and Singapore, where the bulk of the division was taken prisoner following the surrender to the Japanese in February 1942.

The 9th Division spent more time fighting in the Second World War than any other Australian division. The Division was the mainstay of the defence of Tobruk during the first part of the siege from April to October 1941 at a cost of 3,164 Australian casualties, and took part in both Battles of El Alamein (1–27 July 1942 and 23 October–4 November 1942). In the Second Battle, under Montgomery's command, the 9th were given the tough task of smashing through the Italian Trento Division and the German 164th Division in the north of the battlefield. Their success drew German reinforcements northwards, fulfilling Montgomery's hopes and enabling him to execute Operation Supercharge, which clinched the battle. Over a period of four months of fighting in the Alamein sector, the Division suffered another 5,809 casualties. The high regard in which the 9th was held is exemplified by the remark made by General Montgomery's Chief of Staff on the morning of the Normandy invasion: "My God, I wish we had 9th Australian Division with us this morning" (*The Australian Army in World War II* by Mark Johnston, Osprey, 2007). But the 9th had been sent to fight in New Guinea and Borneo.

The 9th Australian Division was the most highly decorated of the four AIF divisions in the Second World War, including seven Victoria Cross winners, six of them posthumous.

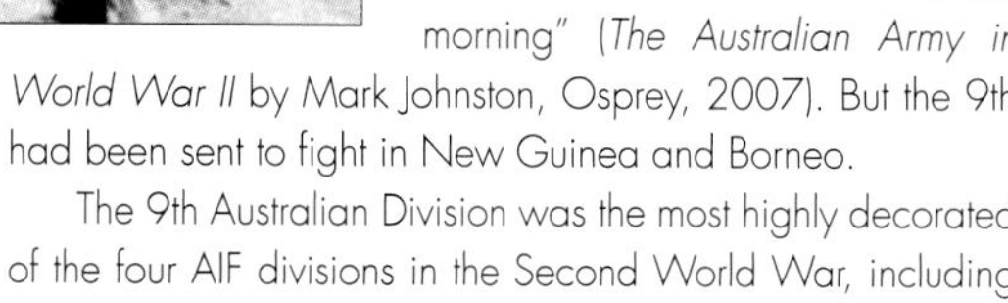

ABOVE: Soldiers of the 9th Australian Division during the Second Battle of Alamein, November 1942.

RIGHT, TOP: The badge of the 7th Australian Division, a Kookaburra perched on a boomerang.

RIGHT, BOTTOM: The 9th Australian Division adopted the duck-billed platypus above a boomerang after leaving the Middle East to serve in New Guinea.

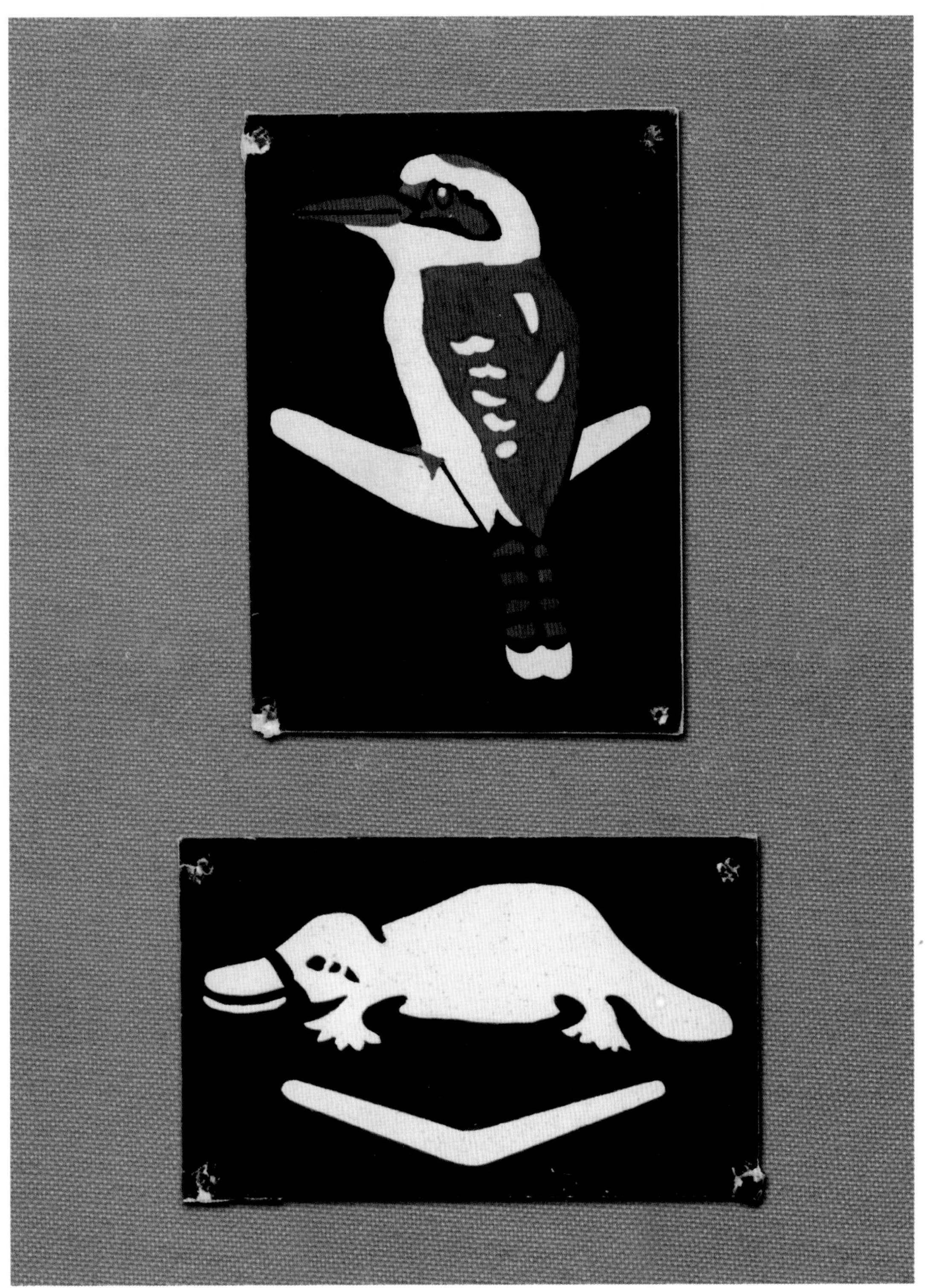

BELOW: Australian infantry displaying the Anzac spirit during house-to-house fighting in Bardia, Libya in 1941.

50 The USS *Enterprise*

At the time of the Japanese attack on Pearl Harbor on 7 December 1941, the US Navy had six large fleet carriers. The USS *Enterprise* (CV-6) was one of two to survive the Pacific War. Ordered with one other similar carrier in 1933, *Enterprise* was built by the Newport News (Virginia) Shipbuilding Corporation and commissioned in May 1938. She was nicknamed "the Big E", and earned the most battle honours of any USN warship in the war with Japan.

Designed from the keel up as an aircraft carrier, *Enterprise* had a standard displacement of 19,800 tons and was 247 metres (810 feet) long by 25 metres (83 feet) abeam, with a normal cruising speed of around 37kph (20 knots). She could carry an air group of up to 80 aircraft plus six utility aircraft, together with a crew and air-group personnel of 2,500. Her defence armament included eight 5-inch/38-calibre guns and assorted 40-mm (1.6-in) and 20-mm (0.8-in) rapid-fire anti-aircraft guns. She also had a special communications suite that allowed her to be the flagship of a task force or carrier group.

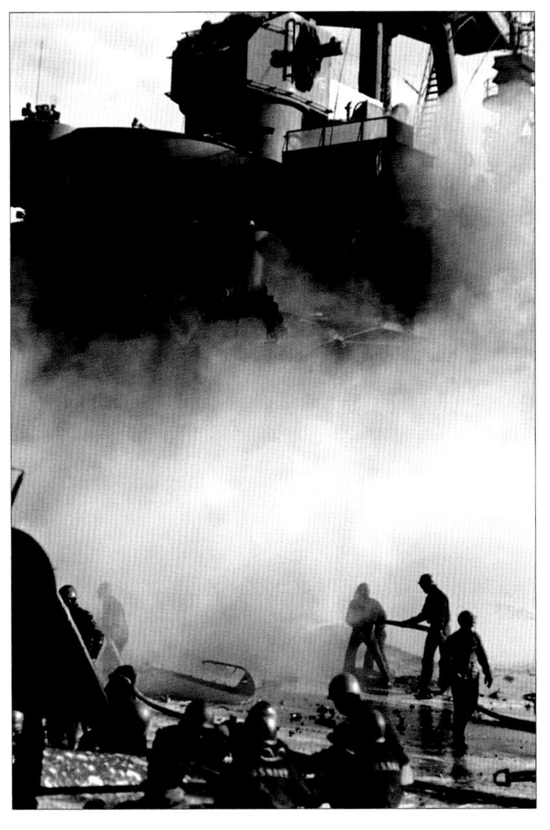

After the attack on Pearl Harbor, the *Enterprise* won the first of her 20 battle stars by participating in carrier raids on the Marshall Islands and providing air cover for the USS *Hornet* when it brought USAAF B-25s close enough to Japan to bomb Tokyo in April 1942. The carrier next engaged the Imperial Japanese Navy in the battle of Midway (4–7 June 1942) as the flagship of Task Force 16 (Rear Admiral Raymond A Spruance), where its dive-bombers helped sink two Japanese carriers.

The *Enterprise* faced its greatest challenge in the Solomons campaign. In the battle of the Eastern Solomons on 24 August 1942, the carrier absorbed three bomb hits that killed or wounded 168 crewmen. After repairs in Hawaii, the ship returned to the Solomon Islands in time for the Battle of the Santa Cruz Islands on 26–27 October 1942 where once more, two Japanese bombs caused serious damage, but the *Enterprise*, repaired enough for sea duty, returned to action in November. Some of her air group operated from Guadalcanal when she again had to go to Noumea for repairs. She then returned to the United States for an overhaul, bearer of a coveted Presidential Unit Citation. The Japanese had by now twice reported that the carrier had been sunk.

Returning to the Pacific War in November 1943, the *Enterprise* participated in the Gilbert and Marshall Islands campaign, and her air group played important roles in the Battles of the Philippine Sea and Leyte Gulf in August and October 1944. She continued to mount air attacks on China and Formosa in 1944–45 but it was off Okinawa on 14 May 1945 that a kamikaze struck her forward flight deck and elevator, which forced her to sail back to the United States for more yard works. For the third time, the Imperial Japanese Navy reported the *Enterprise* sunk.

Replaced by larger, modern carriers, the *Enterprise* finally left the fleet in February 1947 and she was scrapped in 1958. A newer nuclear carrier now bears her name.

LEFT: Shrapnel and fires pepper the *Enterprise* as a result of an anti-aircraft shell from another ship helping her ward off a kamikaze attack off the caost of Japan.

ABOVE: Aerial shot of USS *Enterprise* underway, with aircraft on deck; 12 April 1939.

51 The Long Range Desert Group Vehicle

The Long Range Desert Group (LRDG) was founded in June 1940 by Major Ralph A Bagnold, an officer on the staff of General Sir Archibald Wavell, Commander-in-Chief Middle East Command. When Italy came into the war on the side of the Germans, the large Italian garrison in Libya posed a threat to the British bases in Egypt and the Suez Canal. Bagnold suggested to Wavell that a reconnaissance force be formed to penetrate behind enemy lines to see what the Italians were up to. According to the Imperial War Museum Sound Archive, when Wavell asked, "What if the Italians are doing nothing?" Bagnold replied, "How about some piracy on the high desert?" Wavell was delighted and immediately gave Bagnold permission to raise a force from volunteers among the British and New Zealand troops in Egypt.

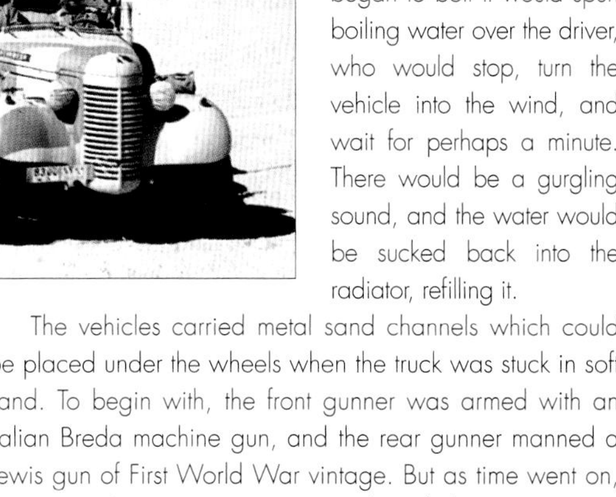

Bagnold had spent several years in Egypt before the Second World War, and had pioneered the art of driving and navigating in the desert. The selection of vehicles was made by Bagnold; he was looking for a total of 33. Nothing the British motor industry produced at the time was suitable, so he tested a variety of American vehicles, and selected the commercial two-wheeled drive Chevrolet 30-cwt. He could only find 14 so he had to beg the remaining 19 from the Egyptian Army, plus some sun compasses.

A magnetic compass was unreliable because there was so much metal in a truck. If you wanted to take a bearing you had to stop and walk some distance off, and the delays caused by such frequent stops were unacceptable over a long journey. The sun shone all day and every day, so Bagnold chose a sun compass, a modified sundial. You drove the truck keeping the shadow from the dial's central spike on the requisite pointer. The compass was mounted in front of the navigator who sat beside the driver in the lead truck. Distance travelled was measured with the help of the speedometer. On a twisting journey of 150 kilometres (100 miles), avoiding obstacles, going round the bigger dunes and so forth, the LRDG were very put out if their dead reckoning was out by more than a fraction. The positions were checked by taking sun shots by day and star shots by night using a theodolite, in the same way that a sailor at sea uses a sextant.

To reduce wastage of water when the radiator boiled, a pipe was led from the overflow down in to a can half-full of water, strapped to the side of the vehicle. The steam then condensed in the can. If the contents of the can began to boil it would spurt boiling water over the driver, who would stop, turn the vehicle into the wind, and wait for perhaps a minute. There would be a gurgling sound, and the water would be sucked back into the radiator, refilling it.

The vehicles carried metal sand channels which could be placed under the wheels when the truck was stuck in soft sand. To begin with, the front gunner was armed with an Italian Breda machine gun, and the rear gunner manned a Lewis gun of First World War vintage. But as time went on, a variety of weapons were carried, including Boyes anti-tank rifles, Vickers 770-cm (303-in) medium machine guns, 12.7-mm (0.5-in) heavy machine guns and Bofors 37 mm anti-tank guns.

Initially, a patrol consisted of ten Chevrolets, each

LEFT: Chevrolet trucks of the Long Range Desert Group.

ABOVE: The Bagnold Sun Compass.

able to carry up to three tons of load, and two or three men. They were capable of travelling a distance of up to 2,900 kilometres (1,800 miles), and existing for six weeks on the rations, petrol and water each carried. Communication back to base was by radio, or wireless as it was then known. Eventually the patrols were cut down to five vehicles each in order to cover more terrain. The Chevrolets were replaced in mid-1941 by four-wheel-drive Fords which carried the same load but were not so manoeuvrable. In mid-1942, these were in turn replaced by Canadian 30-cwt Chevrolets.

The LRDG must rate as the most cost-effective special force in history. Between 26 December 1940, its first long patrol, and 10 April 1943, there were only 15 days when there were no LRDG patrols out in the desert.

52 The Commando Dagger

The Commando Dagger is more properly called a Fighting Knife. In 1940 Wilkinson Sword made 500 knives to the specification of two instructors in unarmed combat: Captains William Ewart Fairbairn and Eric Anthony Sykes of the Shanghai International Police. These first knives had a 16.5-cm (6.5-inch) blade with an S-shaped cross-guard, a flat ricasso and a Wilkinson Sword and F-S logo. The leather sheath had tabs so that it could be sewn to the trouser leg, sometimes inside the trouser, with the hilt protruding from a pocket. Around 250,000 similar knives were made between 1941 and 1945. These had a black nickel finish, a slightly longer blade of 17.5 cm (7 inches), and a smaller, straight cross-guard. The sharp edge of the blade was continued to the cross-guard, and the ricasso removed. The blade in both patterns was made of high-carbon, hand-ground steel. The sheath remained unchanged.

The blade was made slim in order that it could enter the rib cage, and long enough to penetrate a body covered by the thickest clothing that an opponent might wear: a greatcoat over uniform, assessed at 7.5 cm (3 ins) of cloth. Fairbairn wrote in his book *Get Tough*:

> *In close-quarters fighting there is no more deadly weapon than the knife. In choosing a knife there are two important factors to bear in mind: balance*

BELOW: The Fairbairn-Sykes Fighting Knife, version three. The top of the scabbard has an elastic strap to prevent the knife toppling out.

*and keenness. The hilt should fit easily in your hand, and the blade should not be so heavy that it tends to drag the hilt from your fingers in a loose grip. It is essential that the blade have a sharp stabbing point and good cutting edges, because an artery torn through (as against a clean cut) tends to contract and stop the bleeding. If a main artery is cleanly severed, the wounded man will quickly lose consciousness and die. (*Get Tough! How to Win in Hand-to-Hand Fighting*, by W E Fairburn, Paladin Press, 1999.)*

Commandos were trained to kill by stabbing an opponent in the throat whenever possible, while holding a hand over the enemy's mouth to silence him. The knife's name is a misnomer, because it was not designed for use in a fight, except in circumstances when the attacker lost surprise, but as a silent killing weapon for use against sentries and enemies taken unaware. The fighting knife was a stabbing stiletto, and was no good for cutting wood or much else except perhaps for severing string or rope. In this respect it was not as versatile as the K-Bar issued to the United States Marines in the Second World War and still in use today. Despite this, most Second World War commandos wore a fighting knife, although as the war progressed and raids became uncommon, the opportunities for close-quarter combat became less frequent. Commandos tended to be employed on the flanks of the main assault or on tasks that required an especially high level of soldiering skill.

The Fighting Knife was soon adopted as the symbol, or logo in modern terminology, for commando badges and formation signs, and is used for that purpose to this day.

53 The Purple Heart

The Purple Heart is a decoration awarded to American military personnel for wounds received in combat. It is also awarded to service members who are killed inaction, who die of wounds or who are missing in action and presumed dead from combat action. It may be awarded to the same person for multiple wounds if suffered on different occasions. Estimates of the number of Purple Hearts awarded during the Second World War and afterwards range between 800,000 and over a million.

Created by the War Department in 1932, the Purple Heart drew its inspiration from a Badge of Military Merit in the form of a purple heart with the word "merit" embroidered on it. This award was established by George Washington in 1782 for combat heroism and distinguished service, and records show that Washington made only three such awards to members of the Continental Army.

The US Army had no official medals or other distinguishing badges to recognize wounds until the First World War, when the War Department created a wound chevron to be worn above the cuff of the right sleeve of the service and dress uniform. This award required the authorization of the Commanding General, American Expeditionary Forces, based on the records of the AEF Medical Department. The wound stripe could be awarded for earlier combat actions. The 1932 regulations dictated that the Purple Heart would replace the wound chevrons, which might be confused with overseas service stripes, also worn on a uniform sleeve. The new model could also be awarded after 1932 to a member of the US Army who had performed an act or acts of merit that reflected "extraordinary fidelity" or provided "essential service".

In 1942 by Executive Order 9277, President Franklin D Roosevelt extended eligibility of the award to all the armed forces, and even to American citizens serving in a civilian capacity in the armed forces, such as a Red Cross worker or war correspondent. The order ended awards of the Purple Heart for anything other than combat wounds, although earlier recipients could exchange their Purple Hearts for other distinguished service medals like the Legion of Merit.

The Purple Heart bears the profile of George Washington to honour the award's founder. The profile is superimposed on a metallic heart attached to a purple ribbon edged in white. Multiple awards are designated either by an oak leaf device (Army and Air Force) or a gold star (Navy and Marine Corps).

To be eligible for a Purple Heart, a service member must be wounded by enemy action and treated for that wound in a medical facility that records that treatment. Many people who might qualify for an award refuse treatment and evacuation and thus have no record of being "officially" wounded; this condition has plagued veterans ever since the Second World War since it may affect current treatment and disability payments.

ABOVE: Five Marines having just received the Purple Heart. From left: Lieutenant Colonel George Mays, Corporal James W Powell Jr, Corporal Arthur John Madden, Corporal Jack Warrens and Corporal Clifford Heinson. Also shown are Private First Class James B Rutledge and Samuel Boyd, who also received the citation.

RIGHT: The Purple Heart medal.

54 Canoes

The first British canoe unit of the Second World War was formed by Lieutenant Roger Courtney as a Folboat section as part of the newly raised Number 8 Commando in Scotland in June 1940, and was designated 1 Special Boat Section (SBS). The early Folboats were canvass-skinned, wooden-framed canoes designed for civilian sporting use mainly on lakes and rivers, and were markedly unsuitable for use in the open sea. They had none of the navigation aids, spray covers, bow and stern buoyancy bags or other fittings found on later versions.

To begin with, the idea of Folboats or canoes as a weapon of war was dismissed by senior commanders, but after experience in the Mediterranean, where Courtney was sent in late 1940, it became apparent that the canoe was a very useful craft for reconnaissance and sabotage operations, and special missions. A canoe could be taken near the target by submarine. After surfacing, canoes could be brought up from below through the torpedo loading hatch and placed on the casing. They could either be launched over the side, or even better, if sea conditions allowed, the crews manned their craft while it was still on the casing, the submarine slowly submerged and the canoe or canoes, complete with crew, floated off. After completing the operation, the canoe would be paddled out to sea on an agreed bearing and for a predetermined distance. The crew would then lower into the water a rudimentary device rather like an old-fashioned coffee grinder with a handle on the top called a "bong stick" or "bongle". Turning the handle made a clattering noise that could be picked up by the submarine hydrophones up to 19 kilometres (12 miles) away. The submarine would home in on the noise, surface and recover the canoes.

Before the Allied invasion of North Africa (8–16 November 1942), Operation Torch, the American Major General Mark Clark was landed on the Algerian coast by canoe on 21 October. The canoes taking Clark, his staff and British escorts from 2 SBS were launched from the submarine *Seraph*. Clark's mission was to find out if the French, still neutral at that stage in the war, would resist the forthcoming landings. Having concluded his visit, Clark was taken out to the waiting *Seraph* the following night, although not without difficulty, as neither Clark nor his staff were familiar with the procedure for launching a canoe in moderate surf at night.

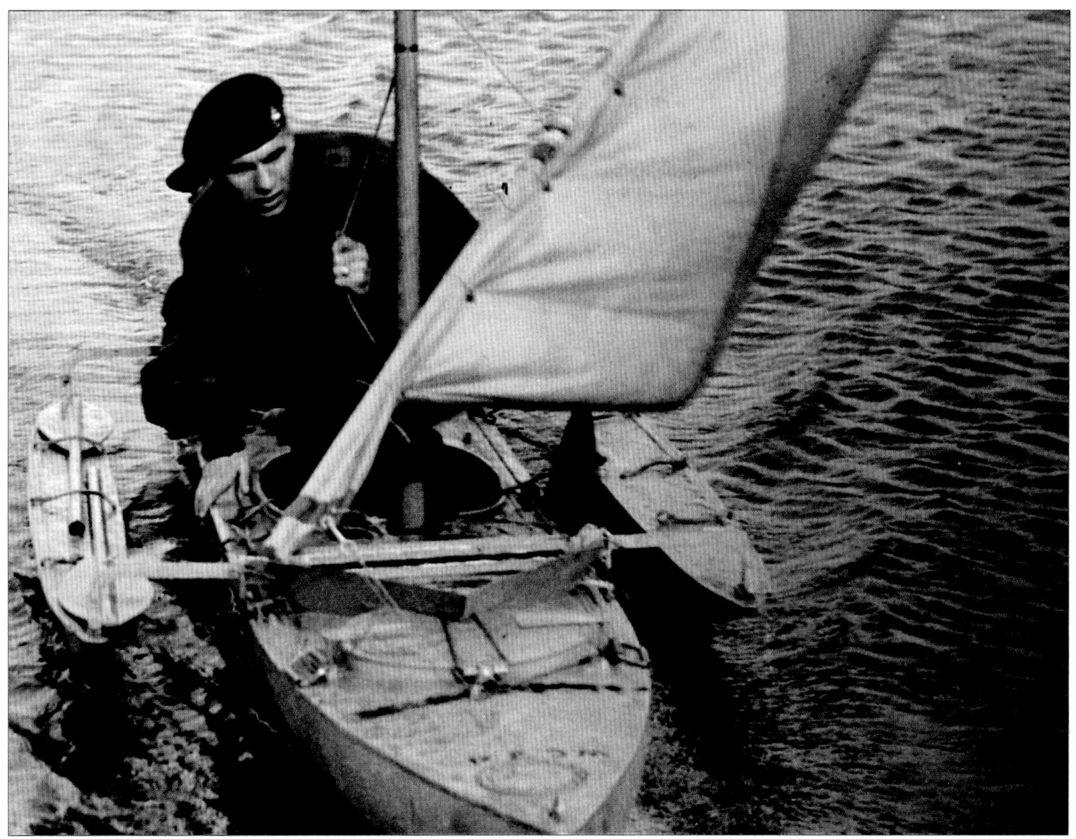

LEFT: The many designs of canoe used by the British in the Second World War included the Mark VI three-man outrigger, which could be fitted with a 4-horsepower two-stroke retractable engine, and a lateen sail. The engine gave the canoe a range of 145 kilometres (90 miles) at 10 kph (5.6 knots). If more stores were required to be taken for a particular task, the crew could be reduced to two.

ABOVE: Two-man outrigger with lateen sail.

A few days later General Henri Giraud was extracted by an SBS canoe party from the south of France. He was to take command of all French troops in North Africa as soon as possible after the Torch landings.

One of the most remarkable canoe operations was by the Royal Marine Boom Patrol Detachment, a cover name for a special force commanded by Major Herbert George "Blondie" Hasler, Royal Marines. Launched from the submarine *Tuna* in the mouth of the Gironde estuary on 7 December 1942, five canoes set out to paddle the 110 kilometres (70 miles) up the river to Bordeaux. Two canoes were lost in a rip tide; a third disappeared. The remaining two continued up river, lying up by day. Three nights later, they arrived at the Bordeaux docks and placed limpet mines on six ships, which exploded after the canoeists had left the docks to make their way overland to Spain. Two made it; the other two were caught and shot.

Canoes were also used for reconnaissance and sabotage in the Far East on numerous occasions. One of the most audacious raids was Operation Jaywick (26 September 1943), in which a force from Australia sank seven ships in Singapore harbour with limpet mines. Singapore lay some 1,925 kilometres (1,200 miles) inside Japanese-held territory. The team of four canoes and its support party were taken to a group of islands off Singapore by a captured Japanese fishing boat, the *Krait*, and from there they paddled in to place their limpets. The *Krait* then recovered the party from another island after the raid. The distances paddled, and the conditions endured, make this one of the most remarkable raids in the history of war.

55 Kamikaze

Kamikaze is Japanese for "divine wind", named after the typhoons that destroyed Mongolian invasion fleets in 1274 and 1281. In the Pacific campaign (7 December 1941–12 August 1945) of the Second World War, the word Kamikaze was applied to aircraft that were deliberately crashed on to the target, sacrificing the aircraft and the life of the pilot.

By October 1944 the air ascendancy that Japan had enjoyed since December 1941 had been reversed. Many of her experienced pilots had been lost, and the United States was producing aircraft that outfought the once-dominant Zero. At Midway on 4 June 1942, the Japanese lost as many aircrew in one day as their training system produced in one year. The inexorable advance of the US Navy across the Pacific towards the Japanese homeland, backed by the massively superior American industrial power, led to the decision to employ Kamikaze.

Early in the war, Japanese pilots had occasionally deliberately crashed on Allied warships, but on 19 October 1944, Vice Admiral Onishi Takijino suggested forming a Kamikaze force to attack American carriers supporting the landings at Leyte in the Philippines. The suggestion was eagerly received and implemented. Commander Asaiki Tamai formed the first Special Attack Force from a group of volunteer student pilots he had trained, and Lieutenant Yuio Seki was asked to command the force. The first Kamikaze attack in the Philippines campaign is thought to have been on the Australian cruiser *Australia* in Leyte Bay on 21 October 1944, killing the captain, seven officers and 23 sailors, and wounding 61 of her ship's company in the area of her bridge and superstructure. However, this attack was not carried out by the Special Attack Force, but by a Mitsubishi of the Japanese Army Air Force; the Special Attack Force was part of the Japanese Navy Air Arm, and flew Zeros.

On 25 October 1944, the Special Attack Force attacked five escort carriers, but succeeded only in damaging one so badly that the bomb magazine exploded, sinking the ship. Subsequent Kamikaze waves totalling 55 aircraft were more successful. Seven carriers were hit, along with 40 other ships, sinking five and damaging 35, including 23 heavily.

Kamikaze sorties were not confined to ship attack. When the USAAF's B-29 strategic bombing offensive began to pulverize the Japanese mainland, the Japanese Army Air Force formed the Shinten Special Unit to defend Tokyo, flying Nakajima Ki-44 Shoki "Tojo" interceptors to ram the US B-29s. Armed with a mix of heavy and medium cannon, the Tojo was a formidable interceptor, but ramming a fast, manoeuvrable target like a B-29 was far more challenging than crashing on a ship. Furthermore, the B-29, with a total of 11 .5-inch (13-mm) and 20-mm (0.8-inch) cannon, was a fearsome adversary. An attack on a B-29 demanded a high degree of airmanship, whereas the concept of the Kamikaze was to use poorly trained and hence expendable pilots. Attacking Allied shipping was a much more profitable tactic and continued right up to the last day of the Pacific campaign.

The most damage inflicted by Kamikaze attacks was during the invasion of Okinawa in April 1945, when massed onslaughts sank 36 ships and landing craft, and damaged 368. It is thought that nearly 1,500 Kamikaze pilots died in these attacks alone. While carriers were the prize target, none were sunk in these attacks, although many were badly damaged. The US carriers with wooden decks were especially easy to damage. One Kamikaze attack on the USS *Bunker Hill* on 11 May 1945 killed 389 men, hugely exceeding the total deaths inflicted on all six Royal Navy armoured-deck carriers by all types of attack throughout the war. During the Pacific campaign five Royal Navy carriers were hit by a total of eight Kamikazes, killing 20 sailors. A Kamikaze hit on a US carrier usually resulted in a long time spent in dock for extensive repair, whereas on a British armoured-deck carrier it was, in the words of a US Navy officer serving on one of these ships, a case of "sweepers man your brooms", push the wreckage over the side and carry on.

The last Kamikaze attack of the war was on 15 August 1945 against Allied ships at Okinawa.

LEFT: A Japanese Kamikaze being shot down while attacking the USS *Hornet* off Santa Cruz Island during the Guadalcanal campaign in the Pacific (7 August 1942–9 February 1943).

ABOVE: Kamikaze pilots with the ribbons showing that they are about to go on a suicide mission.

ABOVE: A Zero Kamikaze aircraft about to plunge into the sea after being hit by American anti-aircraft fire.

RIGHT: The USS *Bunker Hill* burns after being hit by two Kamikaze Zeros on 11 May 1945 while supporting the invasion of Okinawa.

56 Penicillin

One of the paradoxes of warfare is that it has often led to significant advances in technology and medicine that have proved to be of great advantage to humans, and in some cases animals as well. One of the outstanding examples of this is the development of penicillin during the Second World War. Until the early 1940s, bacterial infections resulting from injury and disease were usually treated with sulphonamide drugs. These were effective for the treatment of some conditions, but not in the case of streptococcal infections. Research was therefore carried out into the development of new drugs that acted on the principle that some microbes might destroy others. In 1939, Professor William Florey and Ernst Chain (a Jewish refugee from Nazi Germany), both at the School of Pathology in Oxford, began investigating the anti-bacterial properties of assorted organic matter including *Penicillium notatum*, first noted by Alexander Fleming ten years earlier.

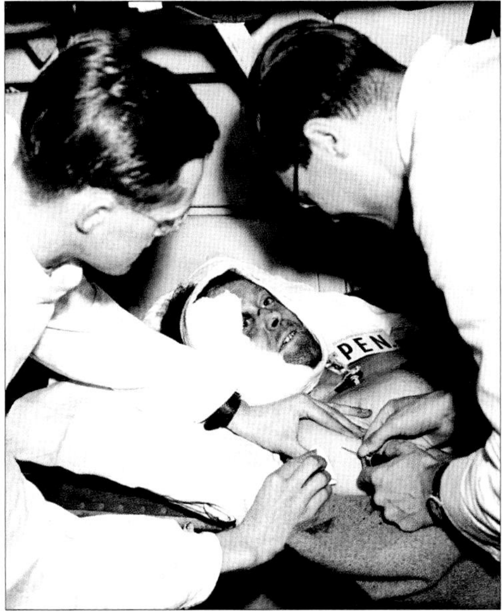

As a captain in the Royal Army Medical Corps, Fleming had seen many soldiers in the First World War die of infected wounds. He maintained that antiseptics killed the patient's natural defences more effectively than they killed the bacteria, especially in deep wounds. After the war he returned to St Mary's Hospital, London, where in 1928 he became Professor of Bacteriology. Here, as he was to later recount, he discovered antibiotics or bacteria-killers by mistake. On return from holiday he noticed that among the cultures of staphylococci on his workbench, one culture was contaminated by a fungus which had killed the staphylococci. He identified the mould as being from the Penicillium genus. At first he called it "mould juice", but he named it penicillin on 7 March 1929. Fleming published his discovery in the same year, but his article attracted little attention.

In May 1940, the results obtained by Florey, Chain and their assistants on the effect of penicillin on streptococcal infections were sufficiently encouraging to lead on to the next stage: clinical trials. These showed that even the most severe bacterial infections could be controlled by penicillin without dangerous side effects. Unfortunately, in a laboratory penicillin could only be produced in infinitesimal amounts, whereas one case of sepsis alone might need around 660 litres (440 gallons) of the organism to be produced. The only way to produce sufficient quantities of the drug would be to do so using the resources of industry, but by now the industrial capacity of Britain was at full stretch meeting the demands of wartime production of medicines and drugs. Fortunately, an approach to the Rockefeller Foundation in the United States led to a suitable manufacturer being found. By 1942, penicillin was in full production in America, and it was first used in field conditions in North Africa in 1943.

The use of penicillin had an important effect on field surgical procedures as the Second World War progressed. In some theatres, because of the terrain (Burma for example) and distances involved, or the speed at which the battle moved back and forth, as in North Africa, it was difficult to operate on the wounded until they had been evacuated to base hospitals. In Burma, this might be by light aircraft, and bad weather or enemy action might impose long delays before the wounded man reached hospital. The requirement was to carry out sufficient surgery to stabilize the patient so that he could survive the journey to hospital. Antibiotics kept the wound free from infection while the patient was awaiting evacuation and during the journey back.

Alexander Fleming and Howard Florey were awarded the Nobel Prize in Physiology for Medicine in 1945, which they shared with Ernst Chain.

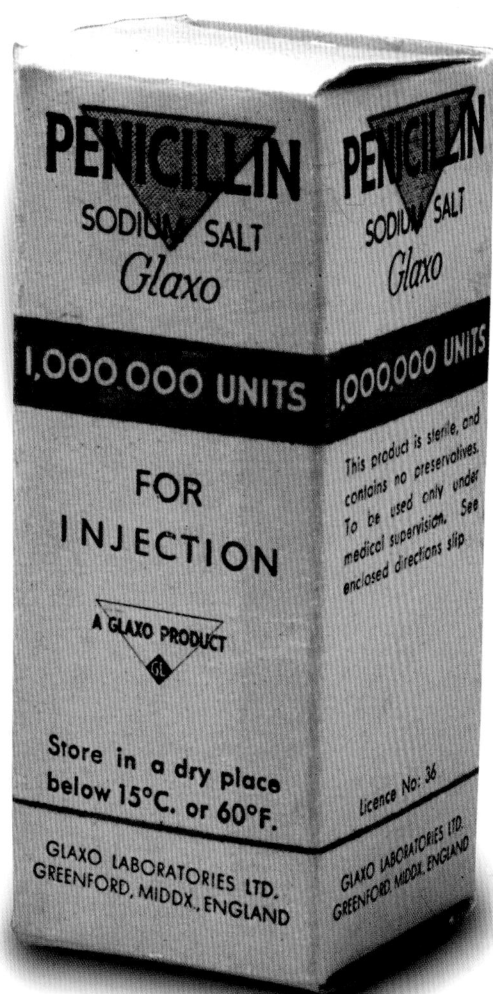

LEFT: A soldier being injected with Penicillin while being transported in a hospital train. His label marked "Penicillin" is to avoid him being overdosed in error.

ABOVE: A penicillin bottle and ampoule.

57 Depth Charge

The object of an anti-submarine weapon is to rupture or pierce the submarine's pressure hull, thereby letting the sea in to sink the vessel. The weapon used by the British (and indeed most other navies) at the outbreak of the Second World War was the depth charge, which was little changed from those used in the First World War. It consisted of a metal canister containing high explosive weighing between 90 and 136 kg (198 and 300 lb), with small patrol craft carrying the smaller ones. A hydrostatic device detonated the charge at a pre-set depth in both kinds. The British heavy Mk VII had a maximum depth setting of 260 metres (850 feet) and a lethal range of 9 metres (29.5 feet).

Usually an attacking ship dropped depth charges in patterns like a five of clubs in a pack of playing cards, with a spacing of 36 to 55 metres (120 to 180 feet); three would be rolled down stern shutes, and one from each quarter would be projected by throwers. The aim was to bracket the submarine both horizontally and in depth. The latter was achieved by using different depth settings on each charge, or by alternating heavy charges, which sank more quickly, with lighter ones.

Depth charges with fins like a conventional bomb could also be dropped from aircraft. In the first years of the war the depth had to be set before take off, and if the hydrostatic pistol was set to detonate the charge at depth, and the submarine was on or near the surface, the depth charge would have little or no effect. The problem was however eventually solved by devising depth charges with a shallow set hydrostatic pistol. The aircraft would carry both types and the right one would be selected for the job.

The disadvantage of a stern-launched depth charge attack was that the attacker's ASDIC lost contact with the submarine in the final 180 metres (590 feet) of the run over the target. That "deaf time", as it was known, together with the time the depth charges took to sink, gave the submarine an opportunity to take evasive action and get sufficiently far away from the explosions to lessen their effect. Despite this, even if the detonations were not close enough to rupture the pressure hull, they could cause damage, frighten the crew and keep the submarine below periscope depth and hence unable to retaliate.

The solution to "deaf time" was the ahead-thrown depth charge. The first type in service was the Hedgehog, which consisted of 24 light mortar bombs on six rows of spigots, the whole resembling a hedgehog and hence the name. Each spigot was slightly angled to spread the bombs over a circular area, about 40 metres (130 feet) in diameter, well ahead of the firing ship to allow the ship to maintain contact with the target. Each row of spigots tilted as the ship rolled to keep the throw straight. The Hedgehog bomb had one disadvantage, however: it exploded only on contact with the target, so if all the bombs missed, there was no explosion to cause the damage and effect on morale that a depth charge could bring about even if it did not sink the boat.

In late 1943, a better ahead-thrown weapon was introduced: a three-barrelled mortar known as Squid, which was fitted in pairs aft of the superstructure. Squid fired bombs filled with 90 kg (200 lb) of a greatly improved explosive called Minol II. The bombs were projected in a high arc right over the ship's superstructure. They sank nearly three times more quickly than a depth charge and exploded at depths set automatically by the improved ASDIC/Sonar, in two depth layers 18 metres (59 feet) apart. A depth charge gave you a six per cent chance of a submarine kill, and Hedgehog 20 per cent; Squid was a huge improvement on its predecessors, raising the kill probability to 50 per cent.

ABOVE: A depth charge on its thrower.

RIGHT: A sailor about to fire a depth charge.

58 C and K Rations

Separated from fresh foods and his company cook, the American frontline soldier depended upon field rations, categorized as C or K rations, for energy and good health. The Army's experience in the First World War dramatized the fact that pure water and available food offset fatigue, disabling gastro-intestinal problems and fear. As Napoleon observed, armies live and fight on their stomachs or, more accurately, on a preferred food intake of 3,000–4,000 calories a day.

The challenge for the Army was to create a ration that individual soldiers and combat Marines could carry and eat under such adverse circumstances as rain, snow, heat, darkness, enemy fire and cold. The ration had to be easy to carry and edible without heating. The "C ration, field, individual" came in a cardboard box that held three small cans and plastic spoons; a well-prepared GI always carried a small can opener, usually on his dogtag chain.

The first can held one of ten different meat-and-vegetable meals (the best meals were pork and beans or frankfurters and beans; ham and lima beans were the least edible, even when heated). The welcome second can contained some sort of fruit like peaches and apple sauce. The third can contained powdered coffee or powdered fruit juice or cocoa, accompanied by candy and chewing gum. A fourth can variant could have cookies, crackers with cheese or peanut butter or a fruit cake or pound cake. Each meal provided 1,000–1,800 calories. The ration also included toilet paper in quantities too little or too great for field use. GIs hoarded toilet paper and ration cigarettes in their helmet liners.

The K ration was a lighter, simpler version of the C ration, packaged to be waterproof. Inside a green, very waxed 16.5-cm (6.5-inch) box, one could find a single survival meal, labelled "breakfast", "lunch" or "dinner", a monument to exaggeration. Breakfast was a fruit bar, powdered coffee with sugar, crackers and a tin of ham and eggs. The other two options had cheese and crackers or a tin of meat, powdered soup, fruit juice powder, sugar, a chocolate bar, chewing gum and some other treats.

Heating a ration with an extemporized stove (usually a ventilated ration can) or a pan of hot water helped improve the ration's taste. C-4 plastic explosives made a nice fire but towards the end of the war, rations came with a smokeless heat tab. GIs also carried individual hot sauce or other condiments. If heat was available, adding the cheese often improved the meat-and-vegetable meal. No one confused C and K rations with Mom's apple pie; living on K and C rations guaranteed weight loss.

The United States armed forces were the best fed in the Second World War. Less than 90 days after D-Day, the Army was feeding hot, prepared meals to 70 per cent of the troops. The C and K ration supply at the same time reached 60 million meals in France. Army meals also fed liberated Europeans as well as the GIs.

LEFT: American army lieutenant Richard K Jones shares his food rations with local children found hiding in an abandoned tomb in Okinawa, Japan, 31 May 1945.

ABOVE: Ration boxes given to soldiers in the US Army, including Type K breakfast box, Type K dinner box and Type K supper box. Also shown are two breakfast tins and a packet of biscuits.

59 The Bridge over the River Kwai

The real bridge over the River Kwai bore no resemblance to the bridge in the film of that name, save that it was built in barbarous conditions, in part by British prisoners of war held by the Japanese. The manner of its building, its appearance and its location in the film are all fiction.

There were actually two bridges built in 1943 over the Mae Klong in Thailand (renamed the Khwae Yai in the 1960s): one temporary, made of wood, and a few months later another of steel and concrete. These formed part of the Japanese railway linking Nong Pladuk in Thailand to Thanbyuzayat in Burma, which enabled the Japanese to move supplies by rail from Singapore to their armies fighting in Burma. The rapid Japanese conquest of South-East Asia had resulted in a serious shortage of shipping to cover a vast area, and the sea route to Rangoon was vulnerable to attack by British submarines and by US and British aircraft.

The construction of this railway was a daunting feat of engineering. The line had to be cut through 420 kilometres (260 miles) of mountainous jungle situated among some of the most unhealthy regions in the world: malaria, dengue, dysentery, cholera and jungle sores were just some of the health hazards faced by those living and working there. The first step in construction of the line began in July 1942 when 3,000 Allied prisoners of war were sent from Changi in Singapore to build a base camp. Eventually some 61,000 Australian, British and Dutch prisoners of war were employed building the line and bridges. In addition, and usually forgotten, the Japanese induced (or more often forced) more than 270,000 labourers from Burma, Malaya, Thailand and the Dutch East Indies to work on the railway. The Japanese regarded the labour force, prisoners of war and labourers alike, as expendable. The minimal diet, lack of medical supplies, atrocious working and living conditions and numerous epidemics resulted in a high death rate. Although figures vary, the most reliable estimates reckon some 12,000 Allied prisoners and 90,000 labourers died. The attitude of the Japanese is encapsulated by the words used by the engineer in charge when addressing prisoners of war, quoted in lectures given by former POW James Noble: "You are rubble. We will build the railway line on your bodies."

Between February and April 1945, a series of attacks by RAF and USAAF Liberators based in India were made on the railway and bridges, resulting in sections of the bridges being destroyed. Both bridges were repaired near the end of the war, but the railway always carried less than the Japanese hoped for. Subsequently the wooden bridge was demolished, but the concrete and steel bridge is still in use today.

The film *The Bridge on the River Kwai* (1957) fails to portray the full extent of the appalling conditions and suffering endured by the prisoners of war, and omits the native labourers entirely. While the senior British officer in the film, played by Alec Guinness, collaborates with the Japanese, the real senior British officer, Colonel Philip Toosey, most certainly did not. In fact he did as much as possible to delay the building of the bridge, including organizing the collection of termites in huge numbers to eat the structure of the wooden bridge and encouraging acts of sabotage such as mixing concrete as badly as possible. Not content with getting just about everything else wrong, the film portrays the Japanese as being so technologically backward that they are unable to build the bridge without British engineering expertise.

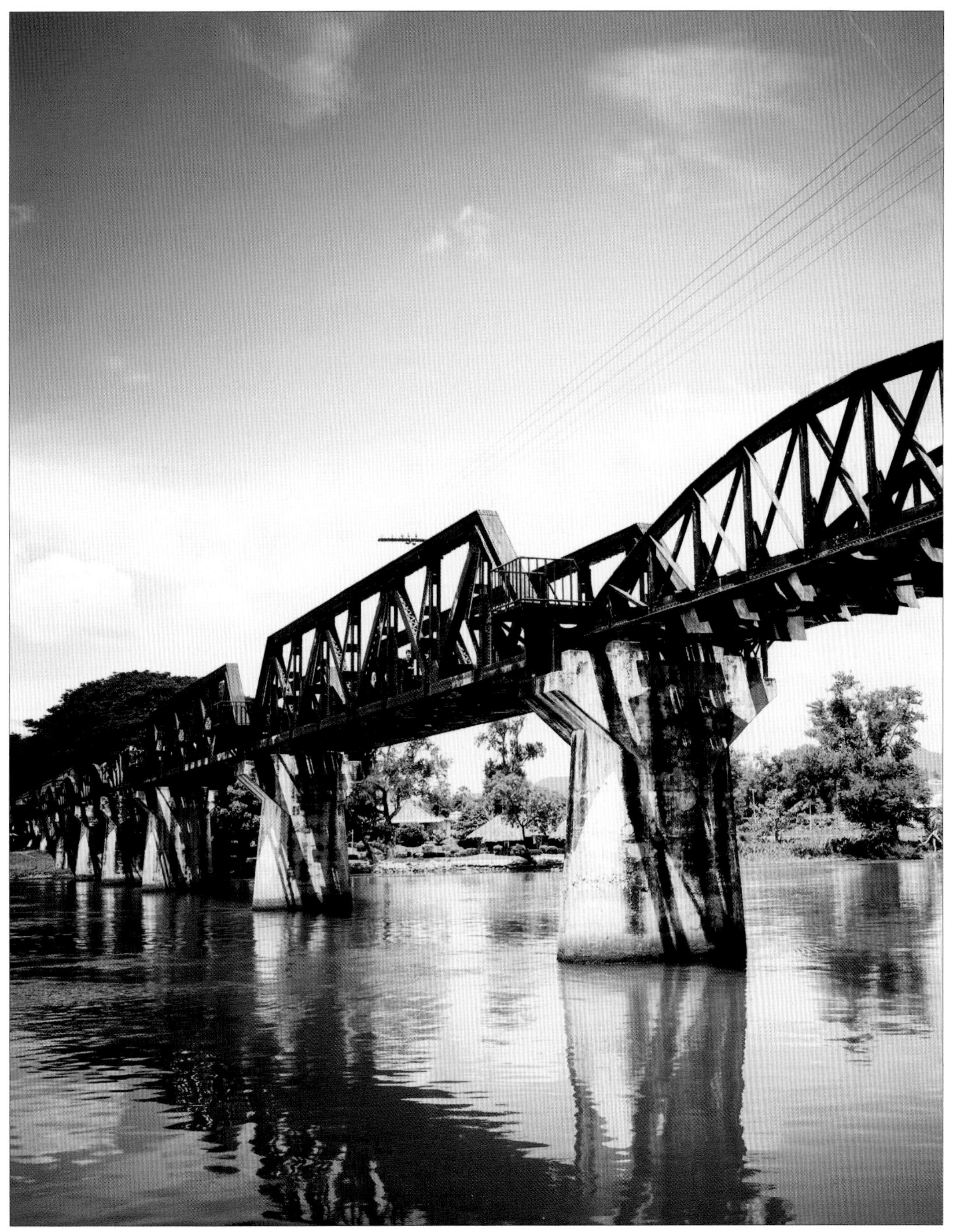

LEFT: A drawing of the bridge over the Mae Klong under construction.

ABOVE: The modern bridge over the Khwae Yai.

60 CAM Ships

In late 1940, Catapult Aircraft Merchantmen (CAM ships) were conceived in response to two threats to convoys out of range of land-based fighter protection. The first threat was long-range Focke-Wulf Condors flying from occupied French and Norwegian bases to bomb convoys far out in the Atlantic west of Iceland. Secondly, Condors signalled the position, course and speed of a convoy to Admiral Karl Dönitz, whose headquarters controlled all U-boats, enabling him to position them in the path of the convoy. The Royal Navy did not have enough carriers to provide air cover for convoys at this stage in the war.

In December 1940, the first fighter catapult ship, HMS *Pegasus*, a converted First World War seaplane carrier, accompanied a convoy. She carried three Fulmar fighters, and was followed by three more Fighter Catapult Ships, *Springbank*, *Maplin* and *Ariguani*, converted from merchantmen to carry one fighter each. On 3 August 1941, a Condor was shot down 640 kilometres (400 miles) off the coast of Spain by a Hurricane piloted by Lieutenant Everett RNVR, catapulted from the *Maplin*. After shooting down the Condor, Lieutenant Everett landed his Hurricane on the water and was rescued before it sank.

In April that year, catapults began to be fitted to 50 merchantmen, the CAM ships, and they began to go to sea in the summer. The CAM ships remained merchantmen flying the Red Ensign, unlike the fighter catapult ships. Except for the pilot and technicians on loan from RAF Fighter Command, CAM ships were crewed by merchant seamen and carried a cargo. The aircraft carried in CAM ships was a single Hawker Hurricane Mk I converted to a Sea Hurricane Mk IA. The ship was not fitted out to recover the aircraft like a carrier, so after a sortie, the pilot would ditch, unless within range of a friendly airfield. The pilots were volunteers and joined the Merchant Ship Fighter Unit under Wing Commander E S Moulton-Barrett. Each team consisted of one pilot, or two for longer voyages, a fitter, a rigger, a radio operator, a flight deck officer and a Royal Navy torpedoman/electrician who maintained and operated the catapult.

The Hurricane was launched only when an enemy aircraft was sighted. The catapult was rocket-fired. The pilots were extraordinarily courageous, because once launched, the only way back to the ship was being rescued by boat after parachuting into the water or ditching. The Atlantic was cold even in summer, and the water in the Arctic in winter could kill within minutes. Between November 1941 and July 1943, CAM ships carried out nine combat launches. Eight Hurricanes and one pilot were lost for eight German aircraft destroyed and one damaged.

In June 1941, the British completed the first escort carrier, a captured German grain ship, the *Hannover*, renamed *Audacity*. It was fitted with a flat deck, like a true aircraft carrier, and carried six American Grumman Martlet (F4-Wildcat) fighters designed for carrier operations. The American-built *Archer* followed in November. As more escort carriers were completed, CAM ships were withdrawn from Atlantic and Arctic convoys. Some 16 CAM ships continued on the Mediterranean and Freetown runs until September 1943. By the end of the war, 44 escort carriers of various classes were operated by the Royal Navy, and 19 merchant aircraft carriers: bulk carriers with a flight deck, sailing under the Red Ensign. These aircraft carriers helped turn the tide of the war at sea, which the pilots of the Hurricanes launched from CAM ships had so gallantly played a key part in beginning.

LEFT: A shot taken from astern of a Hurricane on the catapult of the Catapult Armed Merchant (CAM) ship SS *Empire Darwin*.

ABOVE: A posed publicity photograph of a pilot climbing into his aircraft on a CAM ship at anchor at Greenock, near Glasgow. For a successful launch, the ship had to be steamed into wind, so the aircraft could not be launched from a ship at anchor.

61 The Atlantic Wall

Up to the end of 1941, German fortifications along the French coast consisted of seven heavy coastal batteries between Boulogne and Calais, built to bombard England in the prelude to Operation Sealion, the invasion of England. In addition some fortified U-boat pens had been built with a few naval coastal batteries to protect them.

Following the cancellation of Sealion, Hitler ordered Dr Fritz Todt, his Minister for Arms and Munitions, to continue construction of U-boat pens and fortify the French Atlantic coast, especially at Brest, Lorient and Saint Nazaire. Over the succeeding 18 months additional fortifications were erected and in September 1942, Hitler ordered the construction of defences along the length of the French coast similar to the Siegfried Line along the Franco–German frontier. This new wall was to consist of 15,000 concrete strongpoints manned by 300,000 men. Hitler designed many of these strongpoints himself, each housing 30 to 70 men equipped with machine-guns and anti-aircraft weapons. The intervening ground was covered by interlocking fire from these strongpoints, which were planned to withstand air and sea bombardment. The U-boat pens were to be strengthened first, followed by the fortification of harbours suitable for Allied landings, and finally those beaches most appropriate for amphibious landings. The wall would also be extended to include the Belgian and Dutch coasts.

The task was now undertaken by Albert Speer, the new head of Organization Todt following Todt's death in an air crash on 8 February 1942. Although the Wehrmacht High Command believed the Channel coast to be the most likely place for Allied landings, Hitler decreed that priority be given to portions of the Atlantic Wall defending the V-1 rocket-launch sites. As a result, even the strongest sections of the wall never became the impregnable fortress that existed in Hitler's imagination. He himself never inspected the wall.

Hitler decreed that the German armies in the west must give priority to holding the wall when the attack came. This was also the view of Field Marshal Erwin Rommel, who had been appointed to command the initial phase of resistance to any Allied landing under the overall command of Field Marshal Karl Rudolf Gerd von Rundstedt.

On the eve of D-Day, 6 June 1944, there were 73 large-calibre guns in concrete emplacements, with mines and other obstacles on and behind likely beaches. In late 1943, von Rundstedt, whose views on tactics differed sharply from Rommel's, had ordered a second line to be built a short distance inland to give some depth to the wall – this was in addition to installing stakes in all likely glider-landing zones – but in April 1944, Rommel ordered work to cease on the second line and concentrated on beach defences. In spite of this, of the 50 million mines needed to provide a continuous belt along the whole coast, only five million had been planted by D-Day. The string of smaller fortifications was still incomplete, especially on the east coast of the Cotentin Peninsula. For example, in the 352nd Division's sector overlooking Utah Beach, only 15 per cent of the positions had been bombproofed. Because of Hitler's delay in initiating construction, and shortages of labour and material, the Atlantic Wall was never completed. This was a major factor in contributing to Allied success on D-Day.

One Allied Formation assaulted the Atlantic Wall twice: the 4th Special Service Brigade of Royal Marine Commandos. Having landed in Normandy on 6 June 1944, on 1 November the same year they assaulted the island of Walcheren, which guarded the entrance to the River Scheldt, capturing a series of massive coastal batteries in the process.

ABOVE RIGHT: One of the four 380-mm (15-in) guns at the Batterie Todt near Cap Gris Nez. This part of the wall was never assaulted by the Allies.

RIGHT: The construction of part of the Atlantic Wall.

62 Liberty Ships

The United States made a critical contribution to Allied victory in the Second World War by building a merchant fleet that could carry men, war materiel, food and scarce resources like oil to the Allied trans-oceanic battlefronts. As Winston Churchill wrote to Franklin Roosevelt in 1941: "The oceans, which were your shield, threaten to become your cage…" The Liberty ship, a 14,000-ton general cargo carrier, played an important role in breaking out of that oceanic cage.

The merchant fleet sinkings of 1940 showed that German U-boats threatened to make American aid to the British war effort irrelevant. The US Maritime Commission accepted the challenge of building a simple cargo ship that could be assembled rapidly in vast numbers. In December 1940, President Roosevelt authorized $36.5 million of emergency funds to allow the Maritime Commission to develop a general cargo ship on an emergency basis. Congress authorized additional money in February 1941 to build 200 special merchantmen, dubbed "Liberty" ships. By the end of the Second World War, the Maritime Commission had built and sent 2,710 Liberty ships to sea. This programme of "emergency cargo" ships peaked in 1943 when "Liberties" made up 13 million tons of an annual wartime high of 18.5 million deadweight tons of new merchant ship construction. There was no longer any doubt that American ship construction would outpace U-boat sinkings.

Although the Liberty programme began slowly (only seven ships were commissioned in 1941), the Maritime Commission learned that it could not build ships the old-fashioned way and still meet its 19 million-ton goal for 1943. First, it had to finance 107 new shipbuilding sites and encourage production innovation from its prime contractors, most notably six companies anchored on Henry J Kaiser Industries of the San Francisco Bay area. Speed of construction demanded radical changes in building Liberty ships; accepting advanced technology was not one of them. Instead Liberty ships were "retro" in design. The key to rapid construction was the production process: to build a Liberty-type cargo ship in 1941 took 355 days, but by 1943 shipbuilders could produce a Liberty in 56 days. The key time savings came from simultaneous modular construction, the introduction of welding over riveting to join sections, the creation of a skilled and well-treated workforce, and the lure of high profits for good management. The basic limitation was the availability of steel.

The Liberty ship programme had its share of problems. The ship itself was slow at 20.4kph (11 knots) and thus an attractive target in convoys that could travel no faster than their slowest ships, almost always Liberties. The ship could not be loaded and unloaded rapidly because of the outmoded boom-and-winch system. And although Kaiser-built Liberty ships were dependable, others were not.

To encourage rapid production, the Maritime Commission used unbid, cost-plus contracts which could be exploited by unprincipled managers to enlarge company profits and their salaries. A Congressional investigation found shocking examples of fraud and mismanagement that threatened the entire Liberty programme in 1944, but by that time the shipping crisis had passed, and the Maritime Commission could cancel some of its contracts. Liberty ship production fell to 7 million tons in 1944 and 1.5 million tons in 1945.

During the course of the war, the US Maritime Commission accepted delivery of 45 million tons of new shipping. Almost 30 million tons of this fleet were Liberty ships.

LEFT: One of the Liberty ships being fitted out in 1943 prior to being sent to war.

ABOVE: The bow of one of the Liberty ships at Bethlehem-Fairfield Shipyards, Inc, after she had ran arground.

63 The Bouncing Bomb

The Bouncing Bomb was conceived by Dr Barnes Wallis, the chief designer at Vickers, who had a reputation as an aircraft designer dating back to the 1930s. At the outbreak of the Second World War, he began designing very big bombs to knock down buildings and other large structures. At that time, the RAF, along with all other air forces, preferred to drop quantities of small bombs rather than one big one. During the course of his work on this project, Wallis set about designing a bomb that would be capable of destroying the dams that supplied water to the population and armaments factories of Germany's Ruhr valley: the Eder, Möhne, Sorpe, Ennepe, Schwelm and Diemel. The first dam-busting bomb envisaged by Wallis, in 1940, was far too heavy for any aircraft then in service or even on the drawing board. He realized that if a 2,720-kg (6,000-lb) bomb could be placed right by a dam wall, the water would multiply the effect of the charge and blow a hole in the 34-metre- (112-foot-) thick wall of the Möhne Dam and the even larger Eder Dam. The Lancaster could carry such a bomb, but the problem was dropping it exactly in the right place. This led Wallis to design a barrel-shaped bomb, actually a mine or depth-charge, that would bounce across the water like a stone thrown in a stone-skipping game. Before the bomb was released, a mechanism started it revolving, imparting back-spin so that when the bomb hit the dam wall it would roll down it and sink to a predetermined depth where a hydrostatic pistol would set it off. It had to be dropped at an exact height, speed and distance from the wall. The bomb, it must be emphasized, was designed for use against concrete dam walls, not the earth dam of the Sorpe.

Contrary to popular belief, Wallis was not the only person with designs on the dams. An attack on the Ruhr valley dams had been on the RAF's target list since 1938, but when the proposal was put to the C-in-C Bomber Command, Air Chief Marshal Sir Arthur Harris in early 1943, he said:

> *This is tripe of the wildest description. There are so many ifs and buts that there is not the smallest chance of its working.* (*The Right of the Line: The Royal Air Force in the European War 1939–1945* by John Terraine, Wordsworth Editions Ltd, 1997.)

Nonetheless, Harris was won over. Barnes Wallis's power of persuasion seems to have been the critical factor. It is arguable that the bouncing bomb was used because it existed – on the principle, by no means rare in war, "we've got it, let's use it".

A special squadron, 617, was formed, under Wing Commander Guy Gibson. Rigorous training in low-level flying at night over water took its toll: in one rehearsal, six out of 12 aircraft were damaged. The attack on the night of 16/17 May 1943, resulting in the destruction of the Möhne and Eder Dams, is the stuff of legend, described by the official historian of the RAF's strategic bombing campaign, himself a Bomber Command navigator, as the "most brilliant feat of arms which has been carried out by any air force", a judgement that no one can dispute (*Royal United Services Institute Journal*, May 1962, page 103). Unfortunately the heavy losses (eight out of 19 of the RAF's best crews) did not justify the result. The Sorpe Dam had to be destroyed to cut the Ruhr's water supplies. It was only damaged. Wallis's bomb was not suitable for this dam, and he knew it. The official historian is clear that neither the special bomb nor the resulting floods were of any importance. What mattered were the low-level and master-bomber techniques devised and executed by Gibson and his crews. These, when adopted by the rest of Bomber Command, were to transform its tactics from about mid-1944 onwards.

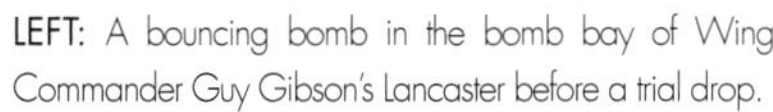

LEFT: A bouncing bomb in the bomb bay of Wing Commander Guy Gibson's Lancaster before a trial drop.

ABOVE: A bouncing bomb salvaged from Flight Lieutenant Barlow's Lancaster, which crashed, killing the whole crew, after hitting an electricity pylon on its way to attack the Sorpe Dam. A German official standing by the bomb gives a good indication of its size.

RIGHT: A Lancaster of 617 Squadron carrying out a practice drop at Reculver range in Kent.

OVERLEAF: The breach in the Möhne Dam four hours after the raid.

64 Ration Books

All combatant nations in the Second World War imposed rationing of food and other key materials, but the United Kingdom was the first to do so because the country relied so heavily on imported food and other materials, including oil and petrol, all of which was transported by sea. In 1939, the United Kingdom imported 20 million tons of food a year, amounting to 50 per cent of all meat, 70 per cent of cheese and sugar, 80 per cent of fruit and 70 per cent of cereals. This was a vulnerability of which the Germans took advantage by attacking shipping in an attempt to cripple British industry and starve the population. After the experience of the First World War, when German U-boats had brought the United Kingdom close to being starved into surrender, the British government had plans for rationing ready before the outbreak of the Second World War.

Once war was declared, the first commodity to be rationed was petrol, but this was followed on 8 January 1940 by food rationing: first bacon, butter and sugar, and soon after meat, tea, jam, biscuits, breakfast cereal, cheese, eggs, lard, milk and tinned fruit. A Ministry of Food was established which laid down the system by which rationing was controlled. Every inhabitant of the United Kingdom, including children, was issued with a ration book.

Most ration books held by adults were buff-coloured. Pregnant women, nursing mothers and children under five years old had a green book, which entitled them to first choice of any fruit available, a daily pint of milk and a double ration of eggs. Blue ration books were issued to children between the ages of 5 and 16, which gave them a higher priority in obtaining fruit than adults, a better scale of meat ration and half a pint of milk a day.

In order to buy the majority of rationed goods, everybody had to register with a particular shop. The details were stamped in the ration book, and you had to buy from this shop and no other. This enabled the shopkeeper to stock the amount of items required to supply the number of people registered. The coupons inside the book were either torn out or stamped by the shopkeeper each time a rationed item was purchased.

Food wasn't the only thing rationed in Britain. For clothes there was a points system, and the number of points allocated per person was reduced from 66 per year in 1942 to 24 in 1945 (a man's suit took between 26 and 29 points, depending on the amount of lining). No points were required for second-hand clothing or fur coats. Lace and frills on knickers were banned, and the number of buttons, pockets and pleats on clothes was regulated. Soap was also rationed, to around three bars a month per person – reduced if you also bought soap flakes or powder for washing clothes and dishes. Coal was rationed, and central heating was prohibited in the summer. Paper was also rationed, with newspapers being limited to 25 per cent of their pre-war consumption, and wrapping paper forbidden altogether for most shop purchases.

Although the Germans imposed some food rationing in September 1939, Hitler did not introduce full rationing until 1943. This was partly because he did not believe the war would last long, and also because he thought it would damage his popularity. Furthermore, any shortages in Germany could be made up by food requisitioned in large quantities from conquered nations; for example 15 per cent of French food production was siphoned off. In mid-1943, however, with the war beginning to go badly for Germany, strict rationing was imposed there, with the lowest, almost starvation, scales reserved for the millions of forced labourers and prisoners of war. These people did much of the heavy work in factories and on the land.

The inhabitants of Leningrad during the 900-day siege suffered one of the most stringent rationing regimes of the Second World War. During the winter of 1941–42 the daily ration was reduced to 225 g (8 oz) of all types of food for manual workers and 112 g (4 oz) for all other civilians. Birds, rats, dogs and cats were eaten, and there were even reports of cannibalism.

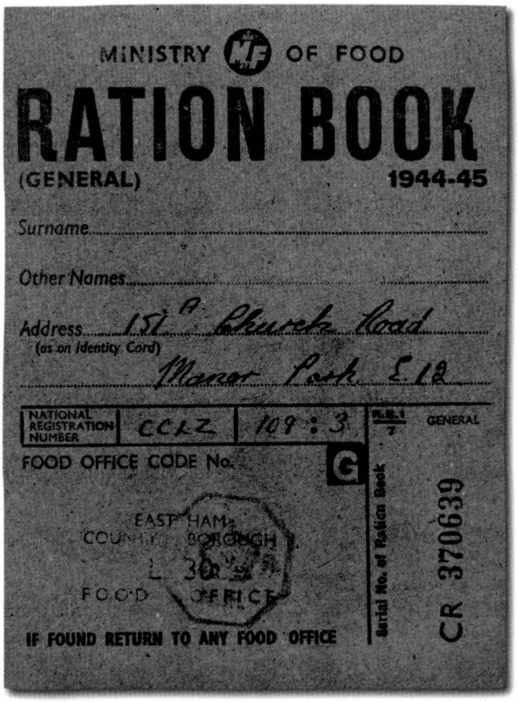

MINISTRY OF FOOD

RATION BOOK

(GENERAL) 1944-45

Surname

Other Names

Address 151A Church Road
(as on Identity Card)
Manor Park E12

NATIONAL REGISTRATION NUMBER CCLZ 109 3

R.B.1
7
GENERAL

FOOD OFFICE CODE No. G

EAST HAM COUNTY BOROUGH L 30 FOOD OFFICE

IF FOUND RETURN TO ANY FOOD OFFICE

Serial No. of Ration Book CR 370639

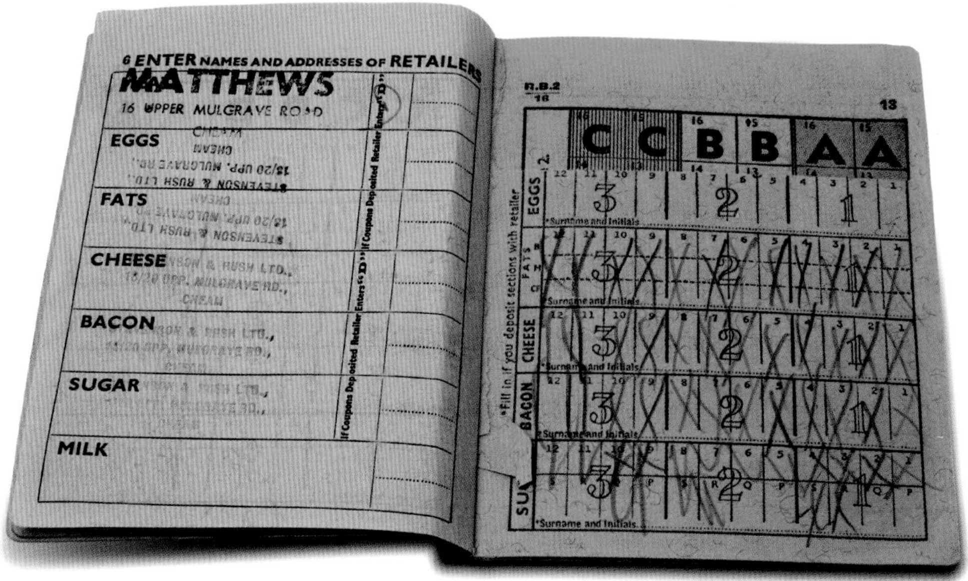
6 ENTER NAMES AND ADDRESSES OF RETAILERS

MATTHEWS
16 UPPER MULGRAVE ROAD

EGGS

FATS

CHEESE

BACON

SUGAR

MILK

If Coupons Deposited Retailer Enters "D"

R.B.2
16

13

C C B B A A

EGGS

FATS

CHEESE

BACON

*Surname and Initials

*Fill in if you deposit sections with retailer

LEFT: A still life of a variety of rationed items. The picture includes a buff (adult) ration book, a red clothing ration book, a packet of powdered eggs and a tin of SPAM (processed ham).

ABOVE: The outside cover and inside pages of a ration book.

65 The Owen Gun

The Owen Gun, or Owen Machine Carbine to give it its official army name, was the only such weapon designed by an Australian in the Second World War. Evelyn Owen, the 24-year-old inventor, demonstrated a 5.6-mm (.22-in) calibre prototype to the Australian Army Ordnance Board six weeks before the outbreak of the Second World War, but the Board decided that there was no use for such a weapon in the Australian Army. When war broke out, Owen joined the Australian Army as a private soldier.

In September 1940, Vincent Wardell, the manager of the Lysaght steel works in Port Kembla, New South Wales, returned home from work to find a sack sitting by his garage door. In it was the prototype sub-machine gun conceived by Owen, the son of Wardell's neighbour. Wardell was impressed by the simplicity of the design, and used his influence to have young Owen transferred to the Army Inventions Board so he could continue work on his brainchild. The army was still indifferent, but Owen was allowed to continue work to modify and improve his machine carbine.

To begin with, the prototypes – made by Lysaght – were fitted with a top-mounted drum magazine. This was replaced by a straight 32-round box magazine, similar to the one fitted to the Sten sub-machine gun but on top of the gun. Sights were fitted to the side in such a way that the firer could line up on the target by sighting alongside the magazine. At the time, there were large quantities of 11-mm (.45-ih) calibre ammunition available in Australia, and initially this round was chosen for the gun. Lysaght, however, made three versions for trials: an 11-mm, a 9-mm and a 5.6-mm. All three were tested against the sub-machine guns with which British and Commonwealth forces were equipped at the time: the 9-mm British Sten and the 11-mm US Thompson (the Tommy Gun). The test included immersing the guns in mud and sand to simulate use in battle conditions. The Owen came through the test with flying colours, in marked contrast to the other two types of gun.

Despite this dramatic test of the gun's reliability, the Australian Army continued to dither over which calibre gun should be brought into service. Eventually, after some chivvying by senior government ministers, the army ordered the 9-mm gun. This was an excellent choice, as the stopping power of the available 5.6-mm round fired from a short-barrelled weapon was inferior to the 9-mm. The 11-mm 32-round magazine was heavy and, added to the weight of the gun, made it less easy to handle and carry than a 9-mm version, especially in thick undergrowth.

The Owen was produced at the Lysaght works at Port Kembla and Newcastle in New South Wales, about 50,000 being made between 1941 and 1945. Although the gun was heavier and bigger than the Sten, it was hugely popular with Australian soldiers. It came into service just as the Australians became engaged in fighting the Japanese in New Guinea. This involved much close-quarter fighting in thick jungle and scrub where the ability to fire several bursts proved invaluable against an enemy who kept coming until he was stopped by death. It proved outstanding in a jungle environment, being able to continue firing after being coated in mud, immersed in rivers and rained on for days on end. The key to its reliability was the top-mounted magazine, so the weight of the ammunition used gravity to help the spring push each round down to the breech of the gun. The design of the breech, which prevented dirt jamming the bolt, also played a part in keeping the gun firing in very muddy or sandy conditions. Not surprisingly the gun came to be called the "Digger's Darling". It was used by the Australian Army until the mid-1960s, seeing service in Korea and Vietnam.

FAR LEFT: The "Digger's Darling" being used by an ANZAC soldier.

ABOVE: The Mk I Owen Gun.

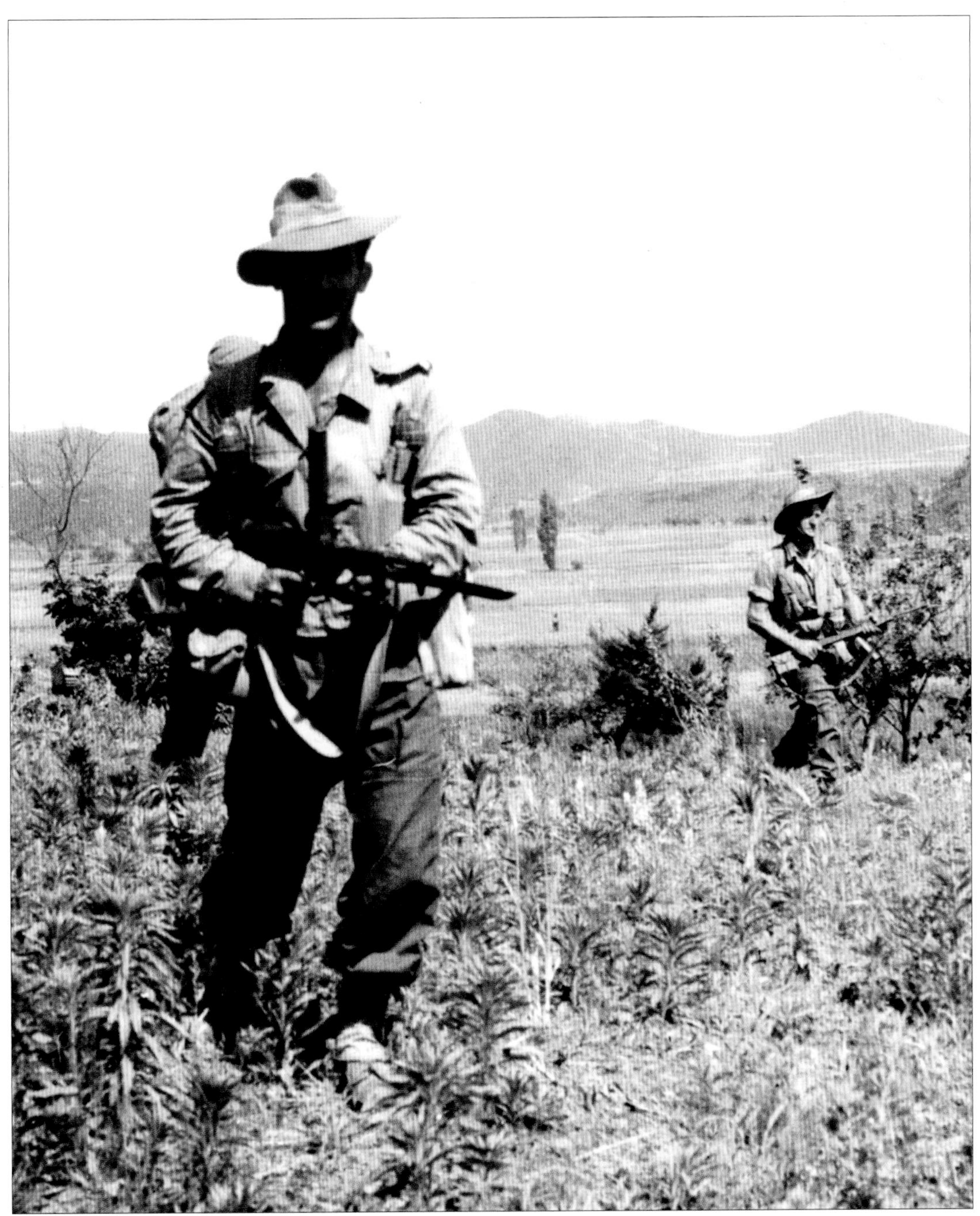

LEFT: The Owen was especially suited to operating in thick jungle, where fleeting targets had to be engaged at close quarters. A longer weapon such as a rifle or carbine tended to catch on undergrowth and vines.

ABOVE: Australian "Diggers" during the Korea War in which the Owen was still in use.

66 The Chindit Insignia

The Chindits were a special force that operated behind the Japanese lines in Burma on two occasions. They were the brainchild of a British Royal Artillery officer, Major Orde Wingate, who had been sent to India at the request of the C-in-C, General Sir Archibald Wavell. Wingate had previously carried out successful guerrilla-type operations in Palestine before the Second World War and in Abyssinia in 1941. He persuaded Wavell to allow him to raise a special force of brigade strength to carry out long-range penetration operations into Burma from Assam.

Wingate, promoted to acting brigadier, was authorized to raise the 77th Indian Infantry Brigade for this purpose. He chose as his brigade formation sign the Chinthe, the mythical beast that stands guard outside temples and monasteries in Burma. His soldiers mispronounced it "Chindit", and the name caught on and endured.

Wingate broke his brigade up into columns, each of about 400 men. Each column would march independently, be self-supporting for a week and be supplied by air. He planned to concentrate two or more columns on specific tasks such as blowing up bridges, or attacking small Japanese outposts. He communicated with his columns by radio.

Wingate's brigade entered Burma in mid-February 1943, cutting the railway between Shwebo and Myitkyina, harassing the Japanese in the Shwebo area and eventually crossing the Irrawaddy with the aim of severing enemy communications with the Salween front where the Chinese were fighting. This last aim was never achieved because after most of the 77th Brigade columns had crossed the Irrawaddy, the Japanese began concentrating their forces against them. Wingate ordered his columns to disperse and make their way back to India.

Of the 3,000 Chindits who entered Burma on the first expedition, 2,182 returned four months later. Of those who didn't make it back, around 450 were battle casualties, 210 were taken prisoner (of whom 42 survived) and the remainder were missing. So little was achieved that Wingate thought he would be court-martialled. Instead, he was sent for by Churchill to accompany him to the Anglo–American conference at Quebec. Meanwhile, back in India, the public relations officers busily "milked" the Chindit story as an example of how the British could defeat the hitherto invincible Japanese. It worked.

At Quebec, Wingate so impressed everyone that he was authorized to expand his force massively. He was given two more brigades and a complete infantry division, the 70th, fresh from the desert. He was also supported by a substantial number of aircraft. This allowed him to fly in the bulk of his force by Dakota and glider, although one brigade marched in.

Despite setbacks, the fly-in and the overland march went almost without a hitch, and the brigades started their operations, but a few days after the fly-in Wingate was killed in an air crash. Brigadier "Joe" Lentaigne commanding the 111th Brigade took over. At first operations went well, especially those at a defensive block called the White City, commanded by the outstanding Chindit Brigadier James Michael "Mad Mike" Calvert.

After some weeks the Chindits were ordered to march north to support the operations of two Chinese divisions commanded by the Anglophobe American Lieutenant General Joseph W Stilwell. During this period, Calvert's brigade captured the town of Mogaung, but Calvert heard on the BBC that Stilwell was claiming that his troops had captured it. Calvert sent a message saying, "The Americans and Chinese have captured Mogaung. 77 Brigade is proceeding to take umbrage."

Eventually the Chindits were withdrawn. Few of the surviving soldiers were fit to take part in operations again. In one brigade alone 80 per cent were unfit for active service.

LEFT: Chindits preparing a bridge on the Mandalay–Myitkyina railway for demolition on their way to join Brigadier Mike Calvert at the "White City" block during the Second Chindit Expedition.

ABOVE: The Chindit badge, based on the Chinthe that guards temples and monasteries in Burma.

67 ASDIC

ASDIC is said by some to stand for Anti-Submarine Detection Investigation Committee, a cover name for highly secret work by the Anti-Submarine Division at the British Admiralty during the First World War that aimed to improve techniques for detecting dived submarines. The best that was available at the time consisted of hydrophones to listen for the sound of the U-boat propeller, but these were ineffective unless the vessel operating them halted before lowering them into the water, and remained stationary thereafter. Analysis after the war showed that the total number of U-boat losses credited to detection by hydrophones was just three; meanwhile, German U-boats had sunk so many Allied ships that there was a very real possibility that imports of food and other vital supplies to Britain could have been reduced to a trickle. Fortunately, since Admiralty staff did not manage to find a technical solution to the detection problem before the First World War ended, the number of sinkings by U-boats was rapidly reduced by the introduction of the convoy system on 26 April 1917. They did, however, recognize that the answer lay in finding a way to emit a pulse of sound under water which would be picked up when it rebounded off a submarine's hull.

In the interwar years, research continued, and by 1938 the technology of bouncing sound waves off a submerged object had been developed by the British into Asdic anti-submarine detection equipment. A transmitter encased in a water-filled metal dome on the ship's bottom sent out a series of "pings". The operator sitting in the Asdic compartment behind the bridge could turn the transmitter head to cover an arc of about 45 degrees each side of the ship's head. When the sound pulse struck an object it "echoed" with a beeping sound, and the operator alerted the officer of the watch or ship's captain, giving a range and bearing.

Before the Second World War, the Royal Navy's faith in Asdic was such that the Naval staff believed the U-boat threat had been largely overcome. There was much discussion in the Admiralty on whether it would be necessary to institute the convoy system in the event of war. Fortunately, merchant shipping was ordered into convoys immediately on the outbreak of the Second World War, because in operational conditions Asdic did not perform as well as had been hoped for a number of reasons: its range was only 1,370 metres (1,500 yards); neither bearings nor ranges could be read accurately – there could be an error of a few degrees in bearings, and a possible error of 23 metres (25 yards) in range; it was usually impossible to discriminate between submarine and non-submarine targets, such as whales; the operator required much skill and practice, which took time to acquire; the efficiency of the set fell off rapidly at speeds above 37 kph (20 knots), in rough weather and in waters with layers of large variations in temperature; crafty U-boat commanders learned to hide under a layer that either bent the sound beam or bounced it back; Asdic could not determine the depth of a submerged U-boat, so it was impossible to set charges to explode at the correct depth; and finally, Asdic could not detect a submarine on the surface. This last was perhaps the most critical failing of all, because the majority of U-boat attacks were at night on the surface, when, as the Naval Staff reported after the war, "the Asdic was practically useless". The answer was more ships equipped with radar, and radar that was able to pick up a small target, such as the conning tower of a submarine and part of its casing on the surface. As the war progressed, escorts were fitted with such radar sets.

Early in the Second World War, British Asdic technology was passed to the US, where work on Sound Navigation and Ranging (SONAR) had been in progress for some years. British and American scientists worked together throughout the war to produce more accurate and reliable Asdic/Sonar equipment for both navies. By the end of the war, Sonar, as the British now called it, was able to locate submarines more accurately, and this, combined with significant advances in depth-charge technology, played a major part in defeating the U-boat.

RIGHT: The officer of the watch and three ratings on the compass platform of HMS *Anthony*, an "A" Class destroyer. The Asdic operator is looking out of the Asdic hut in which he operated.

68 Beach Defences

The Teller mine was the standard German anti-tank mine during the Second World War. Round and plate-shaped (*Teller* is German for plate), it contained about 5.5kg (12lb) of TNT and was exploded by a pressure-operated fuse, usually set to detonate when a vehicle of 90kg (200lb) or more passed over it. This was deliberate, because the mines were laid to damage tanks and destroy lighter vehicles and it would be a waste if one was set off by a person – there were lighter mines for that, which were usually laid alongside anti-tank mines in a mixed minefield, to make clearing it more difficult. Teller mines could be fitted with "anti-lift" devices that detonated the mine if someone tried to move it. This was well known and added to the time taken to clear a minefield.

In the autumn of 1943, Field Marshal Erwin Rommel was commanding Army Group B, responsible for the defence of northern France and the Netherlands, from Nantes to the Zuider Zee. This included the coastal areas most likely to be invaded by the Allies. He had used mines extensively in Africa, and decreed that they should be used in great numbers in his area of responsibility. By October 1943, around two million mines had been laid; by the end of May 1944, the number had risen to more than six million. Not only were mines laid on the ground on all likely beaches, but Rommel also ordered that obstacles be built right out to the low-water spring-tide mark. Wooden or concrete stakes were driven into the sand or clay beach and angled so that they faced seawards. Concrete tetrahedrons 1.8 metres (6 feet) high and weighing nearly a ton were also planted on the beaches. To these were added "hedgehogs" made of 2.1-metre (7-foot) angled girders, riveted together so as to present a sharp point in all directions; when struck they would pierce a craft or turn over, bringing other points up to impale it from beneath. Between these obstacles, or further out to sea, poles on bipods were placed in such a way that craft trying to avoid the outward-facing poles at high tide would impale themselves on these underwater obstacles.

Many of these defences of all types had Teller mines attached. If there were insufficient mines, Rommel made use of captured French artillery shells. The purpose of these devices, either with or without mines and explosives attached, was to rip the bottom out of landing craft approaching the beach and to sink them before they could touch down and disgorge their troops or vehicles.

Ever since February 1944, when the Allies discovered that underwater obstacles were being laid, small teams from the Combined Operations Pilotage Parties (COPPs) reconnoitred selected beaches at night to assess the problem. By day, low-flying reconnaissance produced oblique aerial photographs. As a result of the information brought back, the Allies decided that they would not land at high tide, which Rommel clearly expected, but at low tide so that assault engineers could clear paths in the obstacle belt before the landing craft came in. This they would do by either demolishing them or pulling them aside with tracked vehicles, which could only be achieved when they stood above the tide level or in less than 60 cm (2 feet) of water. Teams from the Royal Navy and Royal Engineers were formed and trained for the task. At low tide the obstacles would be easier for the landing-craft coxswains to see and avoid.

Fortunately Rommel had neither the time nor the equipment to extend the obstacle belt into the lower half of the tidal range as he had intended. In addition, the Allies had at their disposal the specialist armour of Hobart's "funnies", specifically designed to cope with the problems posed by Rommel's obstacles. Landing at low tide would give the troops a longer run up the beach once they had left their craft, exposing them to enemy small-arms fire, mortars and artillery, but this was infinitely preferable to being drowned or cut down in the water, which would certainly happen if lanes through the obstacle belts were not cleared.

LEFT: A German prisoner of war clearing a minefield near Stavanger in Norway fixes a charge to a Teller mine to destroy it in situ; it was deemed too dangerous to move.

ABOVE: A metal "hedgehog".

RIGHT: A naval officer, possibly a beach master, and Royal Engineer officer examining a "hedgehog" with Teller mines attached.

OVERLEAF: "Hedgehogs" and obstacle poles along the Atlantic Wall.

69 The Nebelwerfer

The Nebelwerfer ("smoke-" or "fog-thrower") was a multi-barrelled rocket launcher. The name was a relic of the First World War, when it was used to fire smoke or gas shells in large quantities. In its original form it was a mortar, in essence a large drainpipe out of which a bomb was discharged by a small explosive charge. The impact of the charge was low, so big bombs with thin, light cases and packed with large quantities of explosive could be fired, albeit over ranges that were relatively short compared with a conventional gun. A mortar does not need a recoil and recuperating system, so is lighter and cheaper to produce than an artillery piece. Normally, the recoil mechanism absorbs the rearward momentum of a gun, and the recuperator returns the piece to its original firing position.

The size of the bomb makes the mortar a suitable weapon for delivering large quantities of gas or smoke. Normally mortars are high-angle weapons, fired in the "upper register", ie from an angle of 45 degrees to almost vertical, allowing plunging fire onto targets behind hills and woods, and within fortifications.

In 1934 the Germans designed a 10-cm (4-in) Nebelwerfer, the model 35, to project chemical bombs out to 3,000 metres (3,300 yards), but this was not far enough for the army. The result was the 10-cm Nebelwerfer 40, with a range of 6,000 metres (6,600 yards). But to achieve this performance the original mortar was converted into a breech-loading piece with a recoil mechanism to absorb the shock of discharge, on a wheeled carriage – an artillery piece in all but name. It weighed eight times as much as the Nebelwerfer 35, and cost about ten times more to manufacture.

Also during the interwar period, the Germans had been working on rocket propulsion, and it was recognized that this was a way to deliver large amounts of smoke or gas. The outcome was the 15-cm Nebelwerfer 41, which came into service just after the Battle of France (10 May–25 June 1940), and replaced the 35. It consisted of a six-barrelled launcher mounted on a trailer, firing a spin-stabilized rocket out to 6,850 metres (7,500 yards) and shooting in the lower register like a conventional gun. The 34-kg (75-lb) rocket warhead could be packed with gas, smoke or high explosive (HE). In the event, the Germans never used gas in the Second World War, but used plenty of smoke and HE. A rocket launcher is recoilless, and can therefore dispense with recoil and recuperating systems. The resulting weapon is far lighter than the equivalent calibre artillery piece. Several thousand Nebelwerfer 41s and millions of 150 mm rockets were produced during the war.

Before the invasion of the Soviet Union, two further models were produced: the 28-cmand the 32-cm Nebelwerfer 41. The 28-cm warhead had an HE filling, and the 32-cm an incendiary filling. Both types had a short range: a mere 2,200 metres (2,400 yards). They could be fired from their wooden packing cases, or from a towed launcher. These models were quickly followed by the 21-cm Nebelwerfer 42, which had five barrells, a 112-kg (248-lb) HE warhead and 7,845-metre (8,580-yard) range. It was mounted on an artillery-type carriage, and was therefore highly mobile. This saw service in North Africa, as well as in Russia and northwest Europe. The last model to be produced was the 30-cm Nebelwerfer 42, with a massive 126-kg (277lb) HE warhead. Despite its designation, it was actually introduced in 1943.

Being "stonked" by conventional mortars is an unpleasant experience, all the more so when at the receiving end of a Nebelwerfer barrage. The rocket, fitted with a siren, made a moaning sound as it flew through the air. A multiple launch of a score of rockets produced a long, drawn-out wailing like a pack of banshees; it was extremely unnerving, as the recipients braced themselves for the massive explosions caused by a hail of bombs, each far larger than any Allied mortar bomb with the exception of the later marks of Russian Katyusha rockets.

RIGHT: A soldier loading a 15-cm Nebelwerfer on the Russian Front.

70 The WACO Glider

The WACO Glider, made by the Waco Aircraft Company in the United States was the standard medium glider for use by American airborne forces. It was also used on a number of occasions by British air-landing troops who called it the Hadrian, in keeping with the British glider names: Hengist, Hotspur, Horsa and Hamilcar. It was a 15-seater troop- and cargo-carrying high-wing monoplane with rectangular wings, manually operated flaps and landing gear. The cockpit was hinged along the roof where it joined the fuselage, enabling the nose of the glider to be raised and locked in the open position so that a jeep and trailer, motor-cycles or light guns could be loaded and unloaded through the front of the glider.

The WACO Glider was employed by both the US and British airborne forces for the invasion of Sicily (9 July–17 August 1943), and by Wingate's Chindits in Burma. The first use en masse of WACO Gliders in operations in the Second World War, was the fly-in of the glider infantry, artillery and headquarters vehicles and heavy radios of the United States 82nd and 101st Airborne Divisions on 6 and 7 June 1944.

Most of the attention on the activities of the US airborne divisions during the invasion of Normandy, and indeed elsewhere, centres on the operations by the more "glamorous" parachute infantry, and the glider infantry tends to be ignored. For the Normandy invasion each division had one glider infantry regiment, each of three battalions, as well as two battalions of glider field artillery with 75-mm guns.

Before the introduction of helicopters, the glider provided the only means of flying soldiers and equipment into battle with a reasonable chance of landing them all together, where they could instantly form up into cohesive fighting units. Soldiers and equipment arriving by parachute were often scattered over miles of countryside, taking hours, and occasionally days, to gather together.

In the case of US airborne forces, each glider was towed to the area of operations by a C-47 Dakota. They were released at a designated point short of the landing zone (LZ), to glide down and land. Most, although not all, glider landings by the US airborne were made in daylight. A trip in a glider was far from being a joy ride, and many soldiers preferred parachuting. The glider wallowed in the wake of its tug aircraft; glider soldiers remember that the floor was often awash with vomit long before arrival at the release point. The lumbering tug-and-tow combination was an easy target for enemy flak and fighters, especially in daylight.

Landing in a glider, described as a "controlled crash", was hazardous, especially in wooded country. With luck, trees would rip off the wings, slowing the glider down. If the nose hit a tree, the result could be disastrous, killing or badly injuring the two pilots and the passengers. A glider loaded with a jeep or artillery was potentially lethal: a bad landing could result in the load shooting forward on impact, crushing the pilots.

Despite these drawbacks, the arrival of the gliders on D-Day and D plus one was critical to the success of the 82nd and 101st Airborne Divisions in achieving their objectives in the Cotentin peninsula and the comparative ease with which the US forces landing from seaward came ashore on Utah Beach.

LEFT: The 1st Battalion 325th Glider Infantry in the second wave of the US 82nd Airborne Division's WACO gliders landing at Landing Zone W 3 kilometres (2 miles) south of Ste Mère-Eglise in the US sector on the morning of 6 June 1944. C-47 tug aircraft are overhead.

ABOVE: A WACO glider.

71 The LST

The Landing Ship Tank (LST) provided the backbone of all Allied landings in the Second World War between 1943 and 1945. It could embark tanks, vehicles, artillery and heavy supplies and land them through its bow doors directly on to a beach. The first Landing Craft Tank (LCT) produced by the British in 1940 was too small for anything other than amphibious operations carried out after a short sea voyage. Churchill demanded a bigger and better ship. In order to produce such vessels as quickly as possible, three shallow draft tankers constructed for use on the Maracaibo River in Venezuela were converted. Their bows were cut away, and a new section with a bow door hinged at the bottom was built on. These three ships served throughout the war, including the Normandy landings in June 1944.

However the main type of LCT used in the Second World War by both Americans and British was the LST(2) mass-produced in the USA. They began with the "Atlantic tank landing craft", as they were originally designated, which were designed in 1941 to be able to cross the Atlantic under their own power. These LSTs were designed by John C Niedermair of the US Navy's Bureau of Ships with liquid ballast tanks to allow for deep draft for ocean voyages and shallow draft for beaching.

The LST (2) was powered by two General Motors 12-567 V-12 standard locomotive engines connected to twin screws. Maximum speed was 21.2 kph (11.5 knots) with a cruising speed of 16.2 kph (8.75 knots). It was designed to take 20 Sherman tanks, or up to around120 small vehicles, plus 170 troops. Tanks could be carried only on the lower tank deck, but lighter equipment such as jeeps, small trucks, and towed artillery pieces could also be carried on the upper deck. The LST was loaded and unloaded through the double bow doors and bow ramp. Vehicles were taken up to and down from the upper deck by vehicle lift. The LST could be beached to allow unloading, or loads could be disembarked on to Rhino pontoon ferries, which some LSTS would tow to an area off the landing beach. These pontoons were assembled into 53-metre (175-foot) barges with detachable outboard engines.

Disembarkation by pontoon ferry overcame the difficulty of getting the LST in close enough if the beach was flat with a very gentle gradient. Its use also avoided the problems caused by allowing LSTs to dry out at low tide, like beached whales, thus remaining vulnerable to artillery fire and air attack especially in the early stages of a landing. LSTs were, however, designed to dry out and in the later stages of an operation frequently were allowed to do so, while vehicles drove ashore over the dry sand. Swimming tanks and vehicles, notably the DUKW, were able to disembark straight into the water from the bow ramp and swim ashore. LSTs in British service were fitted with one 12-pounder anti-aircraft gun aft and six 20-mm cannon. American LSTs were armed with up to seven 40-mm anti-aircraft guns and 12 20-mm cannon.

Some LSTs carried a pair of smaller landing craft on davits; on British ships, usually the Landing Craft Assault (LCA), and the Landing Craft Vehicle and Personnel (LCVP) on American ships. These could be used to land infantry, beach parties and other troops on foot.

Selected LSTs were equipped with medical parties to act as forward mobile hospitals where surgical operations were carried out in the tank deck. Large numbers of wounded carried on stretchers in the tank deck were evacuated by these hospital-fitted LSTs.

For the Normandy landings, LSTs were used to tow pieces of Mulberry harbour across the Channel. On the morning of D plus one onwards, LSTs worked a shuttle service from British ports to the beaches, bringing reinforcements, replacement equipment and supplies. One British LST, 416 (LSTs were numbered not named), made 28 Channel crossings between 6 June and 31 September. The LSTs were the forerunners of the roll on/roll off ferries of today.

LEFT: LSTs 22 and 206 in the surf at Leyte in the Philippines on 1 October 1944.

ABOVE: A Sherman tank having driven out of the bow doors of an LST and down the ramp, wades ashore.

72 The George Cross

King George VI instituted the George Cross on 24 September 1940. The German air assault on Britain was just gaining momentum, with attacks on airfields being switched to cities. He felt that there was a need to recognize the growing number of acts of courage either by civilians or by the military not in contact with the enemy. The King proclaimed:

> *In order that they should be worthily and promptly recognized, I have decided to create, at once, a new mark of honour for men and women in all walks of civilian life. I propose to give my name to this new distinction, which will consist of the George Cross, which will rank next to the Victoria Cross.*

At the same time the George Medal was instituted for awarding to those whose deeds were not assessed as meriting a George Cross. An extract from the *London Gazette* of 31 January 1941 announced the George Cross like this:

> *George R.I*
> *George the Sixth, by the Grace of God, of Great Britain, Ireland and the British Dominions beyond the Sea Kings, Defender of the Faith, Emperor of India, to all whom these Presents shall come,*
> *Greetings!*
> *Whereas We have taken into our Royal consideration the many acts of heroism peformed both by male and female persons, especially during the present war*
> *And whereas We are desirous of honouring those who perform such deeds:*
> *We do by these presents for Us, Our Heirs and Successors institute and create a new Decoration which we desire should be highly prized and eagerly sought after.*
> *First: It is ordained that the Decoration be designated and styled "The George Cross".*

The George Cross was intended to replace the Empire Gallantry Medal, and all holders of this medal were told to exchange theirs for the new Cross. It is thought that a substitution of awards in this manner had never been done before. The Warrant for the George Cross states:

> *The Cross is intended primarily for civilians and award in Our military services is to be confined to actions for which purely military Honours are not normally granted... It is ordained that the Cross shall be worn by recipients on the left breast suspended from a ribbon one and a quarter inches in width, of dark blue, [and] that it shall be worn immediately after the Victoria Cross and in front of the Insignia of all British Orders of Chivalry.*

The first recipient of the George Cross was Thomas Alderson, a detachment leader in the Air Raid Precautions organization, for saving people from bombed houses. The George Cross was awarded to three women in the Second World War: Odette Sansom, Violette Szabo and Noor Inayat Khan, all for work in occupied Europe with the Special Operations Executive (SOE). The George Cross was awarded to the Island of Malta on 15 April 1942, in the words of King George VI, "to bear witness to a heroism and devotion that will long be famous in history".

LEFT: Violette Szabo, tortured and shot by the Gestapo. She was awarded the George Cross posthumously.

ABOVE: The George Cross.

73 The Rocket Launcher

Known as a "Bazooka" for its similarity to a musical instrument played by a 1930s vaudeville comedian, the M1/M9 rocket launcher gave the US Army infantry a man-portable anti-armour weapon of modest capability. Its 6-cm (2.36-in) rocket with a small shaped-charge warhead could not penetrate the frontal armour of a German tank, but if fired at the side and rear, it might cripple one. It was very effective at ranges of up to 183 metres (200 yards) against almost all other German fighting vehicles and trucks, and could also be used as a standoff bunker-buster.

The 1.5-metre- (5-foot-) long launcher accepted the rocket at its open rear where a set of electrical contacts ignited the rocket. When the gunner depressed the trigger, it generated electrical power to the rocket engine. The weapon had no recoil, but the loader had to move clear of the backblast, which also identified the weapon's firing position. Skilled two-man teams did not use the same position more than once if possible.

The 1943 table of organization and equipment for a US Army infantry division allocated 557 launchers throughout the division, but the anti-tank rocket teams were most numerous in the headquarters of infantry regiments and battalions where they were paired with anti-tank cannon and mine layers. In actual combat, pairs of rocket launcher teams would be assigned to infantry companies.

Although ordnance experts made modifications to the M-1's sight and trigger mechanism, the M-9 represented the most important change because it divided the launching tube into two parts that could be joined in seconds by twist-locking. This change made the launcher much easier to carry and protected the trigger mechanism.

Impressed by the Bazooka, the German army used it as the model for its own Panzerschreck anti-tank rocket launcher, which fired an 88mm warhead that could penetrate 18 to 20 cm (seven to eight inches) of sloped armour. It had twice the destructiveness of the US 2.36-inch warhead and could destroy American tanks with a frontal shot.

FAR RIGHT: A soldier aims his new Bazooka..

BELOW: A rocket launcher is used by GIs during street fighting in Normandy in June 1944.

FIRE
SAFE

74 The Tunnellers' Trolley

Perhaps the two best-known escapes by prisoners of war (POWs) in the Second World War were from Stalag Luft III. The camp was located in Sagan, in Silesia: then part of Germany, and now in Poland. It was one of several camps for Allied aircrew, but was the biggest. Eventually it held 10,000 POWs and covered 59 acres with 8 kilometres (5 miles) of perimeter fencing. The POWs at Stalag Luft III included Fleet Arm aircrew and USAAF, plus a few non-aircrew soldiers (the reason for this exception is not easy to establish).

The site was selected for two reasons. First, it was in the middle of occupied Europe and therefore any escaper would have to travel a very long way to reach a neutral country: Sweden, Spain and Switzerland being the closest. Second, the sandy soil made tunnelling difficult because it caved in easily and the yellow subsoil stood out clearly against the grey surface dust. So it could not be dumped just anywhere without being seen by the camp guards, and was easily spotted on prisoners' clothing giving away the fact that there was a tunnel being dug somewhere. The design of the camp also hindered tunnelling. The POW accommodation huts were raised 60 cm (2 feet) above the ground making any tunnelling from POW accommodation obvious. Finally, seismograph microphones were placed around the perimeter of the camp to detect sounds of digging, although only to a very shallow depth.

The first successful escape was in October 1943 using a wooden gym vaulting "horse" as cover for the digging. The vibration caused by men running, jumping and landing prevented the microphones from detecting the sounds of digging. The "horse" was positioned quite near the perimeter wire, reducing the length the tunnel had to be.

The next partially successful escape was conceived by Squadron Leader Roger Bushell RAF in Spring 1943 and is now called the "great escape". He planned to dig three, deep, long tunnels: "Tom", "Dick" and "Harry". If one tunnel was found, Bushell banked on the Germans assuming that there were no others. He aimed to get more than 200 POWs out. To avoid the problem caused by the raised accommodation huts, Tom's and Harry's entrances were each dug under a camp stove through the its cement and concrete plinth, which extended all the way from the hut floor to the ground. This was a difficult job taking hours of work with a pick. Dick began in a drain sump in one of the washrooms. The tunnels were 9 metres (30 feet) below the surface in order to avoid the digging sounds being picked up by the seismic microphones.

The tunnel dimensions, 0.6 metres (2 feet) square, were dictated by the material use for shoring: bed boards, just over 60 cm (2 feet) long, 20 under the mattress of each POW's bed. A wooden railway was built along each tunnel. Small wooden trucks or trolleys were pulled along by rope from haulage points positioned at intervals along the tunnel. A ventilation system of empty dried milk (KLIM) tins stuck end to end was laid under the tunnel floor with bellows pumps made from kitbags.

Dick was abandoned when the area planned for the tunnel exit was cleared of trees preparatory to a new compound being built there. It was used thereafter to dump sand from the other two tunnels, to store the huge quantity of escape clothing, false papers and equipment stolen from the Germans, and as a workshop. Tom was discovered in summer 1943, so all efforts were concentrated on Harry, which was finished in March 1944, 102 metres (336 feet) long. But it was not long enough; it did not, as planned, reach the trees some yards beyond the wire: as the escapers would discover,

The breakout occurred on the night 24/25 March 1944. Seventy-six men got out, before a guard spotted a man lying by the tunnel exit, which was well short of the trees. Three escapers reached safety, 50 were murdered by the Gestapo, and 17 were returned to Sagan, four to Sachsenhausen and two to Colditz.

LEFT: The trolley in "Harry" from which 76 men escaped on the night of 24/25 March 1944. The picture was taken in 2011 by a team of archaeologists and veterans who excavated the tunnel and restored part of it.

ABOVE: The restored tunnel.

75 Eisenhower's Unsent Message

Despite his confidence about the cross-Channel attack on 6 June 1944 – Operation Overlord – General Dwight D "Ike" Eisenhower, Supreme Commander of the Allied Forces in Europe, remained concerned about the landings' success. As a student of the history of warfare, and tempered by almost two years of experience as a theatre commander in Europe, Eisenhower knew how easily a well-planned operation could become a disaster and how hard it was to turn defeat into victory unless the enemy made even greater mistakes.

Eisenhower had spent much of his career learning how to plan big operations. Although the D-Day landings had been prepared in great detail and simplified where they could be, he faced uncertainties so daunting that only a stupid, pathological optimist would not have been worried. In the first week of June, the Supreme Commander faced uncertain weather, concern about the status of German panzer divisions in Normandy and some doubts about the air attacks and naval gunfire operations that would precede the landings. He realized that he might be sending three Allied airborne divisions to potential destruction. He weighed all the risks with care, but still commented to an aide: "I hope to God I know what I'm doing." Underneath his serious but outgoing persona, Eisenhower thought about his course of action should Overlord fail.

After a long meeting with his British and American senior commanders and principal staff officers on 4 June General Eisenhower postponed the 5 June landing because of bad weather. When more promising weather reports were received, he called the same officers to another conference at 4.15 pm on 5 June 1944 at his headquarters at Southwick House, just north of Portsmouth. He had his staff meteorologist, RAF Group Captain J M Stagg, present the latest forecasts, which offered a window of moderating wind and rain on 6 June. Should the landing be postponed again, the expeditionary force would have to wait weeks for more favourable tides, moon phase and weather. The consensus of advice was "go". After perhaps a minute of pacing, Eisenhower said, "Ok. We'll go."

At this point, Eisenhower could do little but await the results of the 6 June landings and parachute drops. He fretted through his routine paperwork and tried to calm his anxieties by chain-smoking cigarettes and drinking masses of coffee. Some time during the afternoon of 5 June he wrote a brief note to be used if the landings failed, in which he absolved everyone but himself from the failure. He did not, however, offer to resign, a telling sign of his confidence in his own command. Ike tucked the note in his wallet where it remained for a month until he pulled it out and gave it to an aide. Its message had been overtaken by victorious events.

ABOVE: Although Eisenhower lacked great operational experience, his engaging manner and easy style made him a natural commander.

RIGHT: The day before D-Day, General Eisenhower scribbled a note to be used in the event of failure on the following day, taking all the blame on himself. His state of mind can be gauged by his writing of the wrong date at the end, 5 July instead of 5 June.

Our landings in the
Cherbourg – Havre area
have failed to gain a
satisfactory foothold and
~~I have withdrawn~~
the troops. ~~have been~~
~~withdrawn.~~ ~~This particular~~
~~Operation~~ My decision to
attack at this time and place
was based upon the best
information available. ~~and~~
The troops, the air and the
navy did all that ~~and based~~
Bravery and devotion to duty
could do. If any blame
or fault attaches to the attempt
it is mine alone.

July 5

76 The Tiger Tank

A popular misconception still exists that the German Tiger Tank was produced to provide an answer to the Russian armour (the T-34 and heavy KV-1) which the Germans first encountered when they invaded Russia on 22 June 1941. This is not so. In fact the order for the Panzerkampfwagen VI, Tiger 1, was issued on 26 May 1941. It is true that the shock of encountering the KV-1 and T-34, which were far better than any contemporary German tank, galvanized Hitler into ordering that the production of Tiger be accelerated to provide a counter to the Russian heavy tank. At the same time he ordered a new medium tank, the Panzerkampfwagen V Panther in order to take on the T-34, then the finest medium tank in the world. Although the Panther must rate as the best tank produced by the Germans, or anyone else for that matter, there is no doubt that the Tiger was the most feared.

The Tiger weighed 57 tons, and was mounted with an 88-mm gun and two 7.92-mm machine guns. The 88-mm gun alone struck dread in the heart of most allied tank crews, mounted as it was in a tank whose mobility turned it into a fearsome weapon. The Tiger's frontal armour was 100 mm (nearly 4 inches) thick, and despite a top speed of just over 37 kph (23 mph) it quickly earned a formidable reputation, helped along by clever propaganda on the part of the Germans. Like all German tanks, the Tiger had a petrol engine. It had a crew of five: commander, driver, gunner, loader and radio operator. It had a range of around 190 kilometres (120 miles) depending on terrain and combat conditions, and carried about 80 rounds of 88-mm ammunition.

Any British or American tank could be knocked out by a Tiger (or a Panther) at ranges in excess of 900 metres (1,000 yards), and sometimes more. To knock out a Tiger or Panther, a British or American gunner had to hit the tracks or disable the gun or optics, but a Tiger was usually invulnerable to anything other than a 17-pounder, which only a few British tanks had, or a rocket-firing fighter-bomber. The fear that the Tiger engendered in the British and Americans was known as "Tiger phobia". Word got round that it took five Sherman tanks to destroy a cornered Tiger, and only one Sherman would survive.

The engagement at Villers-Bocage in Normandy on 13 June 1944 provides an example of the deadly nature of a well handled Tiger, especially in the hands of an ace, in this case Lieutenant Michael Wittmann, commanding 2nd SS Panzer Company of 101st SS Heavy Panzer Battalion. By this time, Wittmann was the leading Panzer ace in the Waffen SS, having stacked up 119 armoured vehicle kills in Russia. His company at Villers-Bocage was down to five Tigers. The British 7th Armoured Division had been given the task of seizing the town and the high ground beyond.

The leading British battle group drove through Villers-Bocage and halted on the high ground. Wittmann, leaving four of his Tigers with orders to hold their position, drove down the line of British infantry armoured personnel carriers, knocking them all out. Motoring on into Villers-Bocage he knocked out nine tanks. Here, in a village without infantry support, and vulnerable to anti-tank weapons, his Tiger was finally knocked out by a 17-pounder anti-tank gun. He and his crew baled out and walked back to join his company and at this stage Wittmann's remaining four tanks took a hand. By the end of the engagement, the leading battle group of 7th Armoured Division had been destroyed, losing 60 armoured fighting vehicles in the process. Wittmann with five Tigers had brought 7th Armoured Division, the famous "Desert Rats", to a dead stop.

LEFT: A line-up of Tiger II tanks in the first battalion to receive them. Ordered in 1943 and first issued in May 1944, this Tiger had a sloped armour glacis plate and a re-designed turret with a curved frontal plate, and was able to mount the more powerful version of the 88-mm gun, the L/71. The Tiger II eliminated its opponents easily, but too few were produced to have any significant influence on the outcome of the war.

ABOVE: Tiger Mk I; note the flat glacis plate and front turret plate.

77 Popski's Private Army Insignia

The astrolabe was the cap badge adopted by Popski's Private Army, the nickname for Number 1 Long-Range Demolition Squadron. The founder and commander of this squadron throughout was Vladimir Peniakoff, a Belgian émigré of Russian extraction. He was complex, colourful and had a somewhat mysterious background, particularly during the First World War during which he spent some time at Cambridge, where it was likely that he was a pacifist. He subsequently claimed that he served in the French Army in the latter part of that war. Between 1924 and the outbreak of the Second World War he worked for a sugar company in Egypt. By 1939, he was a tough, stocky 42 year old, and managed to talk his way into becoming a company commander in the Libyan Arab Force (LAF). This force consisted of Senussi Arabs who had fled from Italian suppression in Cyrenaica.

Popski eventually became the commanding officer of the LAF Commando, an offshoot of the Libyan Arab Force. With 22 Senussi tribesmen and a British sergeant, he performed in an intelligence-gathering role in the Gebel Akhdar region of Cyrenaica. He relied heavily on the Long Range Desert Group (LRDG) for transport, and came to admire them. He was absolutely fearless in battle and greatly respected by his men, being feared rather than loved by them. He acquired the nickname "Popski" when working with the LRDG.

After being wounded in a raid on Barca in north-eastern Libya in September 1942, Popksi was found by Lieutenant Colonel John "Shan" Hackett in Cairo, bored and frustrated. His LAF Commando had been disbanded while he was ill. Hackett, in charge of co-ordinating special operations at GHQ, formed a special jeep-borne unit for sabotage work, headed by Popski. Hackett called it Number 1 Long-Range Demolition Squadron but this was such a mouthful that Hackett declared that unofficially it would be called "Popski's Private Army" (PPA).

By the time PPA was ready, events in the desert were moving so fast, as Montgomery's offensive gathered momentum, that there was very little for PPA to do. The Gebel Akhdar had been left far behind, and Popski had no local contacts in Tunisia, where the fighting was taking place. Nevertheless PPA was tasked with operating in jeep patrols behind enemy lines in Italy. To begin with Popski's operations all failed. Penetrating the German lines in the terrain in Italy was usually impossible. Despite this, PPA was not disbanded. Most people in Italy imagined that PPA's spell of ineffectiveness was justified by his earlier legendary desert successes. Few outside the unit knew how short its African career had been, and how little it had achieved. Popski was as adept at fooling the British military system as he had been at slipping through German lines in the desert.

At this stage when nothing was going right, Popski managed to infiltrate behind the German lines by dint of taking his jeeps across what had hitherto been regarded as "impassable" mountain terrain. Operating with partisans, PPA killed several hundred enemy, for the loss of one dead and three wounded. After this PPA did its best work in the last nine months of the campaign, not far behind enemy lines, but working alongside the armoured cars of the 12th and 27th Lancers in a deep reconnaissance role. For example PPA was the first unit into Ravenna in early December 1944. Soon after this Popski was wounded, losing a hand. PPA, now under Major Jean Caneri, one of the originals, was in the thick of the fighting right to the end, its final spectacular achievement being to capture a battery of 88-mm guns and 300 prisoners. PPA's light, manoeuvrable jeeps, its firepower and Popski's ability to achieve rapport with the Italians, made it a valuable asset in the terrain and circumstances in which it found itself.

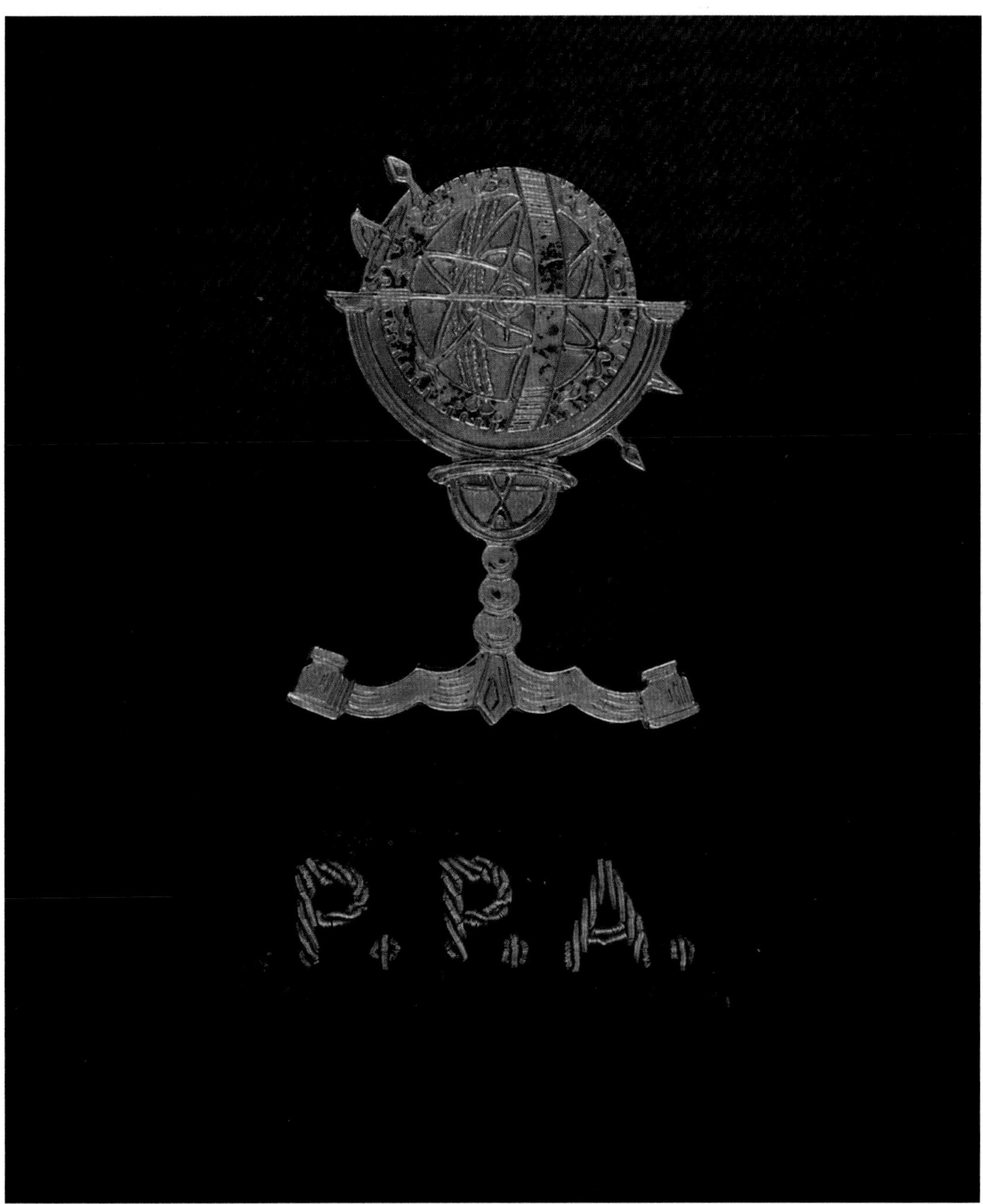

LEFT: Lieutenant Colonel V Peniakoff DSO MC ("Popski") driving his jeep in Italy towards the end of the war. He has a hook on his left hand replacing a hand lost earlier in the war. Beside him is his gunner, Corporal R Cokes.

ABOVE: The Astrolobe badge chosen by Vladimir Peniakoff for his "Number 1 Long Range Demolition Squadron", better known as "Popski's Private Army".

78 Blood Plasma

Among the many medical innovations exploited by the US Army Medical Department that saved the lives of service personnel, the use of blood plasma rates one of the most important. Used to counter-attack the effects of shock and blood loss from traumatic wounds, blood plasma saved thousands of lives. The Army considered plasma, along with sulfa, penicillin, atabrine and morphine, as drugs of the greatest military utility in the Second World War.

In the late 1930s Dr Charles Drew, an expert in blood haematology at the Columbia Medical Center, New York City, experimented in the use of the liquid portion of blood, 55 per cent of its composition, in lieu of whole blood in transfusions. Separated from red and white blood cells, plasma is 90 per cent water and 10 per cent albumin, fibrinogen and globulin, all of which aid clotting, fighting infection and maintaining blood pressure. Plasma's appeal was that it lasted longer in whole form than blood, could be frozen for preservation and travel and could be reduced to dried form and later reconstituted. Military bleeding took place thousands of miles from American blood donors, recruited and processed by the US Red Cross. The development of portable plasma therefore became a high medical priority.

The medical departments of the armed forces adopted plasma for transfusions with a rush and found its use limited only by its supply. The Red Cross eventually turned over 13 million units to the armed forces, which used all but 1.3 million units. Most of the recommendations for improvement focused on the packaging of the liquid plasma and its flow into a patient's veins. One problem was the colour of the labels and the suspension systems of the plasma bottles, cans and flexible pouches. Even the boxes that carried plasma bore too much in the way of white tape and labels; Japanese snipers used these white markings to identify and shoot medics and their patients. All the plasma paraphernalia eventually got a rush coat of olive drab paint.

At the end of the war, General Dwight D Eisenhower praised the Red Cross and its blood donors for their contribution to saving the lives of thousands of GIs. Plasma, he acknowledged, was a tremendous thing.

ABOVE: An American soldier receives blood plasma behind enemy lines in Italy in 1944.

RIGHT: Private Samuel Atherton is given containers of blood plasma at the British blood bank that was part of a US evacuation hospital on Anzio beachhead in May 1944.

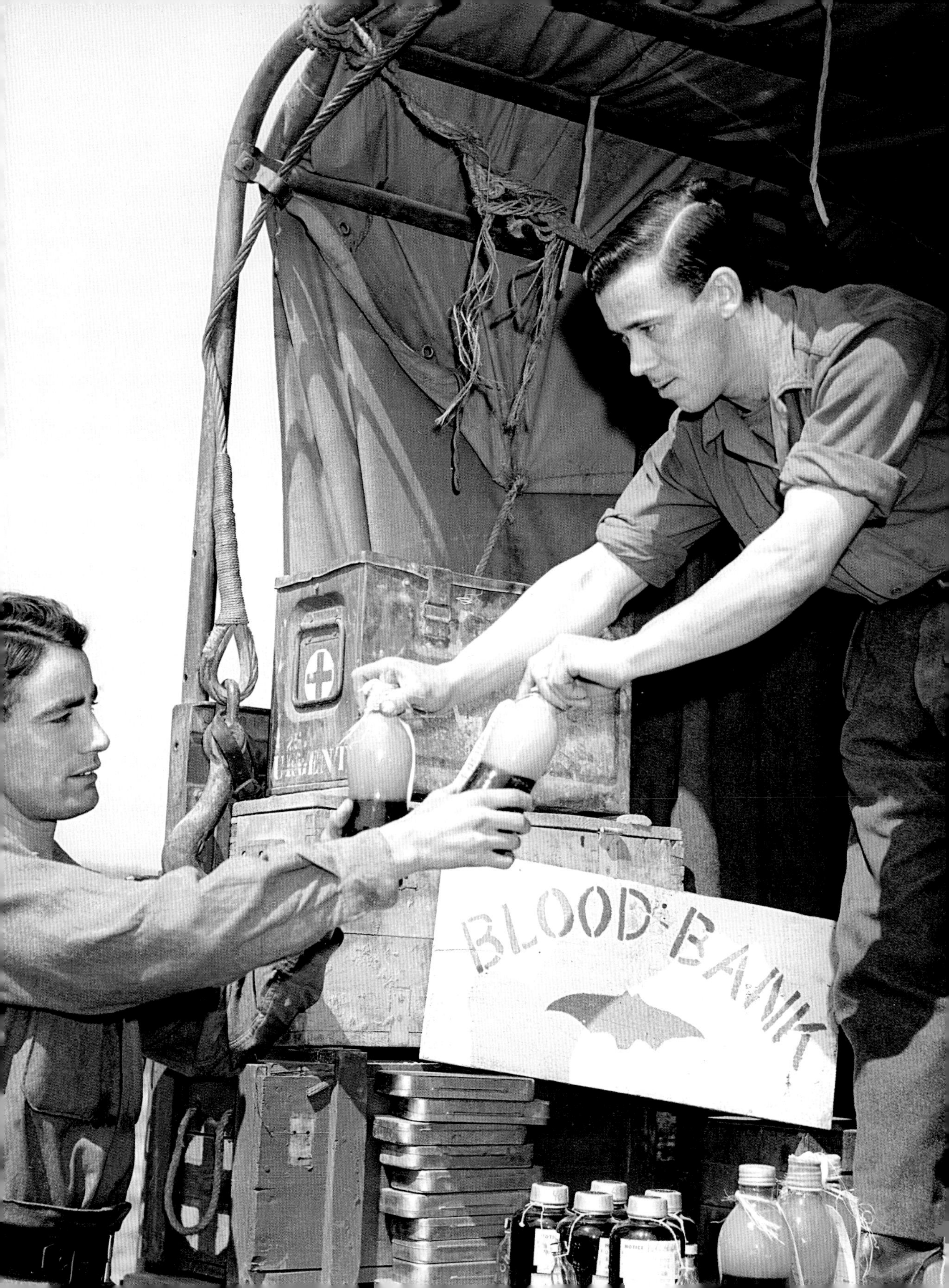
URGENT
BLOOD BANK

79 The Bailey Bridge

During the Second World War both sides frequently needed to bridge rivers or ravines, either because the existing bridges had been destroyed, or because part of an army wanted to surprise the enemy by crossing in a place where there was no bridge. The quicker a bridge is built in the combat zone the better, and engineers are always striving to achieve a design that combines speed of construction with the ability to drive the heaviest vehicles across it. Considerable progress was made towards achieving both requirements in the 1939–45 war.

The outstanding example of this, and a major engineering breakthrough, came with the invention of the Bailey Bridge by Donald Bailey of the British Military Engineering Experimental Establishment at Christchurch in Dorset in early 1942. The Bailey Bridge girders were constructed from identical steel lattice panels held together by metal pins. Each girder could be doubled or tripled for extra length and strength, and could be increased up to two additional storeys for very large spans. The bridge could carry a roadway on the lower transoms. The complete structure could be launched on rollers over the gap to be bridged, using a counter-weight.

The Bailey Bridge was first used operationally to bridge the Medjerda River near Medjez el Bab in Tunisia on the night of 26 November 1942 during the North African campaign. It became the main bridging equipment of the US and British Armies, and later the Soviet Army. To bridge wide rivers, all armies used a system of floating pontoons or boats anchored side by side across the river. The Bailey Bridge would be laid across the "bridge of boats". The British and Soviets used wooden pontoons, while the Americans used more vulnerable, but more easily transported, inflatable rubber boats. For bridges carrying loads up to 9 tons, the British also used easily transported light folding wooden boats on which to lay the Bailey Bridge. For loads up to and including 70 tons, pontoons were used.

The Bailey Bridge was carried in trucks in pieces. When an obstacle was encountered, the parts would be brought forward and the bridge assembled. It was preferable to have some warning that bridging was required in order that the bridging trucks were positioned well forward in the advancing column of vehicles. This was particularly important in the case of Operation Market Garden, the attempt to seize crossings over a series of rivers and canals including the bridge over the River Rhine at Arnhem in September 1944. On the morning of 18 September, the Germans blew up the bridge over the canal at Zon, north of Eindhoven, holding up the Allied advance. The trucks carrying the Bailey bridging were well back in the column advancing on one narrow road, and they had furthermore to be driven through the large town of Eindhoven, whose streets were crammed with Dutch people celebrating their liberation. Eventually, the bridging arrived, the bridge was constructed and the tanks of the Guards Armoured Division crossed the canal. But the delay in bridging the canal at Zon was a major contributor to the failure of the British 1st Airborne Division to hold the vital Arnhem Bridge long enough for the relieving force to arrive.

The biggest bridging operation carried out by the British and Americans was during the Rhine crossings in March 1945, but Bailey Bridges were used in all theatres of war, sometimes as ferries, with bridge sections on pontoons. This was especially useful to get armour across in the initial phase of a crossing, while the main bridge was being built. In Italy and Sicily the British and Americans built over 3,000 Bailey Bridges, the longest being over the Sangro River at 343 metres (1,126 feet); while one built over the Chindwin during the 14th Army's advance to the Irrawaddy and Mandalay in Burma, was 352 metres (1,154 feet) long.

ABOVE RIGHT: Trucks of British Eighth Army crossing the Sangro River in Italy over a Bailey pontoon bridge.

RIGHT: Bailey Bridge spanning sections of bridge destroyed by the Germans during their retreat in Italy, and using the original piers.

80 The DUKW

The DUKW or "Duck" is a dual-drive amphibious truck that provided Allied ground forces with a vehicle for administrative over-the-beach landings and for river crossings. The DUKW did not have enough armour or overhead cover to be a combat vehicle like the amphibian tractor or LVT. It was essentially a 2½-ton truck with a propeller and a boat body (including bilge pumps), that could re-engage its wheels on land and drive its cargo to an inland destination.

GMC and other truck manufacturers produced more than 25,000 DUKWs during the Second World War. Most of them went to US Army engineering and transportation battalions, but the Navy and Marine Corps also used DUKWs as logistical vehicles on Pacific beachheads. DUKWs also appeared in Commonwealth units in every theatre of war.

The basic DUKW weighed eight tons, had six pneumatic tyres and could carry a 2,500-kg (5,512-lb) payload. Powered by a standard 90 hp, six-cylinder truck engine, it could reach a top speed of 9.7 kph (six mph) in water and 80 kph (50 mph) on land with a range of 282 kilometres (175 miles). The hull was designed and built by a commercial builder of barges and utility boats, Sparkman & Stephens Inc, and it had no permanent weapons station.

Whenever someone pressed the DUKW into tactical service, the results were not good. The worst case of misuse occurred during the D-Day landing on Omaha Beach when the Army V Corps attempted to land six batteries of 105mm howitzers using DUKWs. The rough seas and imbalance caused by the heavy guns swamped the DUKWs, sending 17 guns and their crews into the water. The optimal use of DUKWs came from their assignment to US Army Amphibious Special Brigades, where they could be used for over-beach resupply missions, demolition and beach clearance missions, and as emergency ambulances.

As long as DUKWs were not used as combat troop carriers, they provided excellent service. US Navy and Royal Navy Beachmaster units used their DUKWs to rescue broached small craft and to pull stalled vehicles from the surf. The vehicle made an excellent mobile radio station during beach operations. Its ability to move over soft sand made the DUKW a vehicle of choice for emergency missions on beachheads. Today, DUKWs still serve to take tourists on amphibious trips throughout the world.

"Ducks"—amphibious fighting vehicles—used for the first time in the Mediterranean landings.
BACK THEM UP!

ABOVE: A British poster promoting the American "Ducks".

RIGHT: A DUKW in Fort Sheridan, Illinois. Designed in 1942, these vehicles were used to take troops ashore in amphibious operations in the Mediterranean, Pacific and the D-Day landings.

81 The Bangalore Torpedo

The Bangalore Torpedo had been in use since before the First World War. It was invented in 1912 by Captain R L McClintock Royal Engineers, who was stationed in Bangalore, India, attached to the British Indian Army's Bengal Sappers and Miners, and he published details in the *Royal Engineers' Journal* of March 1913. A narrow metal pipe filled with explosive, the Bangalore Torpedo was designed to be pushed under barbed wire obstacles and subsequently detonated; the resulting explosion would then clear a path through the wire. The first record of its use was in clearing obstacles and booby traps left behind after the Second Boer War (1899–1902) and the Russo–Japanese War (1904–05).

It was used extensively during the First World War to clear gaps in barbed wire obstacles, especially on the Western Front. In the Second World War it was also employed to blast a path through minefields.

The Second World War version consisted of light steel tubing 3.8 or 5 cm (1.5 or 2 ins) in diameter, issued in sections 2.4 metres (8 feet) long and packed with 4.5 to 5 kg (10 to 12 lbs) of explosive. These could be fitted together to penetrate the entire depth of the obstacle. As each section was pushed in, the next section was attached, and the whole was pushed forward again. A bullet-shaped nose plug was fitted to the head of the pipe to make it easier to push through barbed wire, and a detonator was inserted in the base of the pipe, initiated by a time-delay fuse. Depending on the type of terrain, undergrowth and so forth, a pipe longer than 7.3 metres (24 feet) was difficult to handle, so deeper obstacles would have to be blown in stages. A Bangalore Torpedo would blow a path about 3 to 7 metres (10 to 20 feet) wide through wire or an anti-personnel minefield; the width depended on the density of the obstacle or the types of mines employed.

Bangalore Torpedoes were normally considered to be specialist engineer equipment, though infantry assault pioneers, US rangers and commandos were all trained to use them. They were deployed in all theatres of war, but perhaps the best-known example of their deployment was at Omaha Beach on 6 June 1944. Here, the soldiers of the US V Corps were pinned down by fire from Germans dug in on top of a 45-metre- (150-foot-) high bluff that dominated the beach. Barbed wire and anti-personnel mines also blocked the small gullies which offered the best beach exits for infantry. In small unit actions made memorable by the film *Saving Private Ryan* (1998), US rangers eventually blasted their way through the obstacles to fight their way on to the top of the bluff and engage the enemy.

Bangalore Torpedoes were packed in boxes and could sometimes be a hazard to those in the vicinity. Lieutenant "Scotty" White, a platoon commander of the 9th Battalion the Durham Light Infantry, part of Montgomery's 8th Army at the Battle of Mareth in Tunisia in March 1943, remembered: "At H-hour the attack started and we were shelled from the beginning. The sappers [engineers] in the truck with the Bangalore Torpedoes were hit by a shell and blown up." (Imperial War Museum Sound Archive.)

If Bangalore Torpedoes were not available, they could be improvised: two two-metre (six-foot) angle-iron pickets, normally used in erecting a barbed wire fence, could be lashed together with wire to form a tube round lengths of plastic explosive. This would be exploded using a detonator and a length of fuse. It was not as effective as a tailor-made Bangalore Torpedo, and could only be used on small obstacles, but in some situations it was better than nothing.

RIGHT: Assault Engineers push a Bangalore Torpedo forward under enemy barbed wire in order to create a space for the advancing infantry to move through.

82 The Tallboy Bomb

Following the success of Barnes Wallis's cylindrical bouncing bomb in the dambuster raid of May 1943, the RAF, who hitherto had rejected his designs for big bombs, showed renewed interest in the idea. Accordingly, Barnes Wallis began work on the Grand Slam, a monster 10,000 kg (22,000 lb) bomb, the heaviest used in the war. The bomb, which was 7.7 metres (26.5 feet) long and 1.2 metres (3 feet 10 ins) in diameter, contained 4,145 kg (9,135 lbs) of Torpex explosive (used for torpedoes, hence its name).

Before the Grand Slam came into service, Barnes Wallis developed a smaller version – the 5,445-kg (12,000-lb) Tallboy, intrinsically the same design. The Tallboy, like the Grand Slam, was designed to be a deep-penetration bomb. It was 6.4 metres (21 feet) long and 97 cm (38 inches) in diameter, containing 2,540 kg (5,200 lb) of Torpex explosive. The streamlined Tallboy could reach the speed of sound during its descent, and its angled fins made it spin rapidly. Like a corkscrew, this spin exacerbated the effect of its weight and speed of descent to enable it to penetrate 5 metres (16 feet) of concrete. Furthermore, the ignition could be delayed by up to 11 seconds, and by penetrating before exploding, the bomb sent out shock waves that wrought massive internal destruction, as well as collapsing adjacent buildings and installations.

Only one of these bombs could be carried at a time, and then only by the Lancaster, which had to be modified for the purpose. The Tallboy was first used operationally on the night of 8/9 June 1944, when Lancaster bombers of 617 Squadron (The Dambusters) attacked the Saumur railway tunnel. The object of the hastily planned raid was to close the railway line to delay the arrival of German armoured reinforcements for counter-attacks on the newly formed Allied bridgehead in Normandy. One Tallboy pierced the roof of the tunnel; the resulting mass of debris blocked the line for several days.

RAF Bomber Command dropped 854 Tallboys on German targets during the Second World War, of which 77 were dropped in three attacks on the battleship *Tirpitz* between September and November 1944. The most successful of these was on 12 November. Between February 1941, when the ship was completed, and the successful raid, there had been no less than ten attacks on her by RAF and Fleet Air Arm aircraft, and by submarines. These had damaged *Tirpitz* but not sunk her. An RAF attack with Tallboys on 15 September 1944 left the *Tirpitz* unfit to go to sea, and she was towed to an anchorage off Tromsø. Another Tallboy attack on 29 October damaged the *Tirpitz* again. Finally, on 12 November 1944, Lancasters of numbers 9 and 617 Squadrons achieved three direct hits on the *Tirpitz*. Smoke and steam rose in a great pillar, the *Tirpitz* began to list, and some minutes later she turned turtle, with only her hull above water.

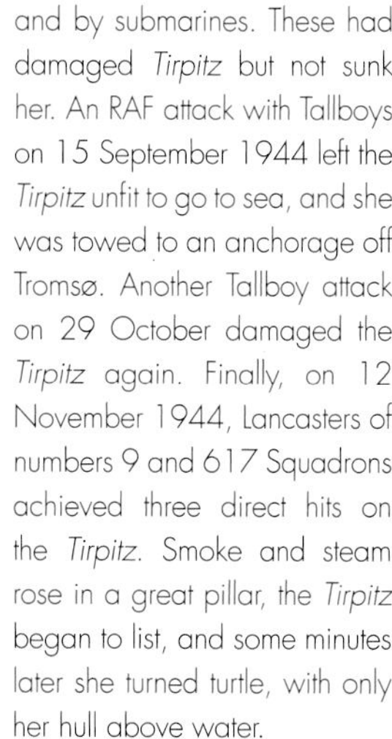

The first Grand Slam raid was carried out by 617 Squadron on the Bielefeld viaduct on 14 March 1945, collapsing more than 9 metres (100 yards) of the structure thanks to the "earthquake" effect of the bomb. On a raid against submarine pens near Bremen, two Grand Slams penetrated over 4.2 metres (14 feet) of reinforced concrete. A total of 41 Grand Slams were dropped during the Second World War, mainly against bridges and viaducts. The accuracy of bombing at the time would not guarantee a direct hit on such slim structures, but with the Grand Slam it did not matter. Provided the bomb landed quite close, and depending on the nature of the soil, the earthquake effect would bring down part of a bridge or viaduct.

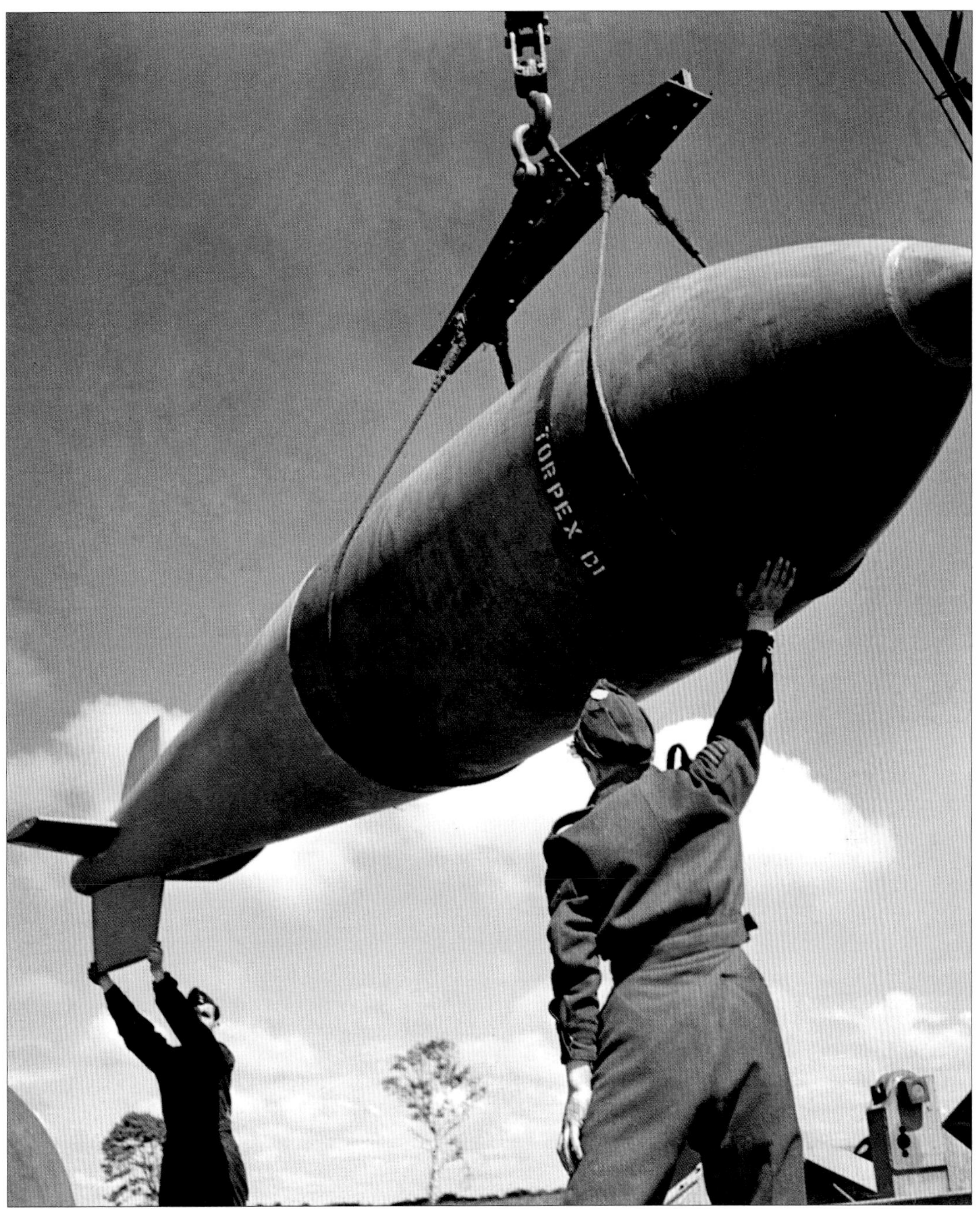

LEFT: The Tallboy bomb in the air.

ABOVE: A Tallboy bomb being lifted from the bomb dump to be loaded into a Lancaster of 617 Squadron RAF for a raid on a V Weapon site at Wizernes France.

83 The Grumman F6F Hellcat

The Grumman F6F Hellcat joined the US Pacific Fleet in early 1943, replacing the Grumman F4F Wildcat as the Navy's standard carrier-based fighter. The first fighter squadron to fly the Hellcat in combat (VF-9) had been assigned to the first of a new class of aircraft carrier, the USS *Essex* (CV-9), the 33,000 ton warship that became the dominant vessel in the Pacific naval war from 1944 to 1945. Designed for extended operations at sea and to destroy the Japanese A6M (Zero) fighter, the Hellcat was powerful, with a 2,000hp Pratt & Whitney engine, and heavy – the maximum take-off weight was 6,800 kg (15,000 lbs). Its normal armament consisted of six wing-mounted .50-calibre machine guns, and it could be altered to carry bombs and rockets for attacks on ships and ground targets.

For taking off and landing on carriers, naval aviators preferred the Hellcat to the Vought F4U Corsair because of its cockpit visibility. During the war, Grumman built 6,500 F6F-5s, the final production model, and 1,200 F6F-5N, a night fighter variant with special avionics. The total of all Hellcats produced numbered 12,275 aircraft. The US Navy and Marine Corps claimed that their pilots flying the Hellcat

ABOVE LEFT: A Grumman F6F Hellcat shown taking off from the USS *Lexington* during operations in the Marshall and Gilbert Islands in November 1943.

ABOVE: The Grumman F6F Hellcat in flight.

shot down 5,156 Japanese aircraft or 75 per cent of all the naval services air-to-air kills.

The Hellcat played the central role in the Pacific War's greatest aerial engagement, the Battle of the Philippine Sea (18–20 June 1944). Task Force 58, which included 15 carriers, engaged a Japanese carrier and a land-based aviation force of 500 aircraft. On 19 June alone, about 500 Hellcats shot down an estimated 400 Imperial Japanese Navy carrier aircraft with a loss of only 29 aircraft. The next day the Hellcats escorted the dive-bombers and torpedo planes that sank a Japanese heavy carrier. After this, Japanese naval aviation ceased to be a major problem since the United States could replace pilots, aircraft and carriers in numbers Japan could not match.

Durable, and armoured to protect the pilot and gas tanks, the Hellcat could survive air-to-air combat with greater ease than the faster, more agile Zero. Almost 1,000 Hellcats served in the Royal Navy's Fleet Air Arm, and towards the end of the Second World War other Hellcats joined the aviation forces of the French navy.

84 The DD Tank

The Duplex Drive (DD) tank was developed in time for the invasion of Normandy. It was designed to meet the requirement for armoured support with high-velocity firepower on the beach as early as possible, to deal with the enormous defence works built by the Germans. Based on the Sherman chassis, it could be propelled by its tracks on land or by twin propellers mounted in the rear in water. A canvas screen mounted round the body of the tank could be raised to enable it to float. Once it arrived on the beach, the screen was lowered to enable the tank to use its gun.

The British were the first to develop the floating tank using a Tetrarch, which was trialled in June 1941 at Brent Reservoir. After sea trials, the go-ahead was given to produce the first operational models, this time based on the Valentine tank. The Valentine was used for training crews and a number were lost, some with their crews. The man most at risk was the driver, because getting out through his small hatch in a hurry was so difficult. Crews were equipped with emergency breathing sets allowing a five-minute "window" to get out and surface. Furthermore, the Valentine tank had to train its gun to the rear to allow the screen to be raised. This led to the Sherman tank being the final selection for this role, because it could swim with the screen up and its gun trained forward, ready to fire as soon as it arrived on the beach.

The base of the screen was fixed to a metal frame welded to the tank's hull. The screen was fitted with horizontal metal hoops and a number of vertical rubber tubes. It was inflated by compressed air, and could be erected in 15 minutes and collapsed quickly on arrival on the beach. Some units discarded the skirt as soon as possible after landing, while others kept it on their tank. DD tanks often supported infantry well inland, both on D-Day, 6 June 1944, and afterwards, with screens still attached. DD tanks could swim at about 7 kph (4 knots). The driver steered under the directions of the commander by swivelling the propellers using a specially fitted hydraulic system. The commander stood on a platform in the turret to enable him to see over the screen and, if necessary, steered using a tiller overriding the driver's control.

It was intended that all DD tanks in the Normandy landings would launch down the bow ramp of LCTs about 3 kilometres (2 miles) offshore, with screens already up, and swim to the beach. The DD tanks should have arrived on the beach first, followed by the AVREs (Armoured Vehicle Royal Engineers), with the infantry arriving next. On all beaches except Omaha, most DD tanks got ashore, although, thanks to rough seas, with varying degrees of success; only some were ahead of the infantry as planned. The DD was designed to swim in waves up to 0.3 metres (1 foot) high, but off Normandy the waves were 1.8 metres (6 feet) high. Some swam in, while others were landed directly onto the beach or in shallow water a few yards off.

At Omaha the lowering position (where landing craft start the run-in to the beach) selected by the US naval commander was so far offshore that craft had to start the run-in in darkness. The confusion was considerable. LCTs carrying DD tanks straggled badly, and in many cases headed well off to the flank of the correct beach, or turned away having launched DDs too early. Of 32 DD tanks launched some 5,500 metres (6,000 yards) from the shore (far too far out), 27 foundered. Without AVREs, which the Americans were offered but rejected, and with most artillery swamped in craft launched too far offshore, the infantry at Omaha suffered badly. Only by their own courageous exertions did the US infantry finally get off the beach to overcome the defenders.

DD tanks were used successfully in subsequent operations in north west Europe and Italy, notably at the 11-kilometre- (7-mile-) wide Scheldt river crossing in October 1944; at the Rhine (23 March 1945) and Elbe (29 April 1945); and at the Po and Adige rivers in Italy in April 1945.

LEFT: A Valentine DD tank with screen raised, alongside a landing craft at the 79th Armoured Division Training School at Gosport in January 1944.

ABOVE: A Sherman Duplex Drive (DD) tank with screen lowered.

85 A German Prison-Camp Watchtower

The popular image of a prison-camp watchtower or guard tower, as portrayed in numerous films and on TV, is of a small open-sided hut on legs, built of wood, or metal, or both. Actually there were a number of designs for Nazi camps – not surprisingly, bearing in mind the number of camps in Germany, Poland and parts of occupied Europe. There were three classes of German camp: POW camps constituted by far the greatest number – counting those in Italy, there were 260 of these, including transit camps and sub-camps (often used as temporary camps for housing working parties from main camps); there were also 23 concentration camps, and six extermination camps.

Concentration camps were instruments of Nazi terror, conceived by Hitler as early as 1921. The original prisoners were political opponents of National Socialism, but in 1939, people from all German-occupied territories began to join them. To start with, the camps were run by the *Sturmabteilung* (SA), but in 1934 the SS took control. They were not built as death camps, although large numbers of people died in them from malnutrition and disease, as well as by execution, and from being used as guinea pigs in "medical experiments". Belsen, for example, was a concentration camp, not an extermination camp. The numbers imprisoned, and subsequent deaths, in concentration camps are not known with any degree of accuracy. The number of registered prisoners is thought to be around 1,600,000, and 450,000 deaths are documented, although a figure exceeding 600,000 is thought to be more likely. The round numbers are an indication of the imprecise nature of the statistics, but in no way exaggerate the scale of the horror.

Death or extermination camps were set up in 1941 for implementing the "final solution", *Endlösung*, the term used for the murder of six million Jews during the Second World War. Six sites for extermination camps were chosen in remote locations: five in German-occupied Poland (Belzec, Chelmno, Sobibor, Treblinka and Auschwitz) and one in occupied Russia (Maly Trostenets, near Minsk). About 300,000 European Jews survived the camps and death marches, but those murdered comprised one-third of the world's Jewish population in 1939.

Some camps, especially the older ones, had brick or concrete watchtowers with rooms underneath. These were to be found in camps such as Dachau, the first concentration camp in Germany, opened 51 days after Hitler came to power. As more camps were created, less permanent structures were erected as watchtowers, of the huts-on-legs type. A common feature of most watchtowers was a sentry or sentries, whose job was to keep a watch on the inmates. Depending on the nature of the camp, he would be armed with a rifle or a machine gun, more usually the latter. Most watchtowers were equipped with searchlights and connected to a central guardhouse by telephone. A handful of camps had only a few watchtowers. The most famous POW camp, Colditz Castle, had just one custom-built guard- or watchtower in a corner of the outer perimeter wire, although sentries with machine guns were posted around the perimeter and on prominent parts of the walls, and the whole of the exterior of the castle was covered by searchlights at night.

Many camps of all sorts had warning fences set up at about knee height several metres inside the perimeter fence. Stepping over this fence usually ended in the person being shot, unless – as occasionally happened, although probably only in POW camps – the sentry shouted a warning, in which case the prisoner made a fast retreat.

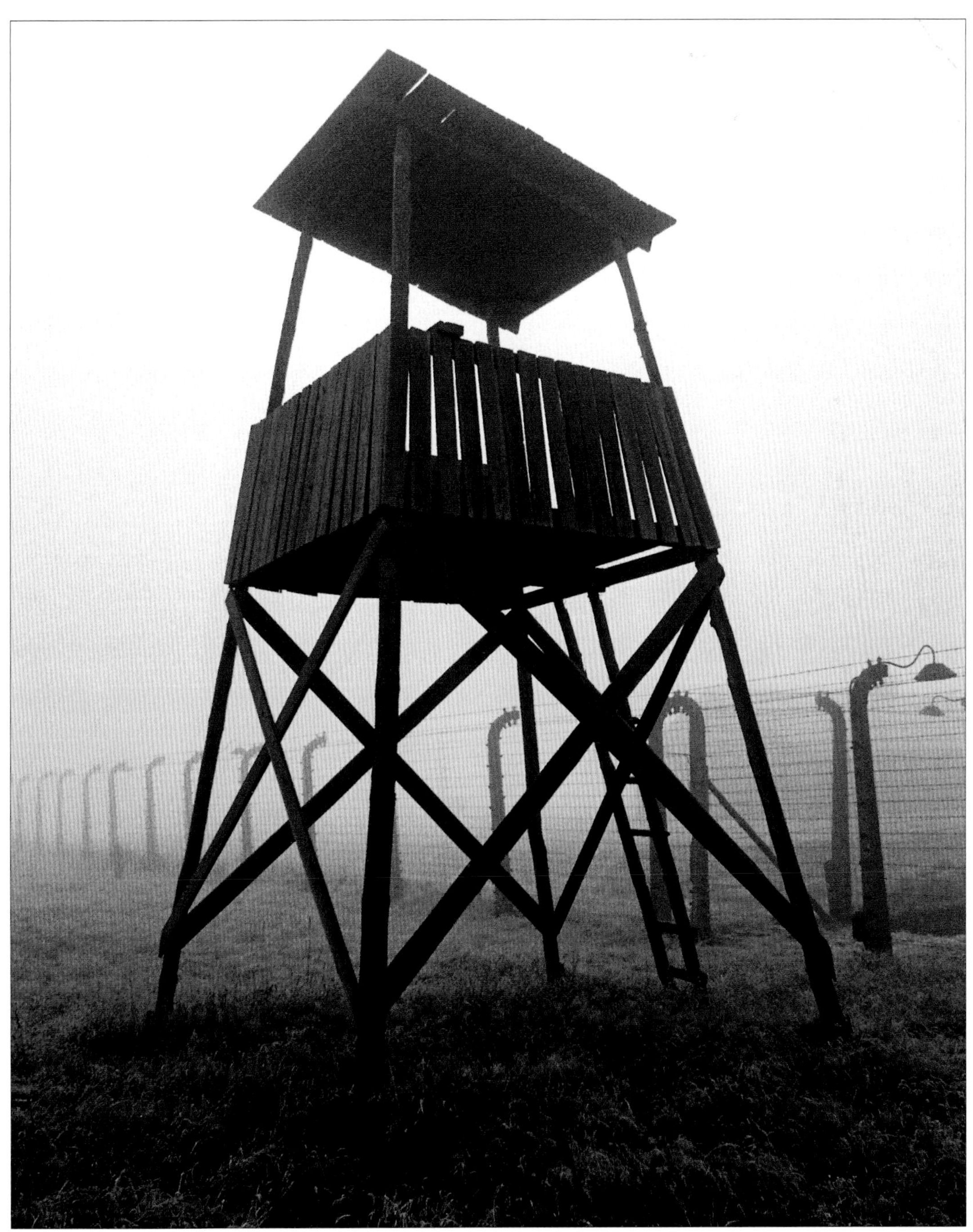

LEFT: A watchtower at Mauthausen concentration camp. This is an example of one of the more permanent types of watchtower.

ABOVE: A watchtower at Auschwitz extermination camp.

86 Hobart's Funnies

In April 1943, the British 79th Armoured Division under its commander Major General Percy Hobart was given the task of training its regiments in the new armoured fighting vehicles that war experience showed would be needed in the early stages of a landing in Europe. By this time flail tanks, equipped with chains on a rotating arm in front of the vehicle, had already been used successfully in the Western Desert to clear paths through minefields. The failure to get tanks off the beach during the Dieppe raid in August 1942 showed the need to clear obstacles and provide trackway over difficult going such as shingle and soft sand.

To overcome these challenges, assault engineer units were formed to lead future landings in special tanks – Armoured Vehicle Royal Engineers or AVREs for short. This special collection of armoured fighting vehicles was dubbed "Funnies" by the British Army. The "Funnies" also included the DD Tank, but as these were not exclusive to Hobart's Division, they are described in a separate chapter. Other than the Crab flail tank, which was based on the Sherman, AVREs were built around the standard Churchill tank weighing 40 tons. Instead of a gun, some AVREs were armed with a petard, which could project an 18-kg (40-lb) bomb a distance of 73 metres (80 yards) to blast gaps and holes in buildings and concrete defences. Each AVRE carried 24 General Wade charges, arch-shaped blocks of explosive weighing 14 kg (30 lb) for destroying concrete obstacles.

AVREs were modified to operate several types of equipment, each designed to deal with a specific type of obstacle. Assault-bridge AVREs carried bridging able to span 9-metre (30-foot) gaps. Some AVREs carried fascines, bundles of chestnut paling or lengths of pipe designed for dropping into anti-tank ditches to allow tanks to cross. Snakes consisting of up to 122 metres (400 feet) of 7.6-cm (3-in) pipe were pushed ahead of the AVRE and detonated to explode mines. AVRE carpet-layers laid carpet from rollers on the tank by rolling forward and unwinding the strip from the roller. Once this was laid, the AVRE uncoupled, leaving the carpet for following vehicles – very useful when sand or boggy ground had to be crossed. Crocodiles, flame throwing tanks, were Churchill tanks which could still use their 75-mm guns but also had a flame projector fitted on the front glacis plate next to the driver's hatch. The Crocodile towed an armoured fuel trailer.

Later in the campaign in northwest Europe, another special vehicle was added to the 79th Armoured Division: the Landing Vehicle Tracked, or Buffalo to the British. This was an American invention developed by the United States Marine Corps after experience of the early landings in the Pacific. The Buffalo was first used by the British at Walcheren in December 1944, again in the Rhine crossing in March 1945 and for the crossings of major rivers in Germany during the advance from the Rhine to the Baltic which ended in May 1945.

Hobart's Funnies played a key part in the success of the landings in Normandy, and in subsequent fighting in the Normandy campaign and the breakout across the Seine. They were much in demand for the capture of Le Havre and Boulogne, as well as in many phases of the fighting in Holland and in the advance to the west bank of the Rhine and beyond. AVREs became an indispensable "club in the bag" in the order of battle of British formations fighting in northwest Europe. When offered support by Hobart's Funnies, the US Army accepted only the DD tank. It is arguable that, had they also included AVREs in their order of battle, they might not have incurred so many casualties at places like Omaha Beach.

LEFT: A Churchill Crocodile flamethrower tank.

ABOVE: A carpet layer tank, on a Churchill chassis.

87 The M-1 Rifle

The standard rifle of American infantrymen in the Second World War, the M-1 designed by John Garand, became the iconic weapon of both the GI "dogface" and the "jarhead" Marine of the US armed forces. It was the perfect individual weapon for a mass army of relatively untrained citizen-soldiers. Before the last M-1 was issued in 1957, the military's armoury in Springfield, Massachusetts, and private manufacturers like Winchester had made 5.5 million of these rifles.

It was a pioneer weapon because Garand designed it for semi-automatic fire, which meant that the rifle reloaded itself without the manual operation of its bolt. Until then, bolt-action rifles remained the global standard for infantry rifles, as they had been in the First World War. The M-1 however could fire a clip of eight .30.06 calibre cartridges. This feature depended upon channelling gases, created by firing from the barrel, to a piston that drove the bolt to the rear (extraction) and then allowed it, with the help of a recoil spring, to ride forward and load a fresh cartridge. When all eight cartridges had been fired, the empty clip sailed clear of the breach with a reassuring "cling".

The M-1 had many attractive features as a combat rifle. It doubled the rate of fire for a trained rifleman from ten rounds a minute with the bolt-action M1903 Springfield rifle, to 20 aimed rounds a minute. It sacrificed nothing in accuracy compared to the older weapon, over open sights to 275 metres (300 yards) and with a peep sight to 460 metres (500 yards). The ammunition was the same for the Springfield 03, the Browning Automatic Rifle and the Browning M1917 and M1919 machine guns. Some GIs found the rifle heavy at 4.3 kg (9.5 lbs), but the weight also reflected durable manufacture and reduced recoil when used with a proper sling. The rifle was also easy to disassemble and clean: it had two compartments in the butt of the stock that held a cleaning rod in sections, and a container for bore cleaner and lubricating oil as well as patches and a bore brush. The moving parts at the breach could be brushed clean without taking the rifle apart. In summary, the rifle had been designed to be "soldier proof".

The rifle could be adapted to more specialized use as well. With a mounted scope and blast suppressor, it could be used by snipers. Using a special clip-on launcher and blank cartridges, it could even launch a grenade with stabilizing fins, turning it into a small mortar.

The M-1 became the most common weapon in a US Army infantry squad in which ten of 12 members carried them. In a Marine squad, this was ten of 13. Cut-down M-1s often appeared in motorized and mechanized units as personal defence weapons, rather than the .30-calibre carbine. The standard US Army infantry division carried over 6,000 M-1 rifles in its table of equipment (1942–45) for a force of around 14,000 officers and men.

LEFT: At Camp McClellan in Alabama in July 1945, a new recruit receives instruction from a sargeant on how to fire the M-1 Garand rifle.

RIGHT: An M-1 as manufactured by Springfield Armory, complete with leather sling.

88 A Mulberry Harbour

One of the problems facing those planning the invasion of Europe was was the unlikelihood that a port could be captured intact early enough to supply the Allied armies during the first days or even weeks of the operation. The landing of supplies over open beaches was likely to be slowed down or even halted completely by bad weather. As early as 1942, Churchill had sent a note to Vice Admiral Lord Louis Mountbatten, then Chief of Combined Operations, telling him to devise piers that would float up and down with the tide, concluding, "Don't argue about it, the difficulties will argue themselves." It was over a year before the problem was solved. Captain John Hughes-Hallett, then on Mountbatten's staff, wrote in 1947 to a civil engineer:

> *You overestimate the part played by Lord Mountbatten... The project was decided upon at a stage when an operational staff headed by General Morgan [Chief of Staff to the Allied Commander (COSSAC)] had been established to plan the invasion. It was this staff, of which I was the naval head, which had responsibility for deciding and advising on such matters... It was either 13.6.43 or 20.6.43 (probably the former) that I decided to rely on a port of some magnitude (The idea came to me oddly enough during the singing of the Anthem at the Abbey)... Between that date and 27 June 1943 the Port was a cardinal point of the COSSAC Plan.*

Hughes-Hallett proposed that an artificial harbour be constructed by sinking blockships off the Normandy coast. A harbour plan was drawn up by Lieutenant Commander I G Steele, who selected a site at Arromanches.

From D-Day on, the intention was to land as much as possible of the stores over the five assault beaches, using an array of craft ferrying from merchant ships anchored offshore. To give some protection to these craft it was decided to establish five craft shelters, codenamed Gooseberries. At each beach 12 old merchant ships were to be sunk in a line in about 4.5 metres (15 feet) of water (at low tide), giving about 1.5 kilometres (1 mile) of breakwater. Without these Gooseberries, if a gale blew in from the north, the craft would be driven ashore and damaged beyond repair, cutting the lifeline to the armies ashore.

Eventually some of the Gooseberries would grow into Mulberries; "no mean agricultural feat", commented a senior naval officer (*The Imperial War Museum Book of Victory in Europe: The North-West European Campaign 1944–1945*, Julian Thompson, Sidgwick & Jackson Ltd 1994, page 4.) The Gooseberries were to be positioned thus:

US

Gooseberry 1	Varreville	Utah Beach
Goosebery 2	St Laurent	Omaha Beach

Gooseberry 2 became Mulberry A

British

Gooseberry 3	Arromanches	Gold Beach

Gooseberry 3 became Mulberry B

Gooseberry 4	Courcelles	Juno Beach
Gooseberry 5	Oustreham	Sword Beach

The Mulberries were to consist of a breakwater made up of large concrete boxes, codenamed Phoenix, sunk in deep water – up to 10 metres (33 feet) at low tide. Outside each harbour it was intended to place 1.5 kilometre (1 mile) of floating breakwater, codenamed Bombardon, to give additional protection to the harbour. There was also an arrangement of piers capable of taking a 25-ton load, and one capable of berthing an LST and bearing a load of 40 tons, the weight of a Cromwell tank.

By D plus 12 (18 June 1944) both Mulberry harbours were in use. A gale on 19 June destroyed most of the American Mulberry, and its remnants were used to repair the British Mulberry, which had not been so badly damaged. However, thanks to the Gooseberries on the US Beach, ships were still able to discharge direct to the open beach if the weather allowed. By mid-July, the British Mulberry had reached its planned capacity of 7,000 tons a day.

During the 10 months that the Arromanches Mulberry was needed, a total of some 2.5 million men, 500,000 vehicles and 4 million tons of supplies passed through the artificial harbour.

ABOVE RIGHT : The artificial harbour in operation at Colville sur Mer near Omaha beach in the US sector on D-Day.

RIGHT: Phoenix concrete boxes being towed into position.

89 The German Half-Track Armoured Vehicle

The invention of the half- or semi-track armoured vehicle was one of the products of German military thought about armoured warfare in the 1930s, and evidence that they were streets ahead of the British, French, Americans and Russians when it came to producing the necessary equipment for this mode of operations. When the concept of the panzer division was being planned in Germany in 1935, it was recognized that there was a need for an armoured personnel carrier (APC) capable of accompanying tanks into battle. The Germans hit upon the idea of fitting an armoured body onto a medium semi-track tractor. Development began in 1937 and production in June 1939. The result was the half-track or semi-track medium APC in three classes – Mittlere Schützenpanzerwagen Ausf A, B and C. The Ausf A and B models were superseded in 1940 by the C, which was produced until 1943. All vehicles had a well-designed and shaped armoured body, and wide-opening double doors at the rear to facilitate a quick exit by the troops. Each had an unprotected mount for a machine gun on top of the crew compartment.

During the late 1930s, trials were also being conducted on assault guns (*Sturmgeschutz*) and it was concluded that these vehicles would need to be supported by an armoured ammunition carrier and an observation post (OP) vehicle for the forward observer responsible for correcting fire. Thus when the *Sturmgeschutz* went into production, these vehicles were also manufactured. The ammunition carrier had a fully armoured body, with pistol ports at the side like many half-tracks. It also normally towed a trailer to increase the ammunition load it carried. The OP half-track was more heavily armoured, with a large circular hatch in the roof. The radio aerial on this vehicle folded into a protective channel when not in use – another example of German thoroughness in thinking through the problems that arise in war, in this case having the aerial torn off by undergrowth or blown off by enemy artillery fire.

Half-tracks were adapted for a large number of roles. In 1938, the 20 mm anti-aircraft (flak) gun was mounted on the D-7 half-track, with a special superstructure and with sides designed to fold down to provide room for all-round traverse of the gun. Eventually an armoured cab was provided, and an armoured shield fitted to the *flak* gun. Ammunition was carried in bins on the sides, and an ammunition trailer towed behind the half-track. Later the heavier 37-mm flak guns and 37-mm anti-tank guns were also mounted on a half-track chassis.

In 1939, the army staff put in a requirement for an APC capable of taking a *Halbgruppe* of infantry (four men) to augment reconnaissance units of the panzer divisions. The result was the Sd Kfz 250 series of half-tracks, which went into production in June 1941, continuing to 1943. This vehicle in its reconnaissance variant had two MG 42 machine guns in a shield mount. As well as the troop-carrying version, there were many others including air-to-ground communications models, medium mortar carriers from which the mortar could be fired without dismounting, various anti-tank and assault-gun models, a telephone cable layer and OP and command vehicles. The Sd Kfz 251, which followed in 1943, was bigger, and again had many variants, including an armoured ambulance version. The well-known photograph of General Heinz Guderian in his command vehicle with an Enigma machine shows him in a 251.

German half-tracked armoured vehicles served in every theatre of war in which they were involved. They were highly successful combat vehicles.

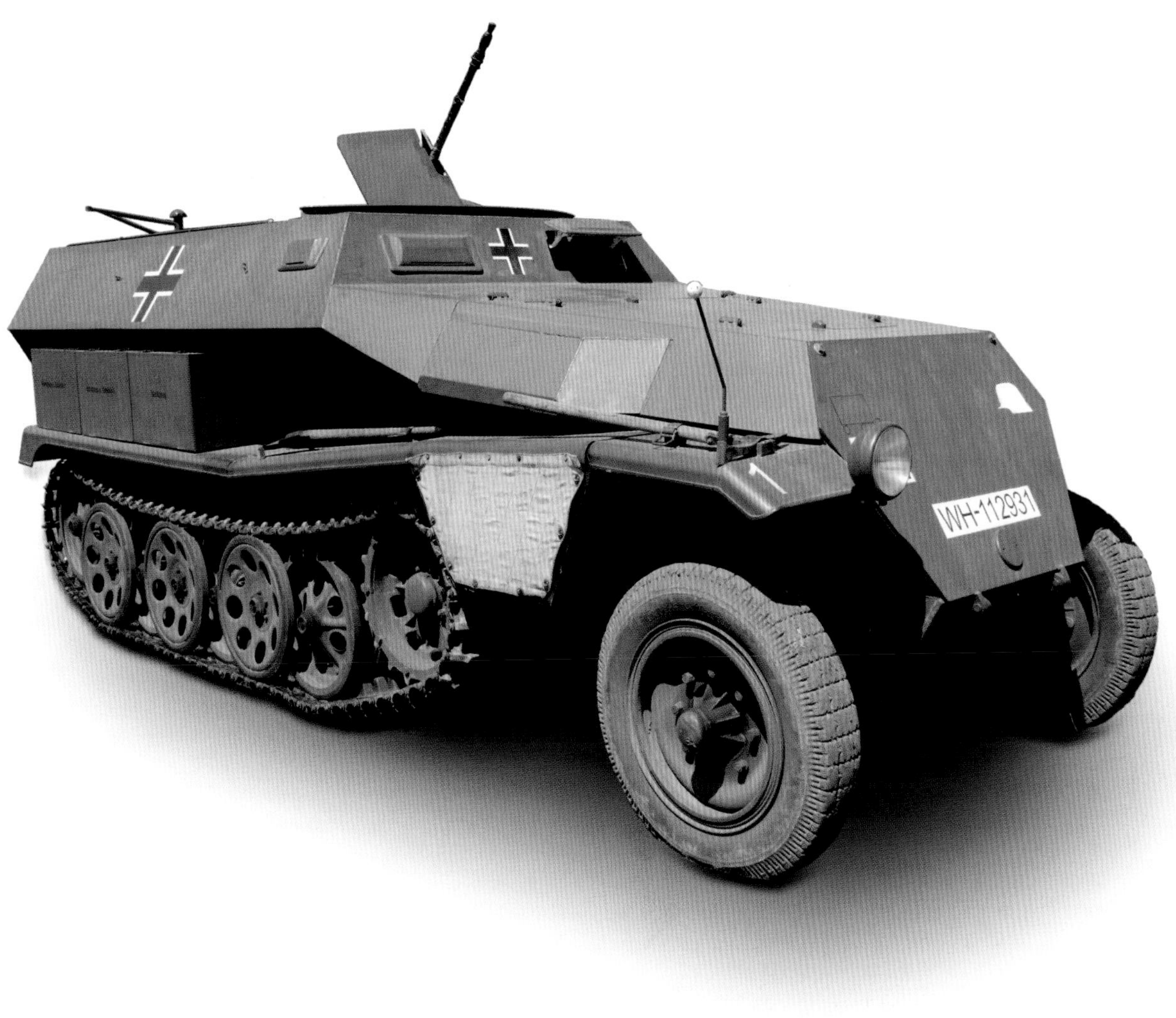

LEFT: A German semi-track Ausf D (Sd Kfz 251), captured by the Polish Home Army from the 5th SS Viking Division.

ABOVE: A German semi-track on display at the War and Peace Show at Paddock Wood, Kent.

90 The French First Army Insignia

The badge of the French First Army marks its advance from the Rhine to the Danube between September 1944 and May 1945, but in the shape of French Army B, it had a rather longer history. On 16 August 1944, this army, headed by General Jean de Lattre de Tassigny, landed in the south of France behind General Alexander Patch's US Seventh Army, which had assaulted the beaches of the French Riviera between Cannes and Hyères as part of Operation Dragoon. Army B largely comprised troops from the Armée d'Afrique (made up of French North and West African soldiers).

After landing, de Lattre captured Marseilles and Toulon before heading north along the west bank of the Rhône. On 11 September 1944, Dijon fell to the French II Corps. Here, a day later, a patrol from Army B met one from Philippe Leclerc's French 2nd Armoured Division advancing after the breakout from Normandy. Leclerc, after mauling 112 Panzer Brigade with its Tiger and Panther tanks between 12 and 14 September, came under de Lattre's command.

At this stage in the campaign, all the Dragoon forces were switched from Supreme Allied Commander Mediterranean, General Sir Henry Maitland Wilson's command to Eisenhower's, and were renamed Sixth Army Group (General Jacob Devers, USA). This included de Lattre's Army B, now re-designated French First Army to bring it in line with British and US practice which assigned numbers, not letters, to armies. At this juncture many, although by no means all, of the African colonial soldiers in French First Army began to be replaced by men of the Forces Françaises de l'Intérieur (FFI). The FFI was formed in February 1944 from nearly all the existing French resistance groups, and had taken part in operations against the Germans before, but mainly after, the Normandy landings in June 1944. Eventually more than 137,000 FFI troops served under de Lattre. This was done in order that Frenchmen could be seen to be liberating France and taking the fight to the enemy, rather than African troops, good though these were; and of course the FFI were itching to get back at the Germans.

The French First Army advanced towards the Vosges, followed by a breakthrough at the Belfort gap, leaving a German pocket at Colmar. Leclerc went on to take the city of Strasbourg on 23 November 1944, fulfilling a vow he had made after capturing Kufra in the Libyan desert nearly four years earlier. At this point Devers ordered some of his army group north to assist General George Patton, and Eisenhower ordered de Lattre to pull out of Alsace and Strasbourg, which was menaced by enemy in the Colmar pocket. De Lattre's response was, *"Ça non."* Ordering the 3rd Algerian Infantry Division to reinforce Strasbourg, de Lattre stopped the German thrust out of the Colmar pocket in two weeks of bitter combat. He went on to eliminate the pocket, one of the last fragments of German-occupied France, in three weeks of gruelling fighting in freezing weather.

De Lattre dodged the American plan for French First Army to follow US Seventh Army across the Rhine, by seizing his own crossing place. Although short of river-crossing equipment, his II Corps bounced the Rhine between Speyer and Leimersheim, going on to take Karlsruhe, Pforsheim and Stuttgart. Having crossed the Danube on 21 April, de Lattre's soldiers entered Ulm and reached the shores of Lake Constance on 24 April 1945. When the Germans surrendered, nine French divisions were in Germany. The First Army had liberated nearly one-third of France, and in battle against two German armies had taken a quarter of a million prisoners. The efforts of de Lattre's soldiers played a major part in ensuring that France, having been knocked out of the war in 1940, would sit at the top table with its allies in the postwar political settlements.

LEFT: A soldier of the French First Army on the Vosges Front, 1944.

ABOVE: The Badge of the French First Army Rhine and Danube.

OVERLEAF: Artillerymen of de Lattre's French First Army with American 105 mm howitzers.

91 The Sherman Tank

Assessing tank development in Europe from 1939–41, the US Army's Armored Force Board approved the adoption of a new medium tank, the M4 "Sherman", which married an existing chassis with a new cast hull and a fully rotating turret that mounted a 75 mm gun. The basic consideration was to speed up production of the thousands of medium tanks that the British and the US armies might need to fight German Panzers.

The tank had serious limitations compared with the German tanks they eventually faced – shortcomings which were well understood by US armour officers – but the need for an adequate medium tank was urgent. The men who selected the M4 assumed the basic tank would be modified and improved and indeed, the tank went through six major changes before the war ended. In the meantime, the Sherman in many variants fought in every theatre of the war in the hands of American, Commonwealth and Russian tank drivers. None of them were very happy with the M4 except that they were numerous and easy to maintain. By 1945, the United States had built more than 40,000 Shermans. The Soviets fielded an estimated 40,000 of their basic tank, the T-34. In comparison, Germany produced 10,500 PkW (*Panzerkampfwagen*) IVs and 5,500 PkW Vs, the Sherman's most numerous foes. In the end German manufacturing excellence could not compensate for Allied numbers.

The Sherman weighed 30 tons and had a crew of five. With experience and availability, the power plants gradually improved. The tank engines came from the aircraft industry and from automotive companies: Continental, Wright, General Motors, Ford and Caterpillar. From the crew's perspective, a diesel engine did a better job than a petrol engine since the latter tended to explode and burn too rapidly for the crew to escape; survivability was a serious concern, since the M4's armour was vulnerable to most German tank and anti-tank guns. This reality put a high priority on tank team tactics and the use of terrain for hull-down cover.

The Sherman's main gun could not match German shells of higher velocity and greater penetrating power in frontal engagements, and the tank had to manoeuvre to get killing shots. In 1944, a new M4 variant was introduced with a higher velocity 76 mm gun. The Commonwealth tank corps replaced the 75mm gun with the British 17-pounder anti-tank gun, an even better solution. This "Firefly" M4A4 Commonwealth tank gave Allied tank units greater punch against Panzers.

To improve hull durability, tank manufacturers abandoned cast hulls and joined heavier plates by welding. Another change widened and strengthened the tracks, which gave the M4 improved traction on soft ground and better incline-climbing ability. The vehicle's two .30-calibre machine guns could be fired from inside the turret and driver's compartment, though the external .50-calibre machine gun exposed the gunner.

For all its design flaws, the M4 had a battlefield durability that made it an attractive platform for tactical variations. M4s became flamethrowers, mine-clearers, rocket-launchers and command vehicles. Some M4s acted as troop carriers with the turret removed; others carried forward air controllers. One variant exchanged a tank gun for a 105mm howitzer and became a self-propelled artillery piece. An M4 with a bulldozer blade or "hedgecutter" became a standard part of Allied armour units in Europe in 1944. In the end, the M4 proved as versatile as its sponsors hoped.

LEFT: Sherman tanks move through the bombed town of Flers, following the D-Day invasion.

ABOVE: The late war M4A4 "Firefly" with the British 17-pounder anti-tank gun mounted on the new turret.

92 The Victoria Cross

By the start of the Second World War, the Victoria Cross had been established for 83 years as the highest award for bravery by a member of the armed forces of the United Kingdom, British Empire and Commonwealth. A holder of the Victoria Cross takes precedence, irrespective of rank, over holders of all other orders including the Garter.

The Victoria Cross was authorized by Royal Warrant in 1856 by Queen Victoria, who wanted the bravery of her sailors and soldiers, regardless of rank, to be recognized by the award of a medal. The warrant made the award retrospective to include the war against Russia in the Crimea and Baltic (1854–56), the conflict which had kindled the Queen's concern. Until then, only officers were awarded decorations for gallantry. Between 1858 and 1881, the Victoria Cross could be awarded for acts in circumstances of extreme danger. The regulation was changed in 1881 to award it only for gallantry in the face of the enemy. There have been occasions over the years when it has been open to debate whether the enemy was present or not. If there is doubt, the Victoria Cross is not awarded. This led to the institution of the George Cross during the Second World War.

The Victoria Cross has been awarded 1,356 times to 1,353 people, three of these having been awarded a bar to the medal denoting an award for two separate actions. Only one of these VC-and-bars was awarded during the Second World War, to Charles Upham, a New Zealander; thus during the Second World War the Victoria Cross was awarded 182 times to 181 people.

The first Victoria Cross of the Second World War was awarded to Lieutenant Commander Gerard Roope, captain of the destroyer HMS *Glowworm*, for an action on 8 April 1940. The *Glowworm* was on patrol off Norway, and having attacked and put to flight two German destroyers, encountered the German heavy cruiser *Admiral Hipper*. Roope attacked with torpedoes, and scored one hit, but the *Glowworm* was sunk, with heavy loss, including Roope. Although awarded later, the Victoria Cross received by Commander John Linton was for his command of the submarine *Turbulent* from September 1939 to March 1943, when he sank one cruiser, one destroyer, one U-boat and 28 supply ships, and destroyed three trains by shell fire.

The last Victoria Cross of the Second World War was posthumously awarded to Lieutenant Robert Gray, Royal Canadian Naval Volunteer Reserve, serving with 1841 Squadron Fleet Air Arm, for his actions in an air strike on Japan. The last Victoria Cross awarded to a soldier in that war was to Private Leslie Starcevich of the 2nd/43rd Australian Battalion in Borneo.

Twenty-six Indians and Gurkhas received the Victoria Cross in the Second World War, the last two on the same day: Sepoy (Private) Ali Haidar, 13th Frontier Force Rifles, and Sepoy Namdeo Jadhao of the 5th Mahratta Light Infantry for their actions on 9 April 1945 during the crossing of the River Senio in Italy.

The only member of the Special Air Service to receive the Victoria Cross to date was Major Anders Lassen of the 1st Special Air Service Regiment attached to the Special Boat Service, for his actions during the Battle of Lake Comacchio on the night of 8/9 April 1945. He is one of only three Danes to be awarded the medal. Thirteen of the 23 Victoria Crosses awarded to air crew of Bomber Command were posthumous, including the last, to Captain Edwin Swales, South African Air Force, serving with 582 Squadron RAF.

Nine submariners were awarded the Victoria Cross in the Second World War, the last two being Lieutenant Ian Fraser and Leading Seaman James Magennis for their successful attack in midget submarine XE3 on the Japanese heavy cruiser *Takao* in the Johore Strait off Singapore on 31 July 1945. Magennis was the only Northern Irishman to win the Victoria Cross in the Second World War.

LEFT: The New Zealander Charles Upham, the only recipient of a VC twice in the Second World War, standing in front of King George VI at the investiture at Buckingham Palace on 7 April 1945.

ABOVE: The bronze Victoria Cross.

93 The Goliath German Mini-Tank

The first German small, remotely controlled, "tank", though not a mini, was the Minenräumwagen (Sd Kfz 300) BI, an expendable mine-clearing vehicle designed in 1939. It weighed 1.5 tons, was radio-controlled and towed mine-detection rollers. Up to May 1940, some 50 of the BI model were produced. This was superseded by the heavier BII, but only prototypes were completed, both types being replaced by the smaller, wire-guided Goliath.

During the Battle of France in 1940, the German army captured some French mini-tanks, and based on these, the Goliath was designed to meet a specification issued at the end of 1940 for a smaller vehicle which could be used for applications beyond minefield clearance. Between April 1942 and January 1944, 2,650 Goliaths were produced, their official designation being Leichte Ladungsträger Sd Kfz 302 (E-Motor), Gerät 67 "Goliath", or expendable remote-controlled tracked demolition charge. It was tracked with four small wheels, a driving sprocket at the front and an idler at the back, weighed .37 tons, and was 1.2 metres (4 feet long), 0.82 metres (2.7 feet) wide and 0.55 metres (1.8 feet) high. Power came from two Bosch 2.5 Kw electric engines, with one forward and one reverse gear, a speed of 9 kph (6 mph), and a range of just under 1.5 kilometres (1 mile). Guidance was via a three-strand wire, two for steering and one to detonate the charge. The hull had three compartments: explosive charge at the front, control unit in the centre and drum of wire at the back. The two 12-volt batteries and electric motors, one for each track, were stowed in sponsons on the side of the tank.

The first units to be issued with the Goliath were the armoured pioneer companies, part of the motorized army engineer battalions, and the armoured storm brigades. The Goliath saw a great deal of service on the Russian Front, being used extensively at Kursk for minefield clearance. It was also used during the Warsaw Uprising of 1944 against the Polish Home Army. Because the Home Army had very few anti-tank weapons, volunteers showing great bravery were sent out to cut the control wires before it reached its target. A few Goliaths were used against the Normandy beaches in June 1944, but Allied troops found most already immobilized before the actual landing. They had been in the zone under heavy preliminary bombardment, which cut their cables; the bombardment had not been planned with them in mind at all.

In 1942 an improved version of the Goliath was ordered, the Sd Kfz 303 (V-motor), to allow a heavier charge to be carried over a greater distance. Two models were built, the 303a and 303b. The 303a was smaller and lighter than the 303b. The latter weighed 0.43 tons. Its 703cc petrol engine gave it a top speed of 12 kph (7.5 mph) and a range of 12 kilometres (7.5 miles), although its battle range was limited by the length of control wire on the drum – just over 640 metres (700 yards). For transport to the battle area, the Goliath was carried on a two-wheeled trailer.

Goliaths were in production until January 1945, but it was not the only remotely controlled demolition vehicle produced by the Germans. The 3.6-ton *Schwere Ladungsträger* Sd Kfz 301 Ausf. A and B were produced from April 1942 to November 1943 and could drop a heavy demolition charge on to or close to a target to demolish fortifications, as well as being used for minefield clearance. After the charge was dropped via radio control, the vehicle was backed off, again via radio control. With a speed of 37 kph (23 mph) and a range of 211 kilometres (131 miles), it was used to great effect for mine clearing on the Russian Front.

LEFT: A Goliath on the Eastern Front in March 1944.

ABOVE: A Goliath.

94 A Parachute Supply Container

In operations undertaken by British airborne forces during the Second World War, most heavy loads such as guns, jeeps, engineer equipment and medical stores, were landed by glider. But before glider-borne air-landing battalions were formed, the parachute battalions had to devise some method of dropping any equipment they might need. Even after the inclusion of gliders as part of airborne forces, there was still a need to drop equipment and stores that were too heavy to be carried by a soldier when parachuting, and which he might need immediately on arrival: wireless sets, motor cycles, ammunition, medium mortars, additional rations and so forth.

The Central Landing Establishment RAF, comprising the Parachute Training School, the Technical Unit and the Glider Training Squadron, experimented with various designs for suitable containers. The first consisted of a quilted mat stiffened with bamboo rods, fitted with pockets into which rifles and other equipment could be slotted. The mat was rolled up and strapped to a steel bar with a 8.5-metre (28-feet) parachute attached to one end, which had to be fitted into a pack the same diameter as the rolled mat so that it could be carried in the bomb bay of an aircraft (which also restricted the dimensions of subsequent types of container). The roll had a number of limitations: only a very small range of arms could be carried, and not many of these; it was difficult to unpack quickly; and it could not stand up to rough use.

The GQ Parachute Company developed the next container, designed to fit into a Whitley bomber bomb bay, and produced a number of them for the SOE. These were 1.8 metres (6 feet) long and 38cm (15 ins) in diameter, and opened at one end only. It soon became apparent that unpacking this container in a hurry, probably in the dark and possibly under fire, took far too long. Subsequently, a metal canister, opening lengthways and able to carry a 270-kg (600-lb) payload, was produced, but even these were no use for radios, as the bulky sets of the time would not fit into a 38cm (15 inch) diameter tube. Eventually, with the arrival of heavier bombers (Halifaxes, Stirlings and Lancasters) and their bigger bomb bays, the 3 metres (11 feet 6ins) by 46cm (18 ins) oblong container was designed and produced.

Special crates were designed for heavy and awkward items of equipment such as 3-in mortar baseplates, spare barrels for the 75-mm pack howitzer and Bangalore torpedoes. Because of their size or shape, certain loads could not be stowed in bomb bays at all, but were carried inside the aircraft and dropped through the jumping hole or thrown out of the door. The success of this method, and the arrival of the Dakota which didn't have a bomb bay, led to the introduction of the wicker pannier, which could be pushed out of the door.

As well as the containers that were dropped with airborne forces, huge numbers were distributed across occupied Europe to partisans, the resistance and SOE. During the Warsaw uprising of 1944, the RAF and Polish Air Force delivered supplies in containers to the "Home Army" between 4 August and 21 September. As the Soviet Union denied use of its airfields for these operations, the supply aircraft had to come from the UK and Italy, so the total

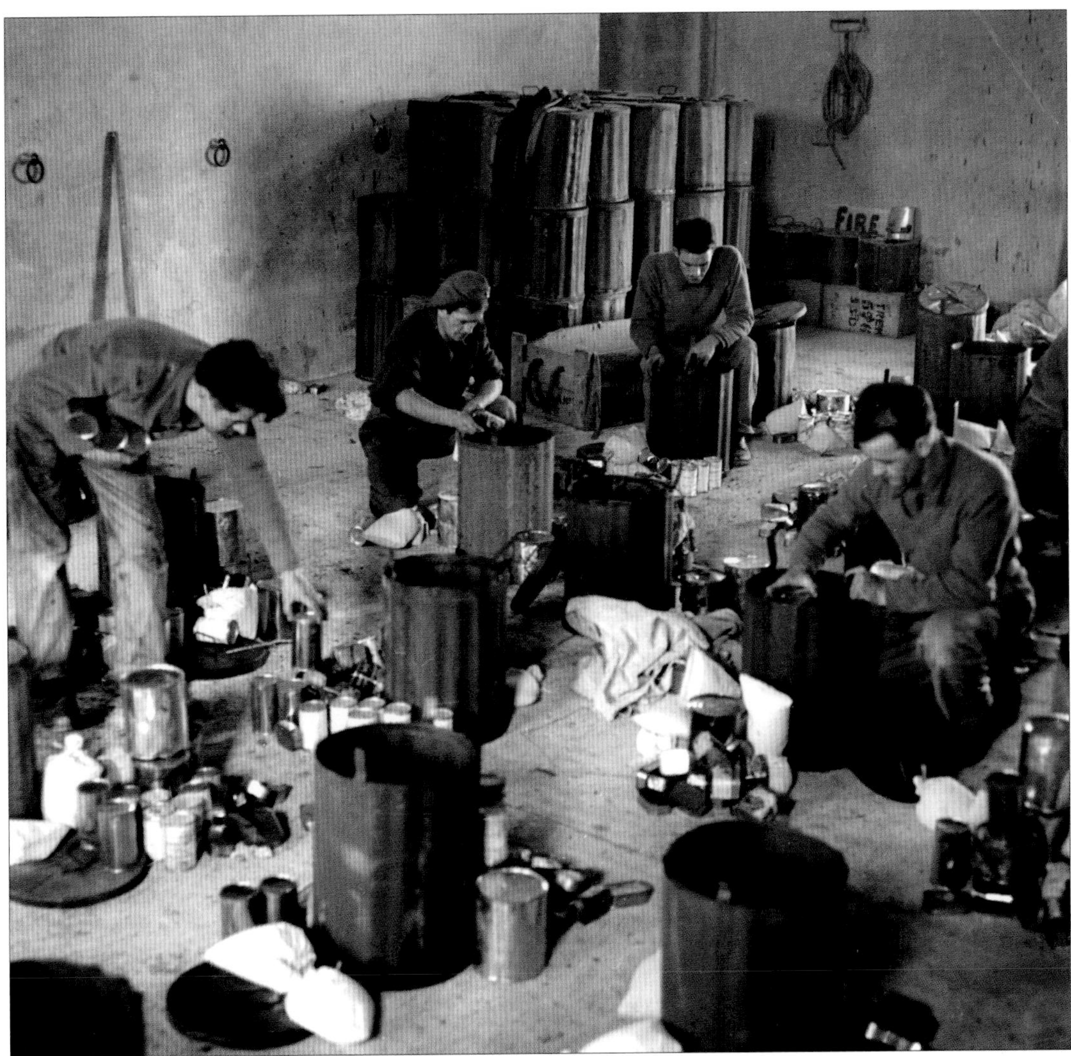

LEFT: A Halifax Mk II of number 148 Special Duties Squadron RAF dropping parachute supply canisters over a dropping zone to partisans in Yugoslavia.

ABOVE: Packing supply canisters in south-eastern Italy for dropping to Yugoslav partisans.

dropped in seven weeks was a meagre 104 tons. Some 12 per cent of the aircraft taking part were shot down while flying the almost 3,220-kilometres (2,000-mile) round trip. To begin with President Roosevelt did not allow the USAAF to take part, but eventually, on 18 September, the Soviet Union allowed 110 B-17s to refuel at their airfields and drop supplies on Warsaw – too little, too late. The Polish "Home Army" surrendered on 3 October 1944.

Other airborne forces including the Germans also used containers of similar size and shape. During the chaotic night drop of the 1st Parachute Brigade on Sicily on 13 July 1943, one British officer who went to open what he thought was one of his battalion's containers discovered it was a German one. It had been dropped in the same Dropping Zone (DZ) as was used German parachute troops reinforcing the island.

95 Canadian Army Insignia

Unlike during the First World War, when Canadian battalions in France simply wore numbers as unit identifiers and a division patch, the Canadian ground forces of the Second World War wore battalion, regimental and special corps badges, as well as division and corps patches on their field uniforms. This system of unit identification mirrored that of the British army and included special headgear, cap badges and other regimental affectations that reflected local, provincial and national pride. The common national symbol was the maple leaf, but the practice of unit identification reflected the influence of the British army regimental system. Since Canadian soldiers wore British-style uniforms and field kit and carried British army weapons, a simple Canadian unit designator was often the only thing that reflected Canadian national identity. The single uniform patch said "Canada".

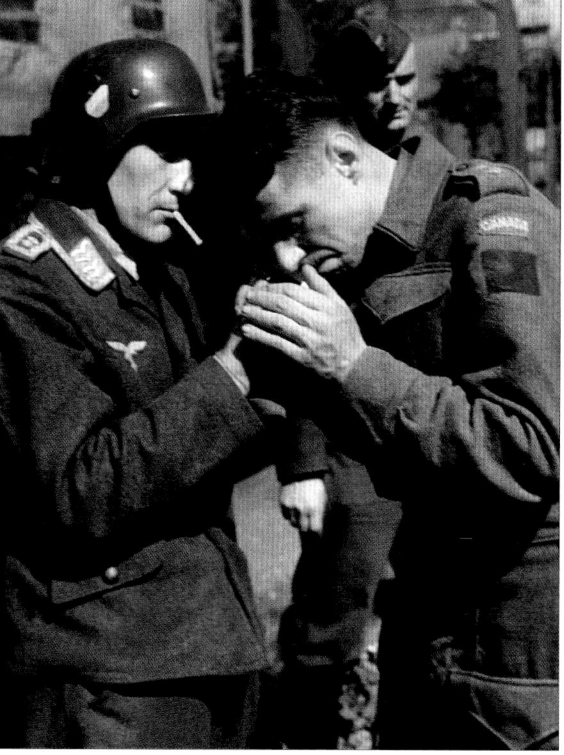

ABOVE: A German sergeant lights the cigarette for a captured Canadian officer in Dieppe, France, on 19 August 1942. Visble on the Canadian soldier's left arm, is the Canadian Army insignia.

The Canadian army provided three infantry divisions, two armoured divisions, two independent armoured brigades, a parachute battalion and many combat support (engineers) and combat service support (medical units) to the Allied expeditionary forces in Europe. The Canadian Army of the Second World War numbered 700,000 of the one million Canadians who served in uniform. Until 1945 this force was all-volunteer and rich in local pride, accommodated by distinctive unit identifiers. Whatever their formal unit titles, Canadians loved particularistic regimental symbols and names.

The standard (meaning most likely) way to show one's "regiment" was the cap badge and the sleeve strip worn just below the shoulder seam that announced that the wearer belonged to a battalion of the Princess Patricia's Canadian Light Infantry or the Highland Light Infantry of Canada or the Fusiliers Mont-Royal. Below the regimental "slash" and above enlisted rank insignia, the Canadian soldier wore colour-coded division patches of rectangular cloth, but without a special division coat-of-arms as became common in the US Army.

Early in the Second World War, Canadian soldiers wore a colour-coded circular patch above the division rectangle to designate which brigade in the division they belonged to. Another modification was for members of specialized units to wear a service corps badge instead of a division patch, for example, the Royal Canadian Signals, a communications service.

ABOVE: The insignia for the Royal Canadian Air Force.

OVERLEAF: Canadian infantry moving slowly through a street in Campochiaro, Italy, in 1943.

96 The *Volkssturm* Armband

Hitler established the *Deutscher Volkssturm* on 25 September 1944. It was first announced in a secret decree on 18 October, the anniversary of the great victory of the Prussians, Saxons, Poles, Swedes and Russians over Napoleon at Leipzig in 1813, dubbed the "battle of the nations". Hitler was fond of identifying himself with selected events in Prussian history that suited his purpose, either for propaganda, or as self-delusion, or both. The Battle of Leipzig marked an important stage in the revival of Prussia after its disastrous defeat by Napoleon at Jena in 1806.

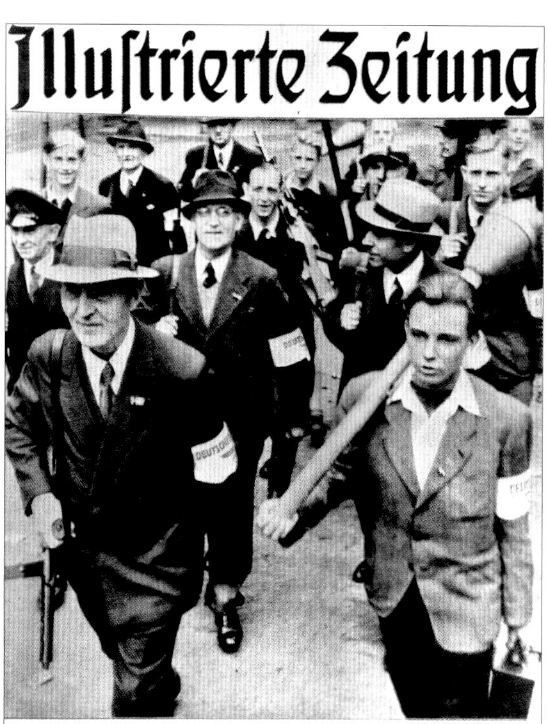

Hitler wished to draw a comparison with the Prussia of then and Germany now, the message being that although the country was being attacked on two fronts, all would come right in the end. A nation under arms would mirror the work of the Prussians who reformed the country and revitalized its army during the Napoleonic war. But the call to arms of the *Volk*, the people, did not strike quite the same chord in 1944 as it had in 1813 when the Prussian *Landsturm* had fought, often as guerrillas, against Napoleon.

Hitler ordered Martin Bormann, Head of the Party Chancellery and his private secretary, to raise six million men. This number was based on the fact that in May 1944, there were over six million men exempted from military service among the German workforce. However, the *Volkssturm* never achieved this strength. The basic unit was a battalion of men ranging in age from 16 to 60. The 16-year-olds were predominantly Hitler Youth, while the older men were mostly veterans invalided out of service or graded as unfit for military duty. They were supposed to be employed only in their own districts, but in fact many found themselves sent to the Eastern or Western Fronts once advancing Allied formations arrived on German soil. The *Volkssturm* was commanded by Heinrich Himmler in his capacity as commander-in-chief of the Replacement Army. While still in their districts the *Volkssturm* came under command of the local Nazi party hierarchy. Once deployed, they came under army command.

War work still had priority, so training was carried out for four hours on Sundays. The men had to bring their own uniforms if they had them, otherwise they wore civilian clothes, and trilbys or flat caps. Arms and ammunition were in short supply. The most numerous weapons were panzerfausts, the German hand-held anti-tank weapon. During the final months of the war the Germans produced a *Volkssturmgewehr* (People's Assault Rifle). There were several marks of this weapon; most were crudely manufactured bolt-action rifles, some without a magazine, so each round had to be loaded manually after the previous one was fired. Some had fixed, ie non-adjustable sights. From January 1945 to the end of the war a more sophisticated semi-automatic rifle was beginning to be produced with a magazine. It is not known exactly how many were made though the figure of around 10,000 seems credible. Few exist today.

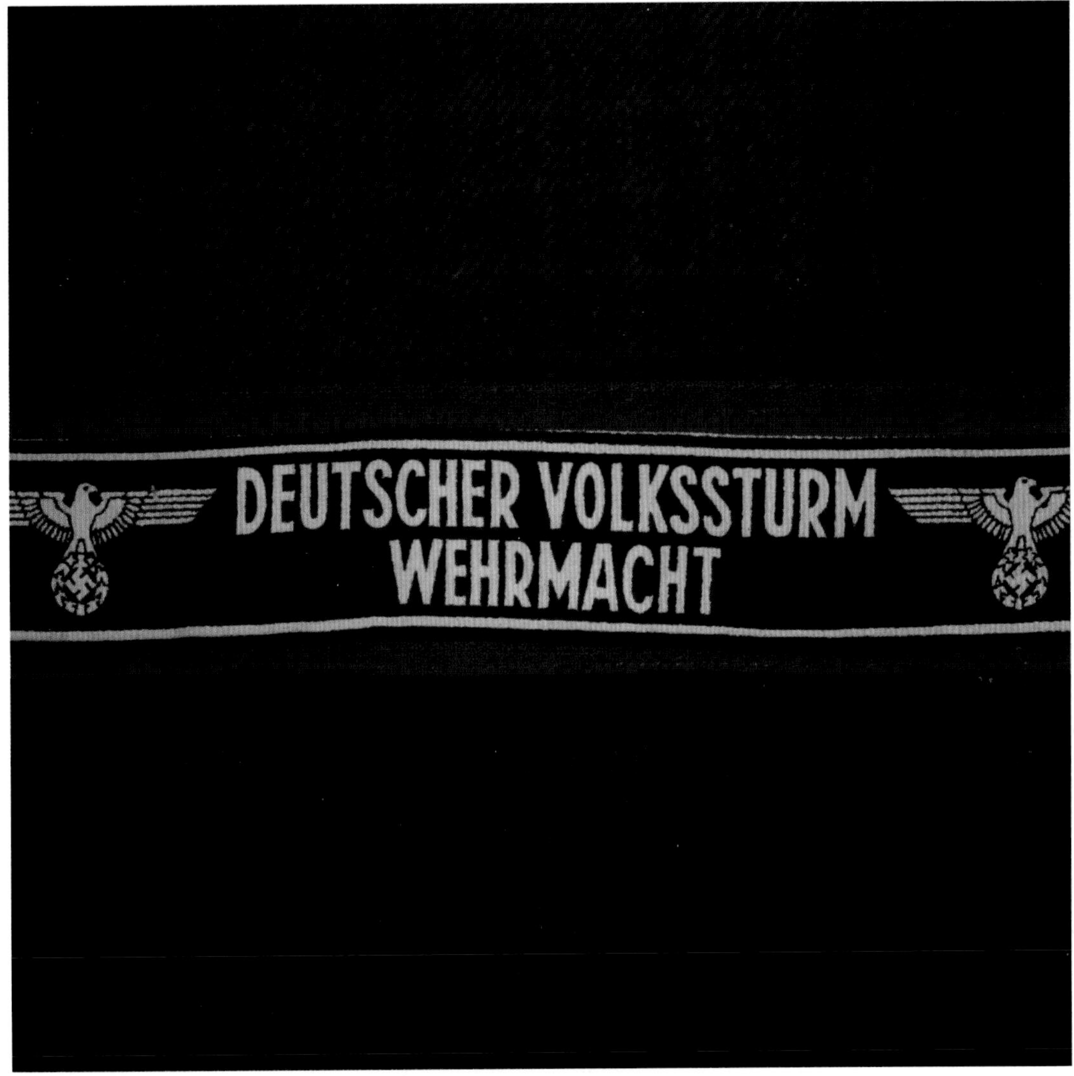

LEFT: The cover of the *Berliner Illustrierte Zeitung*, 2 November 1944, announcing *"Das Volk steht auf"* ("the people arise").

ABOVE: The *Volkssturm* Armband.

OVERLEAF: These *Volksturm soldiers* are not wearing armbands, because all are in uniform, perhaps because they are being inspected by Goebbels, pictured here shaking the hand of a boy.

The *Volkssturm* units in East Prussia were the most effective. It was here that the Landsturm had been raised in the previous century, so there was already a tradition for a people's army. Furthermore, it was in the east that the territory of the German homeland was first threatened in the Second World War, by the Red Army, and they were guarding their homes against the invaders. Right to the end, many Germans clung to the belief that the Red Army might be held at bay while an accommodation was arrived at with the Americans and the British in order that the war should end with the smallest possible portion of Germany occupied by the Russians. All these factors combined to make the Landssturm fight harder in East Prussia than elsewhere, though there were also cases of them putting up a stout resistance in the west.

97 The P-51 Mustang

Conceived by the Royal Air Force as a ground attack fighter-bomber in 1940, the P-51 Mustang became one of the best air superiority fighters – designed specifically to engage enemy aircraft – of the Second World War. It turned into the mainstay of the US Army Air Forces' 8th and 15th Fighter Commands, which escorted American bombers deep into Germany to strike urban-industrial targets in 1944–45 and thus weaken the Third Reich. In one or another of its three basic models, the Mustang saw action over six years of global warfare in every theatre.

With its own industrial facilities overtaxed producing Hurricanes and Spitfires for Great Britain's air defence, in April 1940, the Royal Air Force and British Purchasing Commission negotiated with North American Aviation in the United States to produce a single-engine, single-pilot aircraft that ensured air superiority over the battlefield and also attacked ground targets.

Based on earlier design experience, North American produced an advanced aerodynamic airframe in 117 days, but construction of an 1100hp Allison engine slowed testing. The engine problem also ensured that the Mustang I (or Model A) had limited use except as a ground attack aircraft. It had many marvellous combat flight characteristics – speed, range and manoeuvrability – and eight .30 calibre machine guns. The aircraft looked so promising that the RAF ordered 320 before it had evaluated the aircraft. After the Mustang's initial use in a ground reconnaissance role for the Army Cooperation Command, the RAF ordered 300 more aircraft.

Testing and operational experience during 1940–41 however, dramatized the Mustang's basic limitation, which was that it lost power and speed as it tried to reach 6,100 metres (20,000 feet). The Mustang could fly into Germany but only at low altitudes on reconnaissance missions. When the USAAF evaluated its own version of the Mustang in 1942, it improved the aircraft within its low altitude missions, with self-sealing wing tanks, four wing-mounted 20mm cannon and better cameras. The USAAF also developed bomb racks for the aircraft and changed the cannon to six .50-calibre machine guns. A slightly improved Merlin engine went under the cowling.

Both the RAF and USAAF saw the need for an air superiority fighter with ranges greater than the Spitfire's, and aerodynamic qualities superior to the USAAF's P-38 and P-47. Engines developed by Rolls-Royce and Packard showed great promise as a substitute for the Allison power plant. A hybrid Rolls-Royce/Packard engine, the Merlin V-1650-3, actually generated greater power (and speed) as the aircraft climbed and reached its maximum airspeed of 910 kph (441 mph) at 530 metres (28,000 feet). It also climbed more rapidly than its competitors.

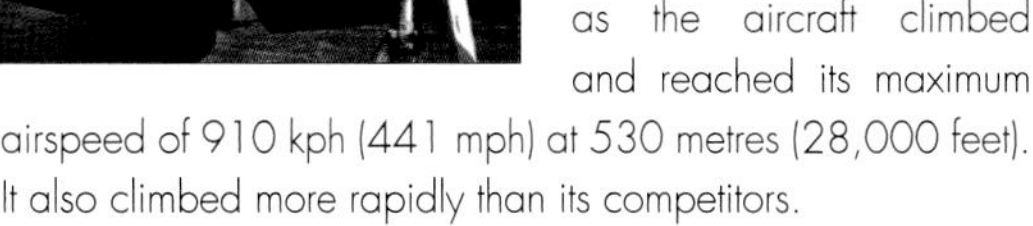

The USAAF desperately needed a long-range air superiority fighter to protect the B-17s and B-24s of Eighth Air Force, a role being pioneered by the P-47 with gasoline drop tanks. On December 1943, the new P-51B and P-51C, identical aircraft built at different plants, entered combat over Europe. More air combat experience brought a D-Model on line in 1944, with a special canopy and other aerodynamic modifications suitable for air-to-air combat. The P-51's final range was over 3,200 kilometres (2,000 miles), and the service ceiling was 12,500 kilometres (41,000 feet). Paired with growing numbers of experienced USAAF pilots, the P-51 ruled the skies in the war's last year in Europe and Asia. Before the war was over, North American built 15,586 P-51s, including 7,956 D-Models.

LEFT: Captain D S Gentile poses for a photograph on the wing of his P-51B Mustang in England on 10 April 1944.

ABOVE: North American Aviation P-51 Mustang fighter planes over France on 20 July 1944.

98 V-Weapons

The Germans called them *Vergeltungswaffen* (retaliation weapons), conceived as revenge for Allied bombing of German cities. The British called them V-weapons. There were three types.

The V-1 flying bomb, a small pilotless aircraft powered by a pulse-jet engine, was an early cruise missile. It could be catapulted from a ramp, or air-launched by a Heinkel III. It first flew at Peenemünde on the Baltic under the direction of Wernher von Braun. The first flying bombs were launched against London on 13 June 1944. By end of June, 2,452 V-1s had been targeted on London. About a third, 800, crashed in Greater London. Another third crashed or were shot down by fighters or anti-aircraft fire before reaching the coast, and the remaining third crashed or were shot down before reaching the intended target.

A minority of V-1s were launched from Heinkel IIIs. Nearly half failed to fly and crashed soon after launch. Those that did stay airborne were very inaccurate compared with ground-launched V-1s. From October 1944 until March 1945, the V-1 effort was switched to Antwerp, the main supply port for the Allied armies in north-west Europe. The attacks on London resumed from launchers in Holland on 3 March 1945, finishing at the end of March when the launching sites were overrun. Just over 10,000 V-1s were directed at England. Of these 7,888 crossed the coast, 3,957 being shot down before reaching their targets. London was hit by 2,419 V-1s, 30 reached Southampton and Portsmouth and one hit Manchester. They caused 6,184 deaths and injured 17,981 people.

The V-1 rocket, also known as the "Doodlebug", or "Buzz Bomb" because of the sound of its engine, would cut out over its intended target, lose flying speed, and dive into the ground. All in the vicinity would hear the sudden silence and wonder where it would hit.

The V-2 rocket was even more terrifying. Not only did it deliver more explosive (975 kg [2,150 lbs] compared with the V-1's 875 kg [1,875 lbs]), but, it arrived without warning, and could not be shot down. It was the forerunner to the intercontinental ballistic missile. It had a maximum velocity of 5.800 kph (3,600 mph), could climb 96 kilometres (60 miles) above the earth, and had a maximum range of 320 kilometres (200 miles). It was first fired successfully in October 1942, but fortunately for the Allies, and Britain in particular, it was hugely complicated to develop and produce. A succession of bombing raids on Peenemünde by the RAF and USAAF seriously delayed work on the V-2 by forcing production to be moved to an underground factory at Nordhausen in the Harz Mountains in May 1944. The first V-2 to reach England landed in Chiswick on 8 September 1944, killing three and injuring 17, the last on 27 March 1945. A total of 1,054 V-2s landed on England, around five a day, of which three a day hit London, killing 2,700 Londoners. Antwerp was hit by 900 V-2s during the last three months of 1944.

The V-2 was launched from a small concrete pad that was easy to hide. All the launch equipment was easily moved from place to place. Even if the sites were found, there was little for attacking aircraft to hit.

The V-3 was a long-range gun, which from two firing sites at Mimoyecques, near Calais, was capable of firing a 10.92-mm (4.3-in) shell at the rate of ten per minute on London. One of the sites was abandoned after an air attack by the RAF in November 1943, and the surviving site likewise in July 1944. Allied troops overran the area soon afterwards. The Germans persisted with work on a simplified version of the gun, which shelled Antwerp and US troops in Luxembourg, but to little effect. Shortly afterwards, the Germans demolished the guns to prevent them from falling into Allied hands.

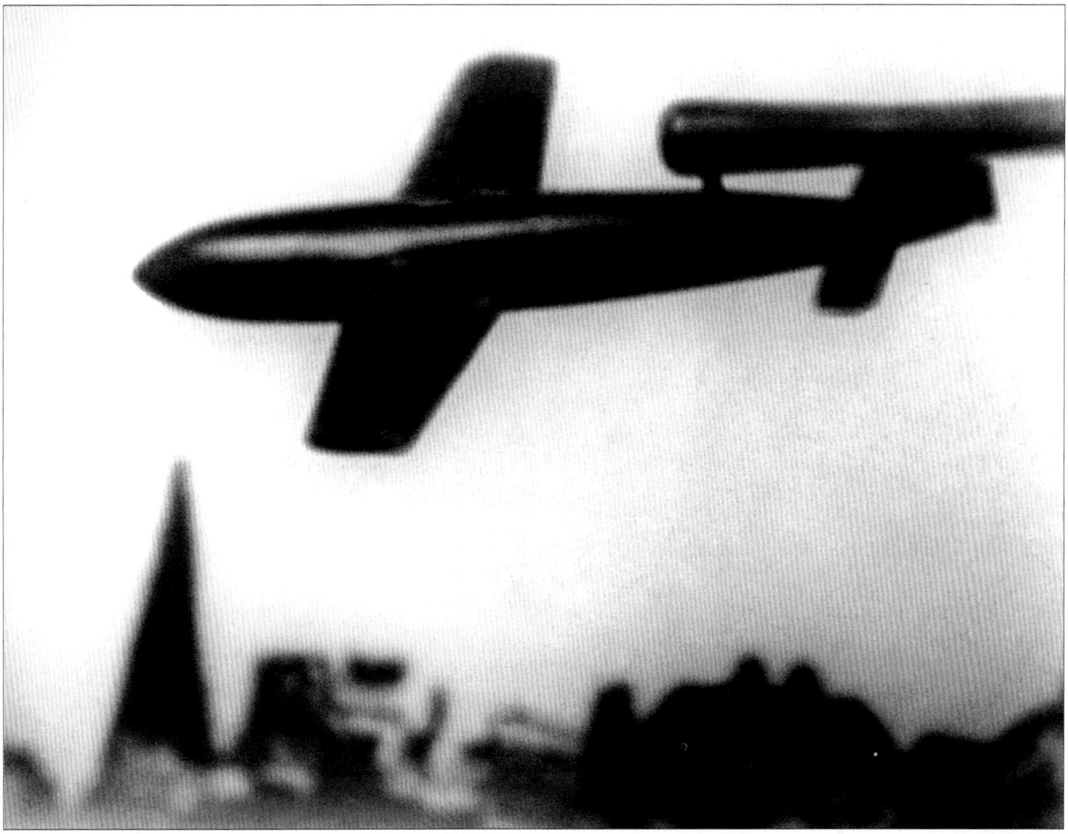

LEFT: A V-2 rocket being placed on the launching site at Cuxhaven.

ABOVE: A V-1 "Doodlebug" in flight.

RIGHT: V-2 rockets being prepared for launch.

OVERLEAF: London 1 July 1944, rescuers working among the ruins of a building demolished by a V-2 rocket.

99 Hitler's Eagle's Nest and the Berghof

The Eagle's Nest and the Berghof were part of Hitler's mountain-top estate in the Obersalzberg, overlooking the town of Berchtesgaden in south-eastern Bavaria. This mountain property was purchased by Hitler using money from sales of his book *Mein Kampf* (*My Struggle*), which set out his political message.

The biggest and original building was the Berghof (Mountain House). Its huge, richly carpeted rooms were designed by the Führer himself, and reflected not only his taste but also his youthful hankering to be an architect, as well as his image of himself as a Wagnerian warrior chief. The buildings, which were constructed by slave labour, consisted of a central chalet situated in the middle of a compound that included barracks for 20,000 troops, and there were five rings of protective fortifications around it. Only the top floor was above ground; like an iceberg, the majority of the space in use, another 12 floors, was dug deep into the mountain rock. On this top floor, which afforded wonderful views of the mountains and the valley floor below, the most impressive of all the rooms was the great reception room, with its vast picture window. Adjacent to this was the banqueting hall. The underground floors contained the guardroom, kitchens, bedrooms, larders and wine cellars.

Hitler's cronies, Hermann Goering, Joseph Goebbels and Martin Bormann, lived in smaller houses nearby. Camps for additional troops were situated within a short distance of the Berghof, and a special road was cut through to the complex from Berchtesgaden.

The Eagle's Nest, also known as the Kehlsteinhaus, was a separate chalet atop the Kehlstein, a peak about 6.5 kilometres (4 miles) from the Berghof. Built as a 50th birthday present for Hitler, it was presented to him on 20 April 1939. The road to the Eagle's Nest went through five tunnels, climbing 79 metres (2,600 feet). Access to the building itself was through a tunnel some 120 metres (400 feet) long bored into the mountain, and thence by lift up the final 120 metres (400 feet). Its official designation was the Diplomatic Reception Haus, or D-Haus for short, sometimes corrupted to "tea house" by English speakers. As a result it is often mistaken for the teahouse at the Berghof, which Hitler walked to after lunch on most days when he was in residence, whereas he rarely visited the D-Haus.

Hitler's regular visits to the teahouse were so well known that the plan to assassinate him while he was at the Berghof was put together by the British SOE. A sniper would be concealed in the forests adjacent to the road, ready to shoot Hitler on his walk. The plan was never put into effect because after the attempt on his life in July 1944, Hitler never visited the Berghof again.

As the war in Europe drew to an end, Allied leaders feared that Hitler, or one of his fanatical Nazi deputies, might command a last stand in the Bavarian Alps from the Berghof complex. On 25 April 1945, Lancasters of 617 Squadron RAF bombed the area, and at least two bombs hit the Berghof itself, smashing the top floor into ruins. In a race between the French 2nd Armoured and the US 101st Airborne Divisions to be first to capture the place, the French won. Four days later, the 506th Parachute Infantry were the first Americans to arrive. On their heels came soldiers of the 321st Airborne Artillery and the 327th Glider Infantry of the 101st Airborne Division, followed by other units of the 101st. The lower 12 floors of the Berghof were almost untouched by the bombing, and although the French had looted the place, there was plenty of the Fuhrer's champagne and cognac left for the American airborne soldiers to enjoy. In one of the lower rooms, soldiers of B Company of the 506th Parachute Infantry discovered a Gruppenführer (SS major general) still in uniform. He refused to surrender and was shot. The paratroopers stripped him of his insignia and decorations, laid his body on a bed and left, telling nobody until years later. He was found by other troops later, leading to a popular myth that he had shot himself.

The Eagle's Nest was undamaged by bombing and was also occupied by the 101st, who followed the example of their comrades in the Berghof and had their photographs taken among the ruins of Hitler's lair.

ABOVE: The Eagle's Nest on the Kehlstein.

RIGHT: Hitler with Dr and Mrs Goebbels and their three children at the Berghof.

BELOW: The entrance to the access tunnel for the Eagle's Nest.

OVERLEAF: The Great Hall at the Berghof.

100 The Atomic Bomb

The first atomic bomb was tested in New Mexico on 16 July 1945. Three weeks later, on 6 August, the first-ever nuclear attack in history took place when the atom bomb codenamed "Little Boy" was dropped on the Japanese city of Hiroshima. This was followed three days later by the dropping of "Fat Man" on Nagasaki. Japan surrendered on 15 August 1945. The Japanese Instrument of Surrender was signed on 2 Septembet 1945, bringing the Second World War to an end.

The idea that atomic fission might form the basis of a large bomb was first proposed by two British scientists, Ernest Rutherford and Frederick Soddy in 1903, but very little progress was made in this field until the outbreak of the Second World War saw a renewed interest in the possibility of such a weapon. Work in Britain began in 1940, assisted greatly by German and Austrian Jewish physicists who had escaped from Nazi Germany. Little research on nuclear fission weapons took place in the USA until 1941 when American scientists visited Tube Alloys, the cover name for the project in Britain. Impressed by the progress made, the Americans set up their own research and development programme, codenamed the Manhattan Project, to which British scientists were transferred when America entered the Second World War.

In the meantime German scientists began working on the production of "heavy water" in Norway, believing that the key to nuclear fission lay in developing this substance.

The Soviet Union also wished to develop a nuclear weapon, devoting much effort to espionage activities in the USA in order to steal the necessary knowledge from the Americans and British. The Soviet Union did not acquire an atomic bomb until 1949, the technology being aquired through spying.

Two major efforts were made to frustrate the German research, although the ending of the war with Germany revealed that they were well behind the British and Americans. The first attack was a successful commando-style raid on the heavy water plant at Rjukan in Norway on the night of 27/28 February 1943, which damaged most of the plant and machinery. Follow-up raids by RAF bombers starting in November 1943 persuaded the Germans to transfer the remaining plant and heavy water to Germany. On 20 February 1944 the SOE planted a bomb on the railway ferry across Lake Tinnsjø in Norway, sinking the ferry.

Meanwhile, joint work by the British Americans (though mainly the latter) resulted in the production of two bombs, "Little Boy" and "Fat Man". Each used different nuclear technology, that of "Fat Man" being an improvement on "Little Boy".

Some 70,000 people, mostly civilians, died in Hiroshima, and around 40,000 in Nagasaki. Also on 9 August, the Soviet Red Army invaded Manchuria, having declared war on Japan the previous day. It is perhaps an indication of the state of mind of the Japanese leadership that, despite these events, it would take until 15 August, six days later, before Japan agreed to accept unconditional surrender terms.

To this day the debate continues on the morality of using atomic bombs on Japan. In fact they caused far fewer casualties than the firebombing with "conventional" weapons that preceded the attacks on Hiroshima and Nagasaki. Starting on 9 March 1945 with an attack on Tokyo that killed 100,000 people and made over a million homeless, the ensuing firebomb attacks resulted in the destruction of large areas of 67 Japanese cities,

LEFT: The mushroom cloud from "Fat Man" rises over Nagasaki. This was the second bomb dropped on Japan.

ABOVE: "Fat Man" the 22 KT atomic bomb dropped on Nagasaki on 9 August 1945.

costing around 500,000 civilian deaths, and about five million homeless in five months. Add to this the thousands of Japanese civilians killed on Okinawa alone, as well as on other islands inhabited by the Japanese during the final months of the war in the Pacific, and the carnage wrought by the atom bombs pales by comparison with what had gone before, let alone the expected losses to civilians had the Allies been forced to invade Japan. In addition, hundreds of thousands of Asians in labour camps, and Allied prisoners of war, would have been put to death had the Japanese not been taken aback by the suddenness with which the war ended — thanks to the two atomic bombs.

ENOLA
GAY

LEFT: Paul Tibbets the pilot of the B-29 Super Fortress which dropped the first atomic bomb "Little Boy" on Hiroshima on 6 August 1945. He named the aircraft after his mother.

ABOVE TOP: The ruins of the cinema in Hiroshima.

ABOVE: Hiroshima after the dropping of the bomb.

Index

Entries in italics refer to pictures

Picture Credits

The publishers would like to thank Getty Images and their photographers/agents for their kind permission to reproduce the pictures in this book.

6. Getty Images/Central Press, 7. Getty Images/Topical Press Agency, 8-9 Getty Images/Popperfoto, 10. Getty Images/Universal History Archive, 11. Carlton Books/IWM, 12. Getty Images/AFP, 13. Getty Images/Galerie Bilderwilt, 14. Scala/BPK, Berlin, 15. Science Museum/Science & Society Picture Library, 16. Corbis, 17. Alamy/Interfoto, 18. AKG-Images/Ullstein Bild, 19. (top) AKG-Images, 19. (bottom) Corbis/Bettmann, 20. Getty Images/Carl Mydans/Time & Life Pictures, 21. Getty Images/Three Lions, 22-23. Getty Images/Three Lions/Hulton Archive, 24. AKG-Images/IAM, 25. Getty Images/Popperfoto, 26. Getty Images/Time & Life Pictures, 27. Getty Images, 28. IWM (HU 40239), 29. Photo12.com/Collection Bernard Crochet, 30. Getty Images/IMAGNO/Austrian Archives, 31. (top) Getty Images/LAPI/Roger-Viollet, 31. (bottom) Getty Images/Keystone, 32. Getty Images/Eric Harlow/Keystone, 33. (top) IWM (PST 13861_2), 33. (bottom) Alamy/John Joannides, 34. Getty Images/Time & Life Pictures, 35. U.S. Air Force, 36. Getty Images/Hulton Archive, 37. Topfoto.co.uk/The Board of Trustees of the Armouries/HIP, 38. Corbis/Hulton-Deutsch Collection, 39. Alamy/ltdarbs, 40-41. Photo12.com/Ann Ronan Picture Library, 42. IWM (H37706), 43. Private Collection, 44. Topfoto.co.uk/EE Images/HIP, 45. Topfoto.co.uk/Roger-Viollet, 46.

Topfoto.co.uk, 47. Topfoto.co.uk/Art Media/HIP, 48-49. Getty Images/Dorling Kindersley, 49. Alamy/Lordprice Collection, 50-51. Alamy/Chris Pancewicz, 51. Corbis/Bettmann, 52-53. Getty Images/Fox Photos, 54. Getty Images/Keystone, 55. Getty Images/Fox Photos, 56. Getty Images/H.F. Davis/Topical Press Agency, 57. (top) Getty Images/Keystone-France/Gamma-Keystone, 57. (bottom) Getty Images/Central Press, 58. Getty Images/Tunbridge, 58-59. Getty Images/Popperfoto, 60. Getty Images/Keystone, 61. Getty Images/Keystone, 62. & 63. Paradata.org.uk, 64. Alamy/The Art Archive, 65. Alamy/Interfoto, 66. AKG-Images/RIA Novosti, 67. (top) AKG-Images/RIA Novosti, 67. (bottom) AKG-Images/Voller Ernst, 68-69. Getty Images/Slava Katamidze Collection, 70. Getty Images/Hulton Archive/Fox Photos, 71. The Churchill Archives Centre, 72-73. Getty Images/Hulton Archive, 74. Getty Images/Keystone, 75. Dumfries Museum & Camera Obscura, 76-77. 7.62x54r.net, 77. AKG-Images, 78. IWM (E 21337), 79. IWM (INS 8116), 80-81. Getty Images/Michael Ochs Archive, 82-83. Getty Images/Popperfoto, 84. IWM (MH 4647), 85. IWM (E_MOS 1439), 86. & 87. Myrabella/Wikimedia Commons/CC-BY-SA-3.0 & GFDL, 88-89. Heritage-Images/National Archives, 90. Getty Images/Hulton Archive, 91. Wilson History & Research Centre, 92. Getty Images/Roger Viollet, 93. Author collection, 95. IWM (EPH 4299), 96. Getty Images/SSPL/Bletchley Park Trust, 97. Getty Images/SSPL, 99. Alamy/Antiques & Collectables, 100-101. Private Collection, 102. Topfoto.co.uk/Ullstein Bild, 102-103. Alamy/Interfoto, 104. Getty Images/Popperfoto, 105. IWM (T 54), 106. Getty Images/Frank Scherschel/Time & Life Pictures, 107. Getty Images/Dmitri Kessel/Time & Life Pictures, 108. Getty Images/Keystone-France/Gamma-Keystone, 109. miltaryheadgear.com, 110. AKG-Images/Interfoto, 111. AKG-Images/Interfoto, 112-113. AKG-Images, 114. Getty Images/Popperfoto, 115. IWM (4000_020_1), 116. IWM (A 30568), 117. (top) Corbis/Bettmann, 118-119. AKG-Images, 120. Getty Images/Popperfoto, 120-121. Getty Images/Hulton Archive, 122. Getty Images/Time & Life Pictures, 123. (top) IWM (INS 7209), 123. (bottom) IWM (INS 7210), 124-125. Getty Images/Keystone- France, 126. IWM (E 14948), 127. (top) IWM (INS 5110), (bottom left) IWM (5499), (bottom right) IWM (5114), 128. AWM (042011_1), 129. (top) & (bottom) Carlton Books/IWM, 130-131. Topfoto/Ullstein Bild, 132. Corbis, 133. National Archives, Washington, 134. Alamy/Interfoto, 135. IWM (FEQ 415), 136-137. Private Collection, 138. Corbis/Bettmann, 139. Getty Images, 140. & 141. Quentin Rees, 142. Alamy/Interfoto, 143. Getty Images/Keystone, 144. Topfoto, 145. Getty Images/Time Life Pictures/US Navy, 146. Corbis/Bettmann, 147. Getty Images/SSPL, 148. Getty Images/Popperfoto, 149. Corbis, 150. Getty Images/Time Life Pictures/US Signal Corps, 151. Alamy/Interfoto, 152. IWM (ART 16884), 153. Corbis/Ocean, 154. IWM (NA 3445), 155. IWM (A 9422), 157. (top) Getty Images/Hermann Harz/Photoquest, (bottom) Getty Images/LAPI/Roger Viollet, 158. Getty Images/Buyenlarge, 159. Getty Images/Frederic Lewis/Hulton Archive, 160. IWM (HU 69915), 161. (top) IWM (HU 62922), (bottom) IWM (FLM 2340), 162-163. IWM (HU 4594), 164. IWM (ART 16345), 165. (top) Getty Images/Popperfoto, (bottom) Alamy/Art Directors & TRIP, 166. AWM (010627-1), 167. AWM (RELAWM30622_008-1), 168. Topfoto.co.uk, 169. IWM (MH 32784), 170. IWM (SE 7921), 171. (top) IWM (INS 43123), (bottom) IWM (INS 43124), 173. IWM (A 22617), 174. IWM (BU 9757), 175. (top) Alamy/Interfoto, (bottom) Topfoto.co.uk/The Granger Collection, 176-177. Topfoto.co.uk/Ullstein Bild, 179. Topfoto.co.uk/Ullstein Bild, 180. Getty Images/Keystone, 181. Corbis, 182. Getty Images/US Coast Guard/FPG/Hulton Archive, 183. Getty Images/Galerie Bilderwelt, 184. Getty Images/Keystone, 185. Getty Images/PjrStudio, 186. Getty Images/Keystone-France/Gamma-Keystone, 187. Getty Images/Hulton Archive, 188. & 189. Rex Features/Geoffrey Robinson, 190. & 191. National Archives & Records Administration, Washington, 192. AKG-Images/Ullstein Bild, 193. Alamy/Jack Sullivan, 194. IWM (HU 1122), 195. IWM (INS 43117), 196. Corbis/Hulton-Deutsch Collection, 197. Corbis/Bettmann, 199. (top) Getty Images/George Rodger/Time & Life Pictures, (bottom) Getty Images/Margaret Bourke-White/Time & Life Pictures, 200. Corbis/Heritage Images, 201. Topfoto.co.uk/Curt Teich Postcard Archives, Lake County HistoryArchives/HIP, 203. National Archives and Records Administration, Washington, 204. Topfoto.co.uk/The National Archives/HIP, 205. IWM (CH 15363), 206. Corbis, 206-207. Getty Images/PhotoQuest, 208. IWM (H 35181), 209. IWM (MH 2210), 210. Getty Images/Imagno, 211. Corbis/Michael St. Maur Sheil, 212. IWM (TR 2313), 213. IWM (H 37860), 214. Getty Images/PhotoQuest, 215. Alamy/Interfoto, 217. (top) Getty Images/Three Lions, (bottom) Getty Images/Popperfoto, 218. Private Collection, 219. Alamy/Maurice Savage, 220. Getty Images/LAPI/Roger Viollet, 222-223. Getty Images/Roger Viollet Collection, 224. Getty Images/Popperfoto, 225. Istockphoto.com, 226. Getty Images/Kurk Hutton/Picture Post/Hulton Archive, 227. Private Collection, 228. Getty Images/Keystone-France/Gamma- Keystone, 229. Deutsches Panzermuseum Munster, Germany, 230. IWM (CNA 3243), 231. IWM (CNA 3566), 232. Alamy/Interfoto, 233. (top) IWM (INS 7993), (bottom) IWM (7994), 234-235. Corbis/Hulton-Deutsch Collection, 236. AKG-Images/Ullstein Bild, 237. Private Collection, 238-239. AKG-Images, 240. Getty Images/Popperfoto, 241. Getty Images/Fox Photos, 243. (top) Getty Images/Keystone/Hulton Archive, (bottom) Getty Images/Roger Viollet, 244-245. Getty Images/Mansell/Time & Life Pictures, 247. (top) Photo12/Cabinet Revel, (bottom left) Getty Images/Three Lions, (bottom right) Getty Images/AFP, 248-249. Photo12/Cabinet Revel, 250. Corbis/Nagasaki Atomic Bomb Museum/epa, 251. IWM (MH 6810), 252. Getty Images/Universal History Archive, 253. (top) Getty Images/Popperfoto, (bottom) Getty Images/Universal History Archive

Every effort has been made to acknowledge correctly and contact the source and/or copyright holder of each picture and Carlton Books Limited apologises for any unintentional errors or omissions, which will be corrected in future editions of this book.

Publishing Credits:

Editorial Director: Piers Murray Hill
Executive Editor: Jennifer Barr
Additional editorial work: Catherine Rubinstein, Philip Parker and Barry Goodman
Design Manager and Cover Design: Russell Knowles
Designer and Production Controller: Rachel Burgess
Picture Manager: Steve Behan